created by EMILIA CLARKE & MARGUERITE BENNETT

Dearest reader,

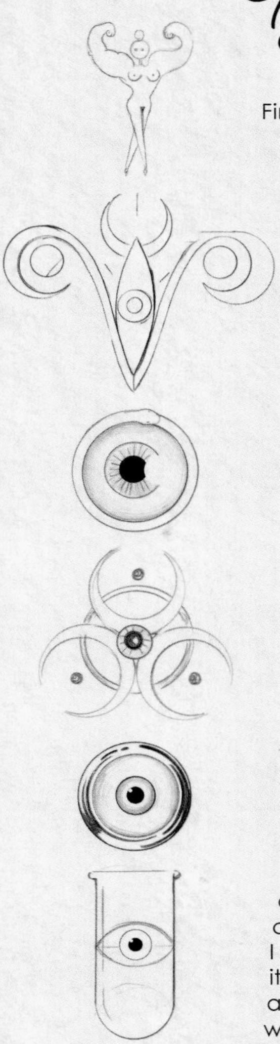

First and foremost, thank you.

By purchasing this hardcover, YOU have decided to embark on the strange journey that is the first arc of MOTHER OF MADNESS. This is my baby. An idea that came whirling out of my mind after one conversation two years ago that started with, "Wouldn't it be funny if...?" Putting it bluntly, YOU have made my dreams come true, so go ahead and give yourself a nice big hug. I will forever be in your debt.

Now why, you might ask, did I decide to write this? Well, I'd be lying if I didn't state for the record that I am an out-and-out feminist. But a very friendly one. There are many things I care about, but one of the biggest is young people and their mental health. I say "young" because, dear reader, I believe myself to be old(-ish). Well, old enough to have been around for the invention of texting, and a LATE teenager for the arrival of Facebook—hell, let's call a spade a spade, I watched *FRIENDS* WHEN IT CAME OUT. So, I missed a lot of the trappings of social media as a very tender young thing, but what I didn't miss was how MTV (remember TV channels dedicated to music videos?) and the magazines I read made me feel TERRIBLE about myself. And thus, a feminist was born. Not to say that this is just for those born pre-1986! That's what makes comics so magnificent—they are for EVERYONE, and so is M.O.M.

I wanted to make something that was, at its heart, about the power of the female form, the magical brilliance of what we, as women, have the joy to call our identity. Remember the first time you learnt about hormones? I don't because no one ever told me, but I DO remember the feelings of shame and self-loathing that accompanied my hormonal evolution as I blossomed into the young woman writing this now (though frankly, I didn't blossom, I exploded, hair, blood, extra water and extra tears).

But why a comic? Well, aside from being too scared to follow my brother into the comic book stores as a kid, I found comics late in life, Daenerys, Sarah, and Qi'ra really brought me to them. There's only so many ComicCons you can attend without starting to read the amazing comics on display, and there I saw all my favourite movie characters (I'm a superhero fangirl) and suddenly it dawned on me, THIS IS COOL. Whilst perusing all the selections on show, I also began to see that the female to male ratios were slightly... off, and it was here that the seeds of M.O.M. were born.

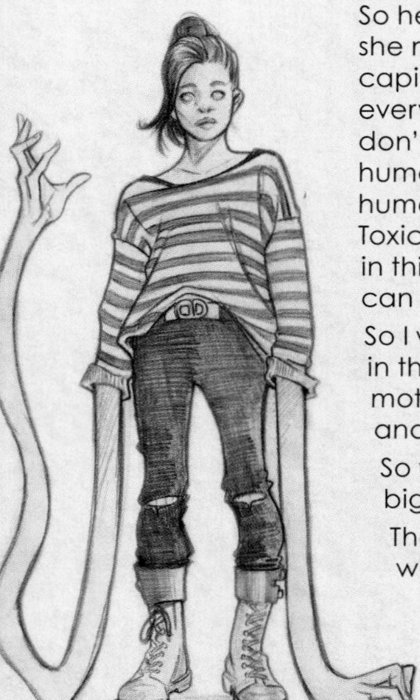

So here we are at M.O.M., a woman, a mother, who finds that all the things she most hated in herself were actually SUPERPOWERED. Set that in an extreme capitalist structure, throw in some very real problems that face women everywhere, and you have the book that is in your hands right now. Now, don't feel that I've forgotten about men. I have not. My dad was a wonderous human, my brother is the best man I know, all my male friends are good, good humans, but the society we live in today doesn't help you boys out one bit. Toxic masculinity is real, and it affects EVERYONE. There are characters a-plenty in this story that address this too. If we can educate our boys young, then we can stand a chance at beating this problem to a pulp.

So I write this letter to let you in, dearest reader, on how I got here. I believe in the power of humans, of our ability to care, and our ability to be badass mothers. I wanted to put a mother at the centre because WE ALL HAD ONE and I think they deserve a superhero makeover.

So young people of the world, I see you, I see your beauty, I see your bright big brain, I see your individuality, I see your soul and it is a miracle.

Thank you for picking up this book, thank you for coming on this journey with me, thank you for BEING AWESOME.

All my love,
EMILIA X

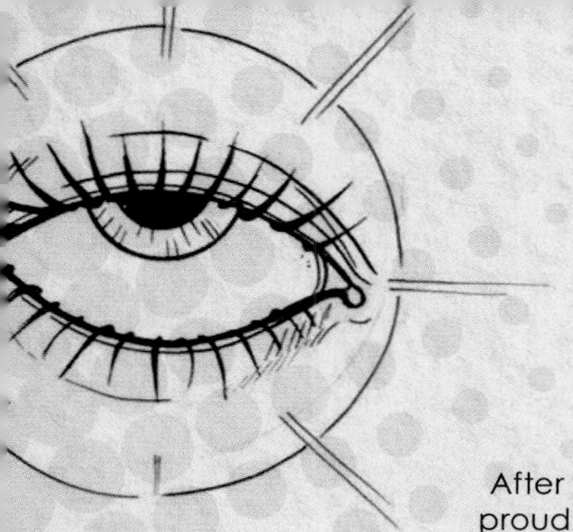

After three years of love and labor, and I am so proud to be able to share this project with the world.

In the Beforetimes, we met in person, Emilia, Isobel, and I. In the pandemic, we met over Zoom. For literal years, we crafted, revised, researched, wrote, edited, reviewed, punched up, and didn't stop until we laughed.

To me, Maya is a patriarchal nightmare, a dark comedy of delightful proportions. Every ugly stereotype about women—our bodies, our emotions, our hormones—has been flipped on its head and given power. We've embraced every trope until it detonated, awesome or absurd.

It was viscerally important to me for this book to be inclusive of women everywhere – trans and cis, queer and straight, privileged and oppressed, of every background and ethnicity, of every body type and ability, the world over. We are too magnificently much, of course, to be contained within any single story. In that spirit, any missteps and absences are my fault alone. Like Maya, I am humbly aware of my failings, past and present. I cannot aspire to perfect, but I do aspire to be messily, clumsily, earnestly better tomorrow than I was the day before, and I thank you deeply for your patience and kindness as I endeavor to deserve them.

I want to especially highlight the tireless efforts of everyone on this team – Emilia and Isobel, our fabulous co-creators, who were present at every step, overflowing with ideas and brilliance with how to make this story at once outrageous and all too real – Leila Leiz, our glamorous and glorious artist, who interrogated every atom of this world, down to its smallest detail, and brought every last impossible character to life – Tríona Farrell, who infused them and their story with radical neons and swirling color, burning yellows and blazing pinks, an undisputed master of her craft – Haley Rose-Lyon, who took the world's chattiest script and fit in every last quip, joke, and pithy one-liner until our panels were bursting with personality and panache – Leila de Luca, our shining knight in equally shining armor, who came splendidly to our rescue in our hour of need. And through all of it, our editor and high priestess, Laurenn McCubbin, who kept us safe, sane, and on target through pandemics and quarantines, protests and elections, political upheavals and personal losses. I'm in awe and in debt to every one of y'all.

As I am in awe and in debt, too, to you, our audience. I hope you've found within this what you were hoping for, and something unexpected, too.

All my love,
MARGUERITE

written & created by
**EMILIA CLARKE &
MARGUERITE BENNETT**

drawn by
LEILA LEIZ & LEILA DEL DUCA
(pages 94, 99, 100, 112-115)

principal contributor & producer
ISOBEL RICHARDSON

color
TRIONA FARRELL

lettered by
HALEY ROSE-LYON

edited by
LAURENN McCUBBIN

logo, covers & costume design
JO RATCLIFFE

additional design
DEANNA PHELPS

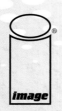

IMAGE COMICS, INC.

Todd McFarlane: President
Jim Valentino: Vice President
Marc Silvestri: Chief Executive Officer
Erik Larsen: Chief Financial Officer
Robert Kirkman: Chief Operating Officer

Eric Stephenson: Publisher / Chief Creative Officer
Nicole Lapalme: Controller
Leanna Caunter: Accounting Analyst
Sue Korpela: Accounting & HR Manager
Marla Eizik: Talent Liaison
Jeff Boison: Director of Sales & Publishing Planning
Dirk Wood: Director of International Sales & Licensing
Alex Cox: Director of Direct Market Sales
Chloe Ramos: Book Market & Library Sales Manager
Emilio Bautista: Digital Sales Coordinator
Jon Schlaffman: Specialty Sales Coordinator
Kat Salazar: Director of PR & Marketing
Drew Fitzgerald: Marketing Content Associate
Heather Doornink: Production Director
Drew Gill: Art Director
Hilary DiLoreto: Print Manager
Tricia Ramos: Traffic Manager
Melissa Gifford: Content Manager
Erika Schnatz: Senior Production Artist
Ryan Brewer: Production Artist
Deanna Phelps: Production Artist
IMAGECOMICS.COM

M.O.M. MOTHER OF MADNESS, VOL. 1. First printing. December 2021. Published by Image Comics, Inc. Office of publication: PO BOX 14457, Portland, OR 97293. Copyright © 2021 Magical Thinking Pictures. All rights reserved. Contains material originally published in single magazine form as M.O.M. MOTHER OF MADNESS #1-3. "M.O.M. Mother of Madness," its logos, and the likenesses of all characters herein are trademarks of Magical Thinking Pictures, unless otherwise noted. "Image" and the Image Comics logos are registered trademarks of Image Comics, Inc. No part of this publication may be reproduced or transmitted, in any form or by any means (except for short excerpts for journalistic or review purposes), without the express written permission of Magical Thinking Pictures, or Image Comics, Inc. All names, characters, events, and locales in this publication are entirely fictional. Any resemblance to actual persons (living or dead), events, or places, without satirical intent, is coincidental. Printed in Canada. For international rights, contact: foreignlicensing@imagecomics.com.
ISBN: 978-1-5343-2093-2
B&N Exclusive ISBN: 978-1-5343-2148-9
Indigo Exclusive ISBN: 978-1-5343-2149-6

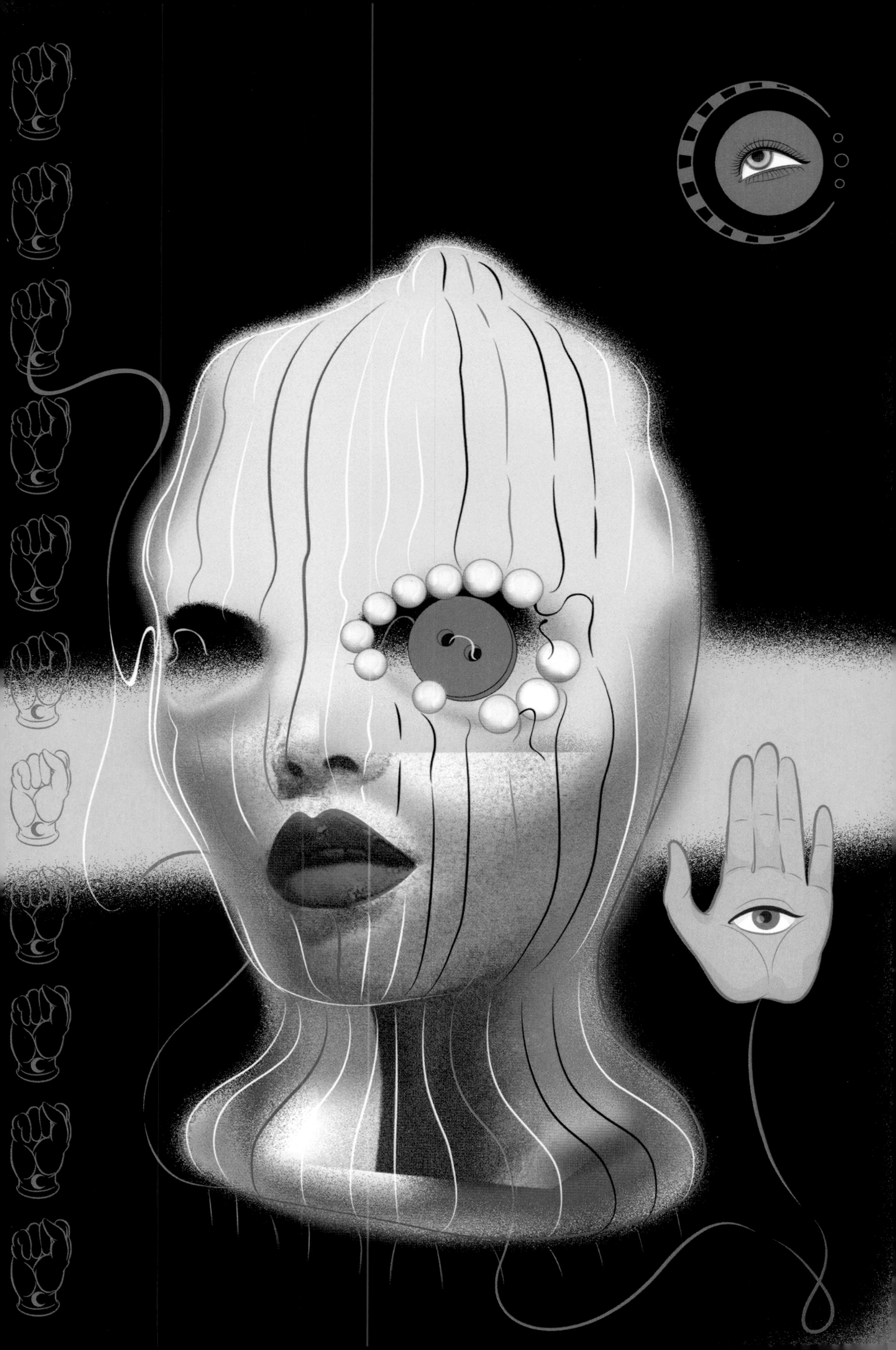

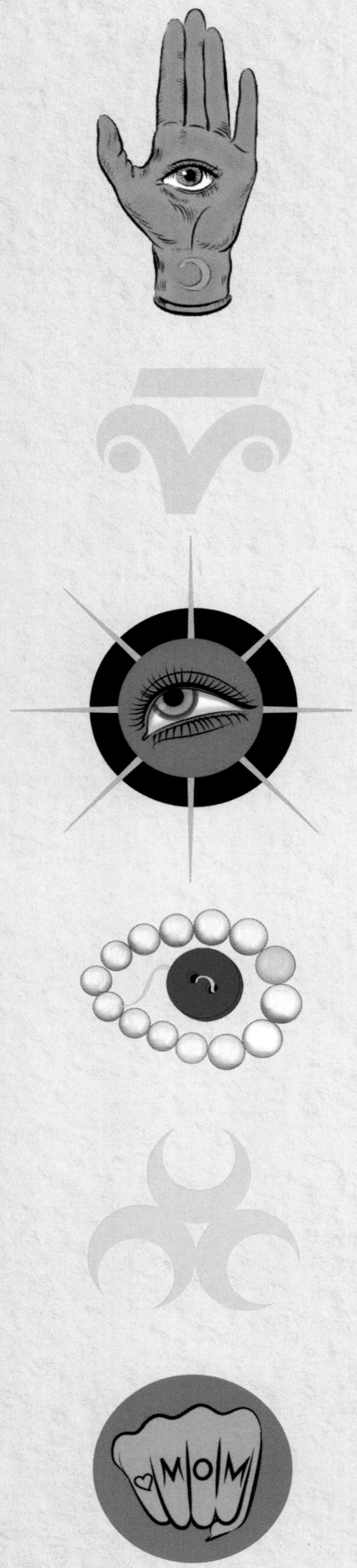
MOM

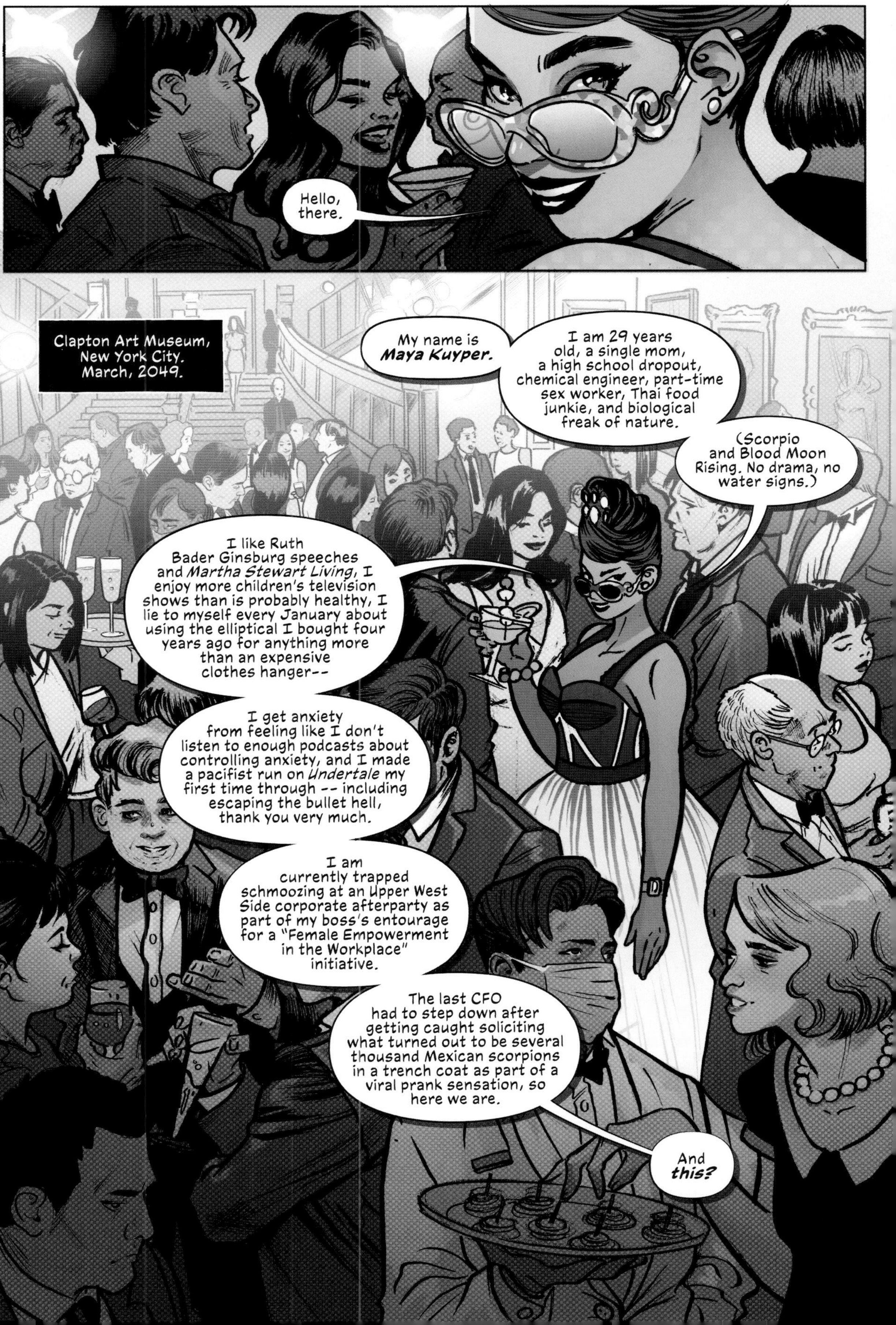
Hello, there.
Clapton Art Museum, New York City. March, 2049.
My name is *Maya Kuyper.*
I am 29 years old, a single mom, a high school dropout, chemical engineer, part-time sex worker, Thai food junkie, and biological freak of nature.
(Scorpio and Blood Moon Rising. No drama, no water signs.)
I like Ruth Bader Ginsburg speeches and *Martha Stewart Living*, I enjoy more children's television shows than is probably healthy, I lie to myself every January about using the elliptical I bought four years ago for anything more than an expensive clothes hanger--
I get anxiety from feeling like I don't listen to enough podcasts about controlling anxiety, and I made a pacifist run on *Undertale* my first time through -- including escaping the bullet hell, thank you very much.
I am currently trapped schmoozing at an Upper West Side corporate afterparty as part of my boss's entourage for a "Female Empowerment in the Workplace" initiative.
The last CFO had to step down after getting caught soliciting what turned out to be several thousand Mexican scorpions in a trench coat as part of a viral prank sensation, so here we are.
And *this?*

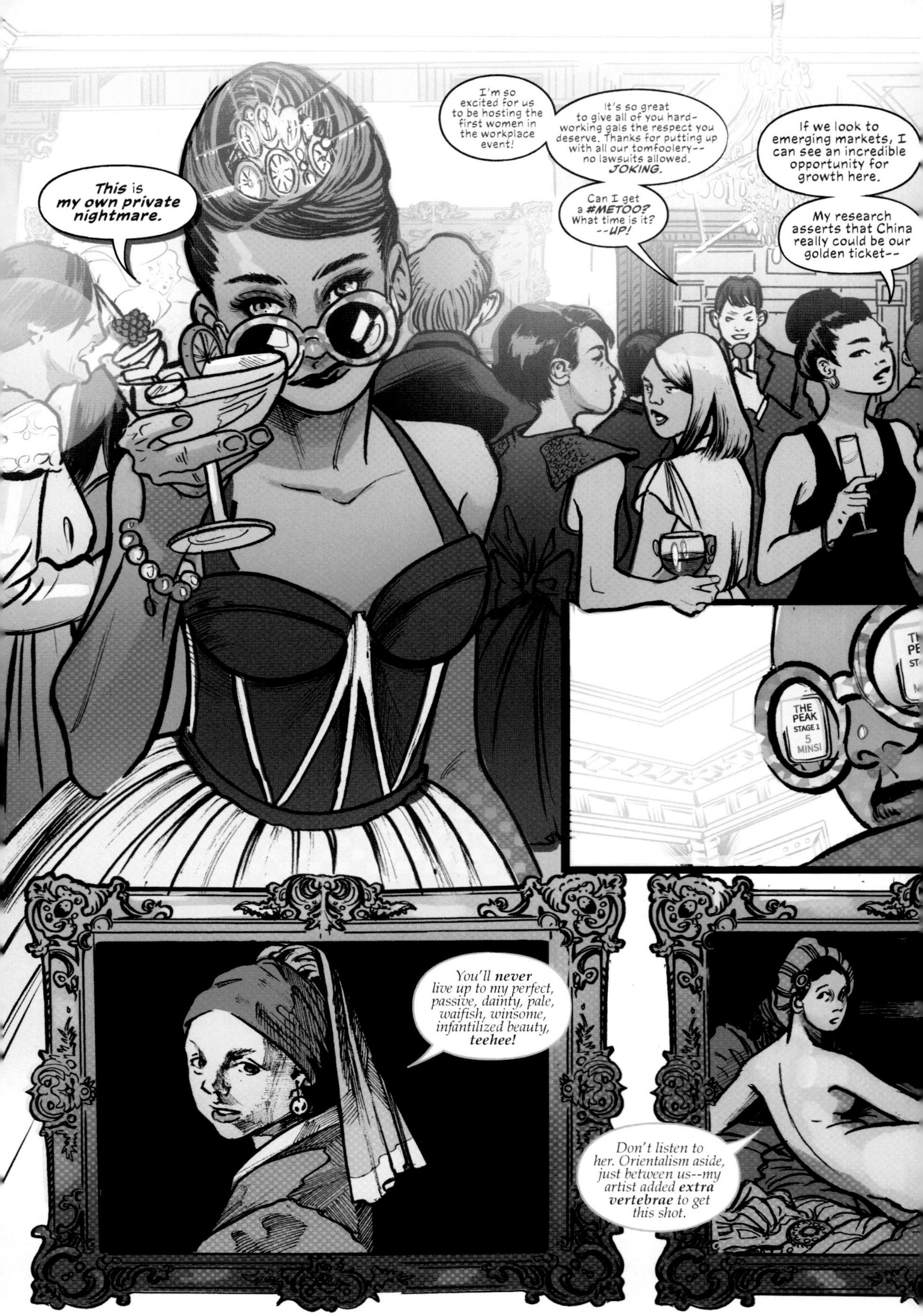
This is my own private nightmare.
I'm so excited for us to be hosting the first women in the workplace event!
It's so great to give all of you hard-working gals the respect you deserve. Thanks for putting up with all our tomfoolery-- no lawsuits allowed. JOKING.
Can I get a #METOO? What time is it? --UP!
If we look to emerging markets, I can see an incredible opportunity for growth here.
My research asserts that China really could be our golden ticket--
THE PEAK STAGE 1 5 MINS!
You'll never live up to my perfect, passive, dainty, pale, waifish, winsome, infantilized beauty, teehee!
Don't listen to her. Orientalism aside, just between us--my artist added extra vertebrae to get this shot.

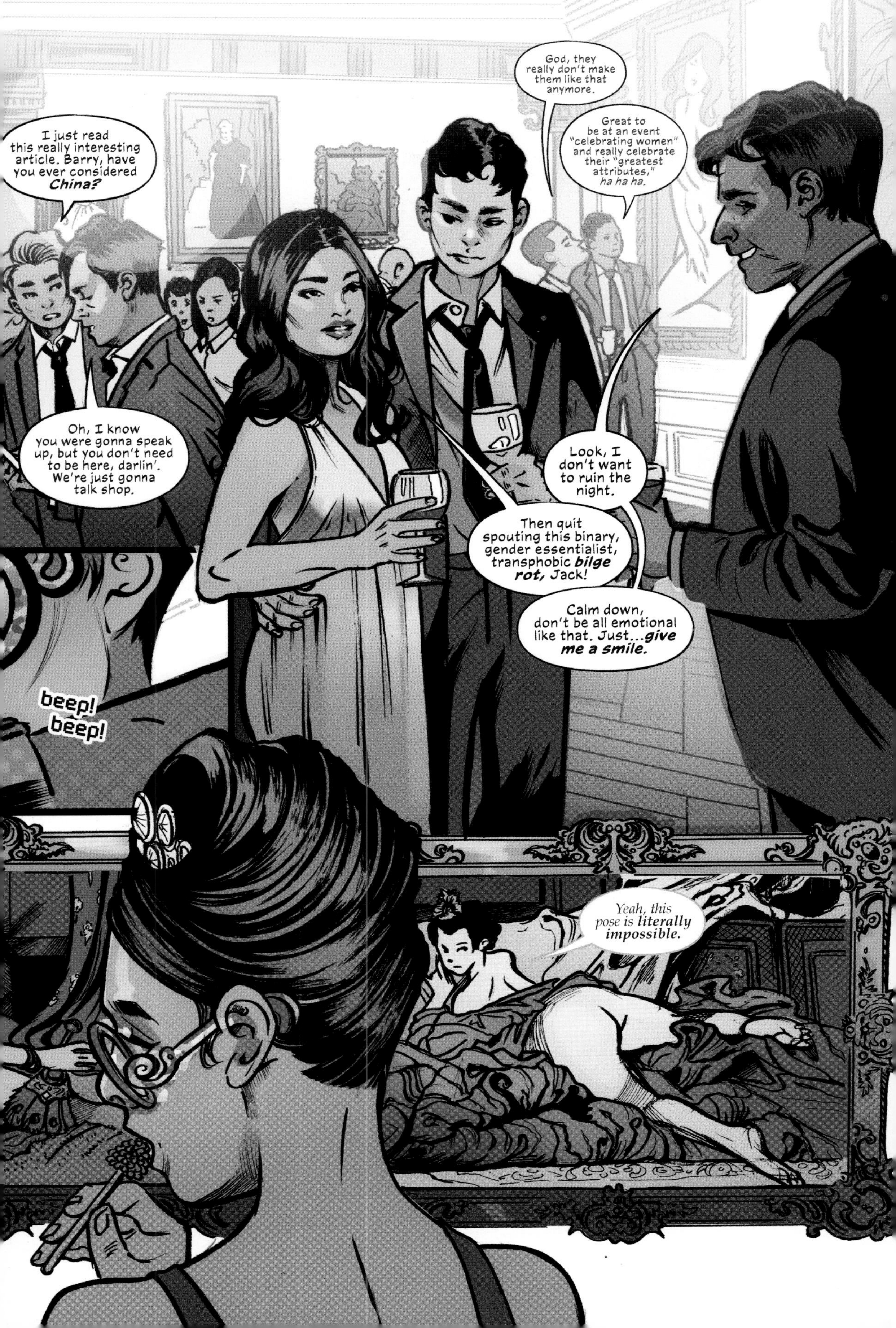

I just read this really interesting article. Barry, have you ever considered *China?*
God, they really don't make them like that anymore.
Great to be at an event "celebrating women" and really celebrate their "greatest attributes," *ha ha ha.*
Oh, I know you were gonna speak up, but you don't need to be here, darlin'. We're just gonna talk shop.
Look, I don't want to ruin the night.
Then quit spouting this binary, gender essentialist, transphobic ***bilge rot,*** Jack!
Calm down, don't be all emotional like that. *Just...**give me a smile.***
beep! beep!
*Yeah, this pose is **literally impossible.***

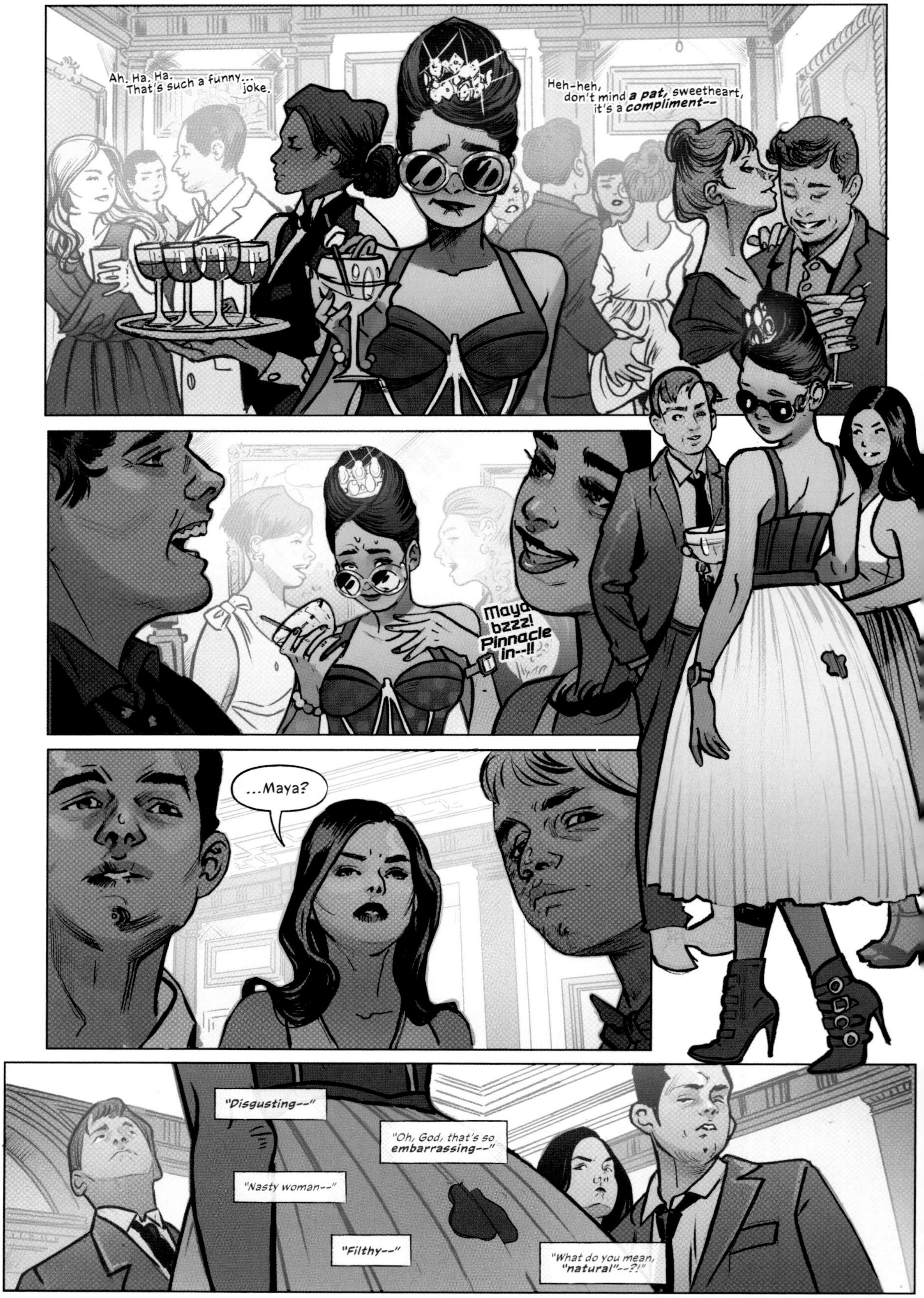
Ah. Ha. Ha. That's such a funny... joke.
Heh-heh, don't mind a pat, sweetheart, it's a compliment--
Maya bzzz! Pinnacle in--!!
...Maya?
"Disgusting--"
"Oh, God, that's so embarrassing--"
"Nasty woman--"
"Filthy--"
"What do you mean, "natural"--?!"

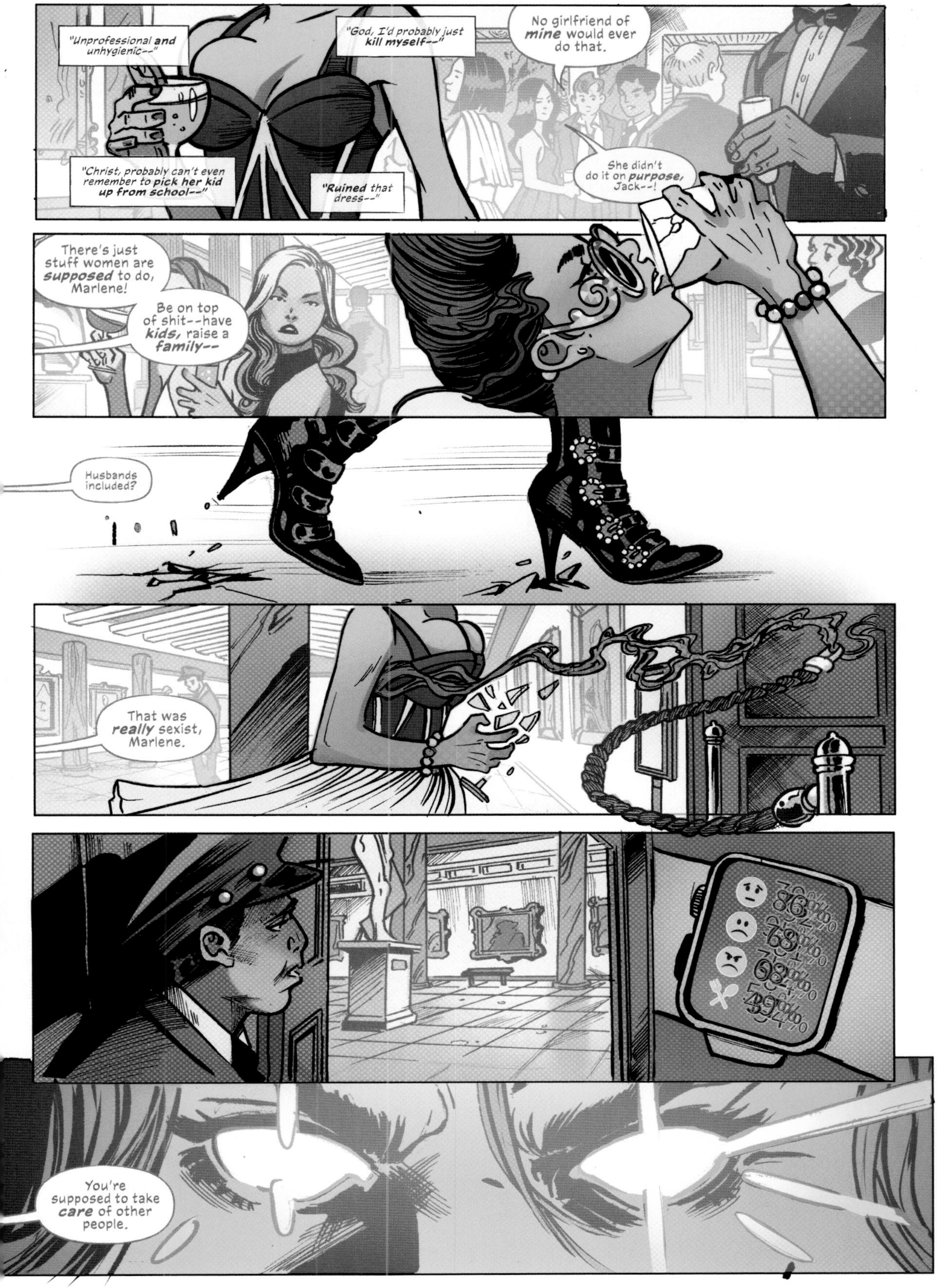
"Unprofessional and unhygienic--"
"God, I'd probably just kill myself--"
No girlfriend of mine would ever do that.
"Christ, probably can't even remember to pick her kid up from school--"
"Ruined that dress--"
She didn't do it on purpose, Jack--!
There's just stuff women are supposed to do, Marlene!
Be on top of shit--have kids, raise a family--
Husbands included?
That was really sexist, Marlene.
You're supposed to take care of other people.

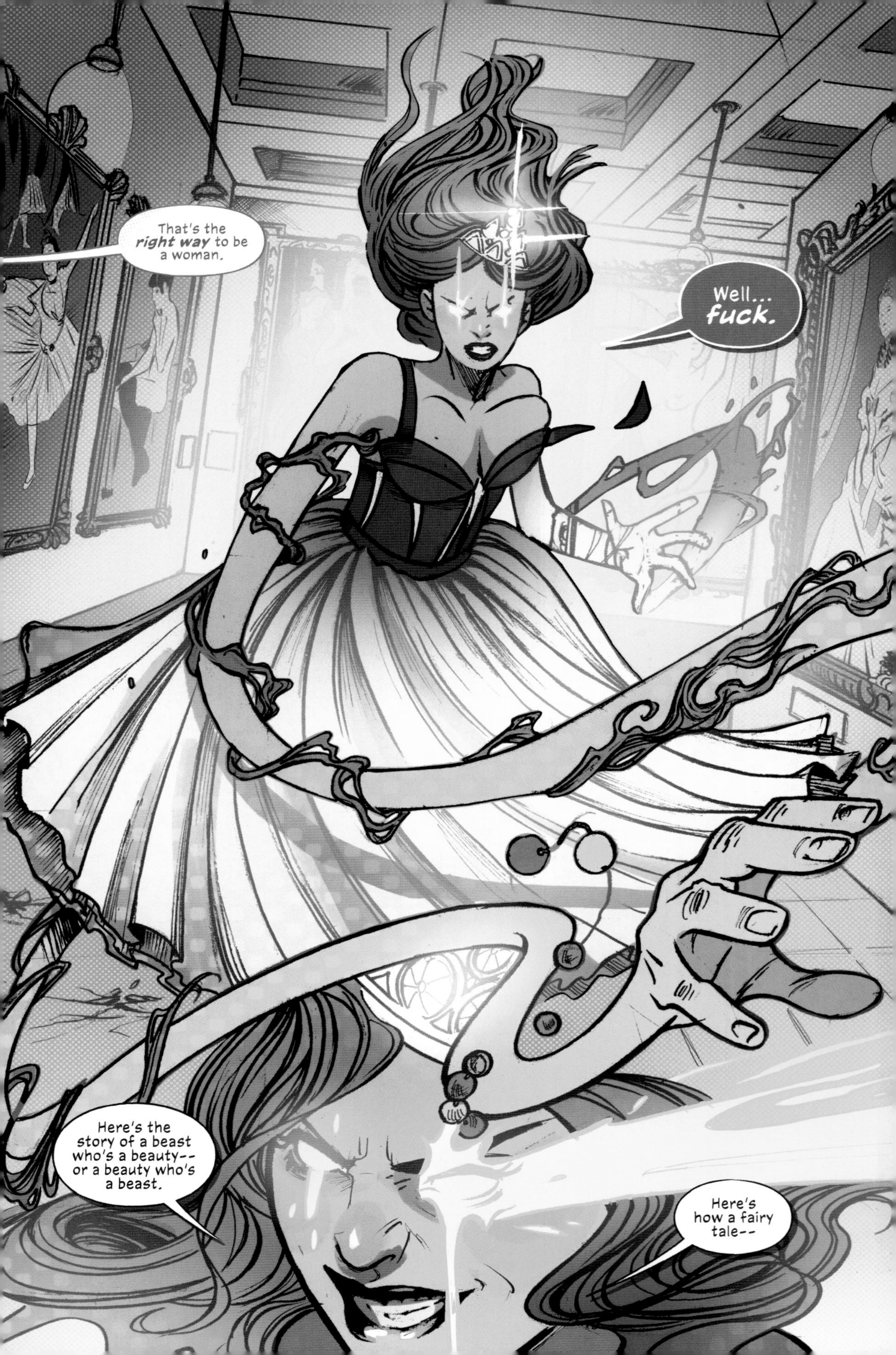
That's the right way to be a woman.
Well... fuck.
Here's the story of a beast who's a beauty-- or a beauty who's a beast.
Here's how a fairy tale--

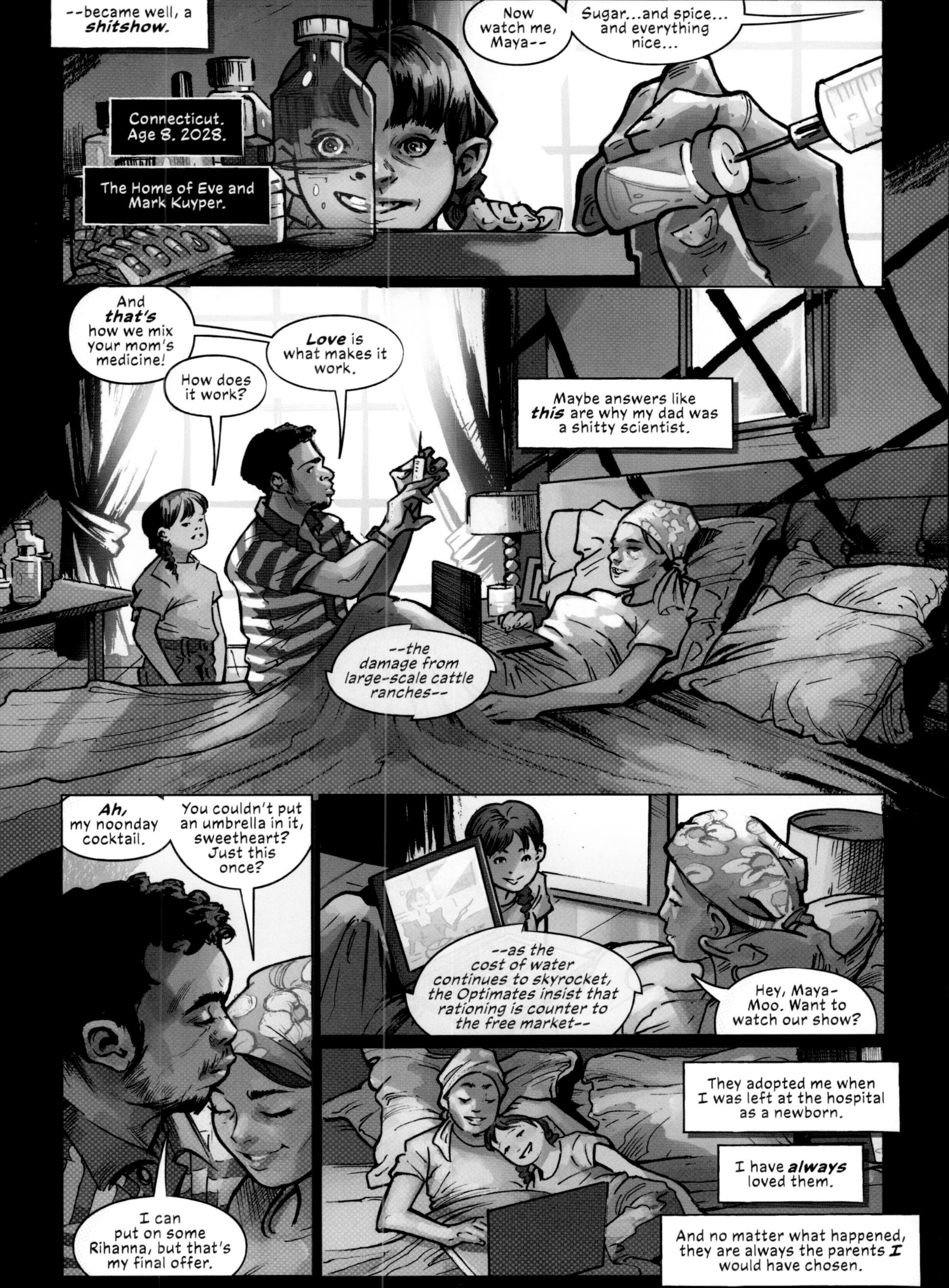
--became well, a *shitshow.*
Connecticut. Age 8. 2028.
The Home of Eve and Mark Kuyper.
Now watch me, Maya--
Sugar...and spice... and everything nice...
And *that's* how we mix your mom's medicine!
How does it work?
Love is what makes it work.
Maybe answers like *this* are why my dad was a shitty scientist.
--the damage from large-scale cattle ranches--
Ah, my noonday cocktail.
You couldn't put an umbrella in it, sweetheart? Just this once?
I can put on some Rihanna, but that's my final offer.
--as the cost of water continues to skyrocket, the Optimates insist that rationing is counter to the free market--
Hey, Maya-Moo. Want to watch our show?
They adopted me when I was left at the hospital as a newborn.
I have *always* loved them.
And no matter what happened, they are always the parents *I* would have chosen.

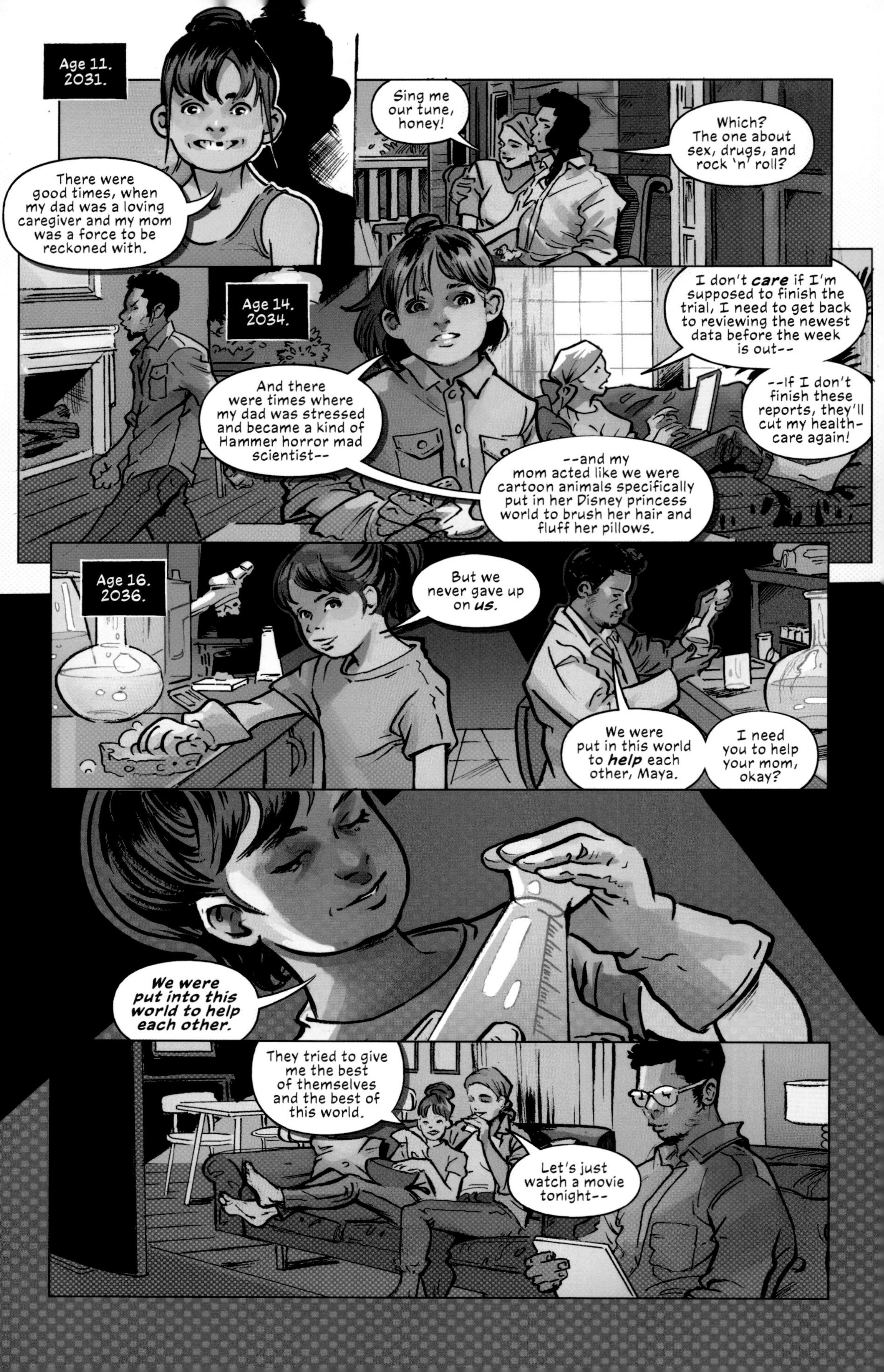
Age 11. 2031.
There were good times, when my dad was a loving caregiver and my mom was a force to be reckoned with.
Sing me our tune, honey!
Which? The one about sex, drugs, and rock 'n' roll?
Age 14. 2034.
And there were times where my dad was stressed and became a kind of Hammer horror mad scientist--
--and my mom acted like we were cartoon animals specifically put in her Disney princess world to brush her hair and fluff her pillows.
I don't *care* if I'm supposed to finish the trial, I need to get back to reviewing the newest data before the week is out--
--If I don't finish these reports, they'll cut my health-care again!
Age 16. 2036.
But we never gave up on *us*.
We were put in this world to *help* each other, Maya.
I need you to help your mom, okay?
We were put into this world to help each other.
They tried to give me the best of themselves and the best of this world.
Let's just watch a movie tonight--

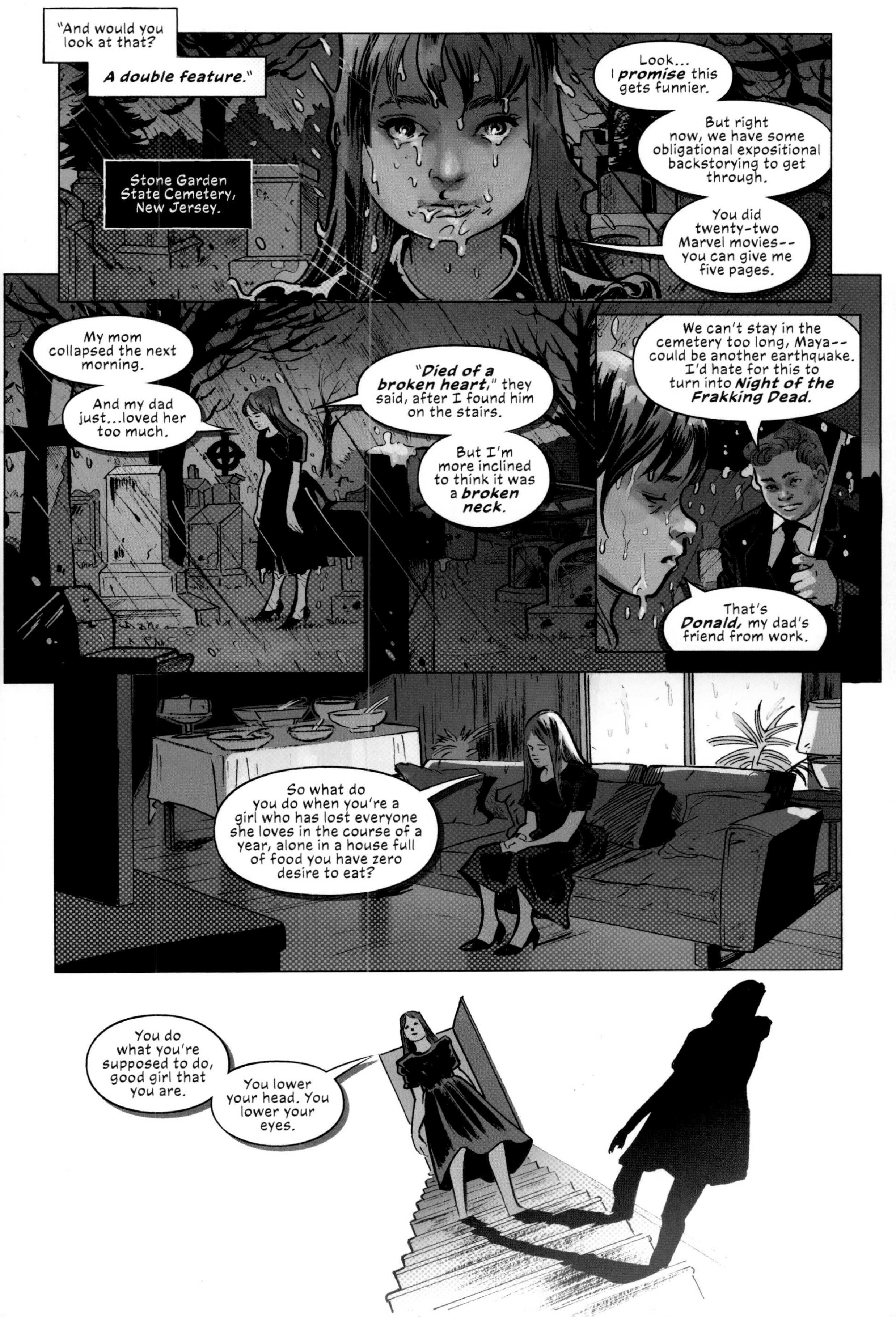
"And would you look at that?
A double feature."
Stone Garden State Cemetery, New Jersey.
Look... I promise this gets funnier.
But right now, we have some obligational expositional backstorying to get through.
You did twenty-two Marvel movies--you can give me five pages.
My mom collapsed the next morning.
And my dad just...loved her too much.
"Died of a broken heart," they said, after I found him on the stairs.
But I'm more inclined to think it was a broken neck.
We can't stay in the cemetery too long, Maya--could be another earthquake. I'd hate for this to turn into Night of the Frakking Dead.
That's Donald, my dad's friend from work.
So what do you do when you're a girl who has lost everyone she loves in the course of a year, alone in a house full of food you have zero desire to eat?
You do what you're supposed to do, good girl that you are.
You lower your head. You lower your eyes.

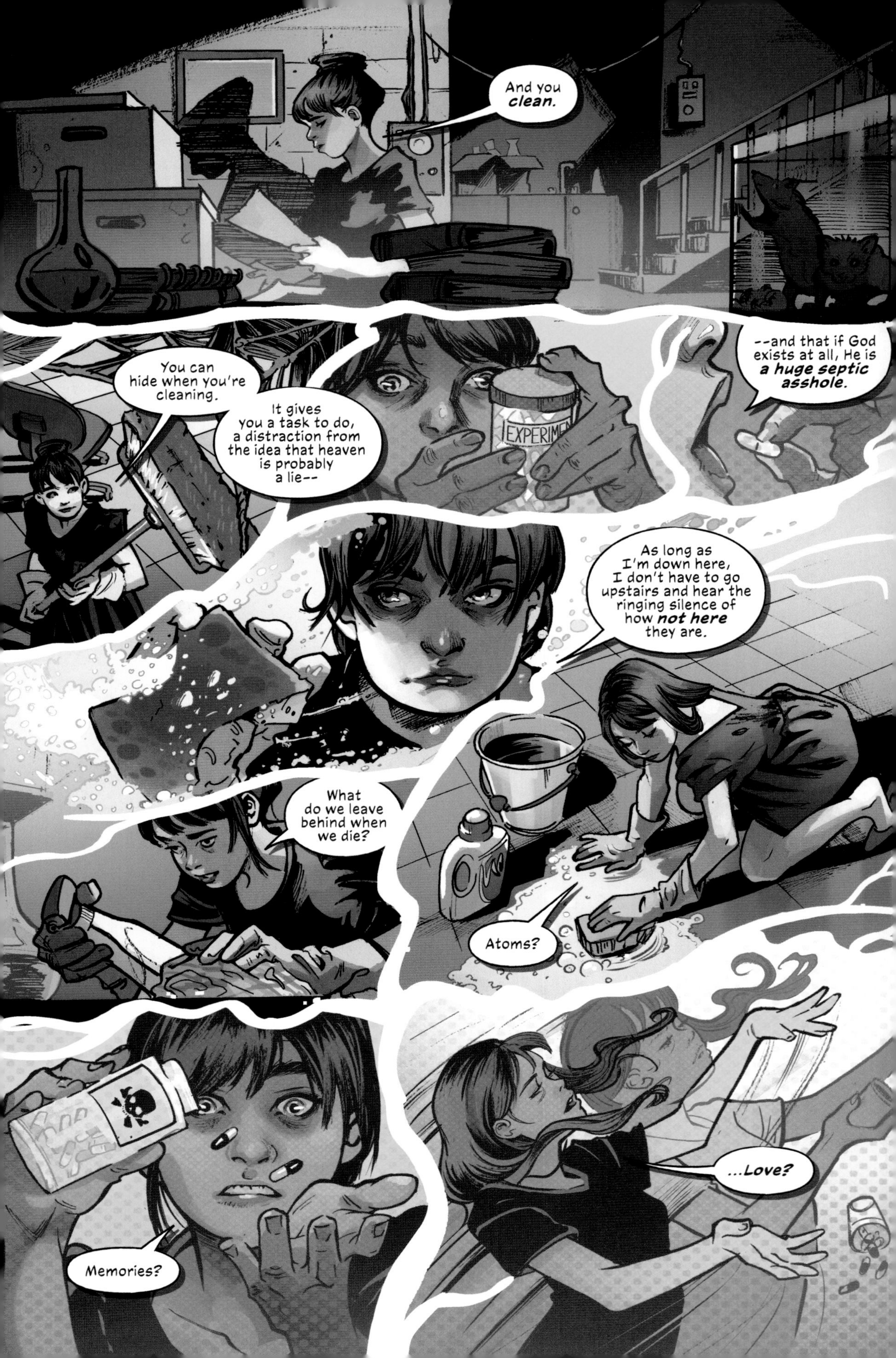

And you clean.
You can hide when you're cleaning.
It gives you a task to do, a distraction from the idea that heaven is probably a lie--
EXPERIMEN
--and that if God exists at all, He is a huge septic asshole.
As long as I'm down here, I don't have to go upstairs and hear the ringing silence of how not here they are.
What do we leave behind when we die?
Atoms?
Memories?
...Love?

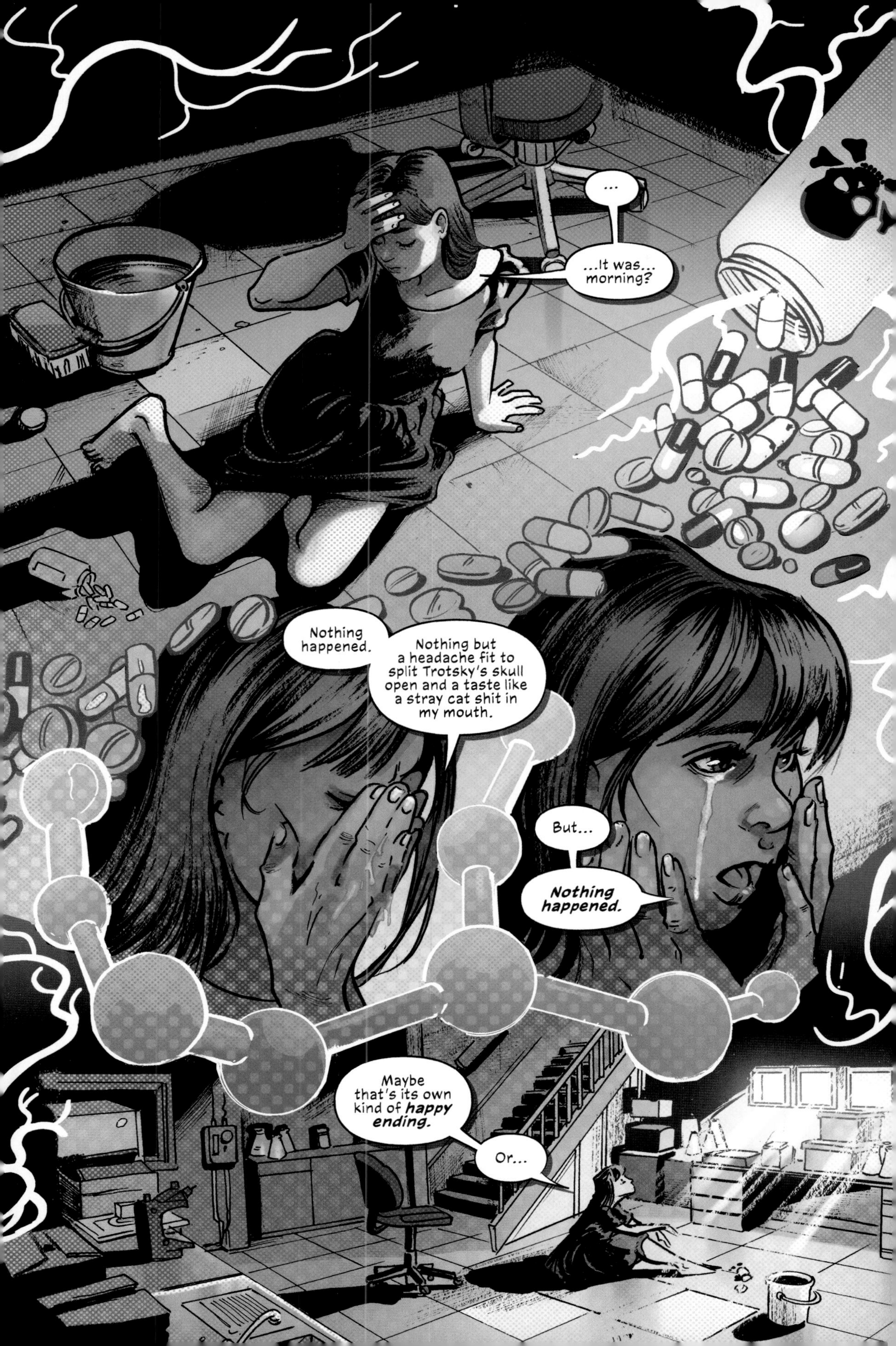
...
...It was... morning?
Nothing happened.
Nothing but a headache fit to split Trotsky's skull open and a taste like a stray cat shit in my mouth.
But...
Nothing happened.
Maybe that's its own kind of ***happy ending.***
Or...

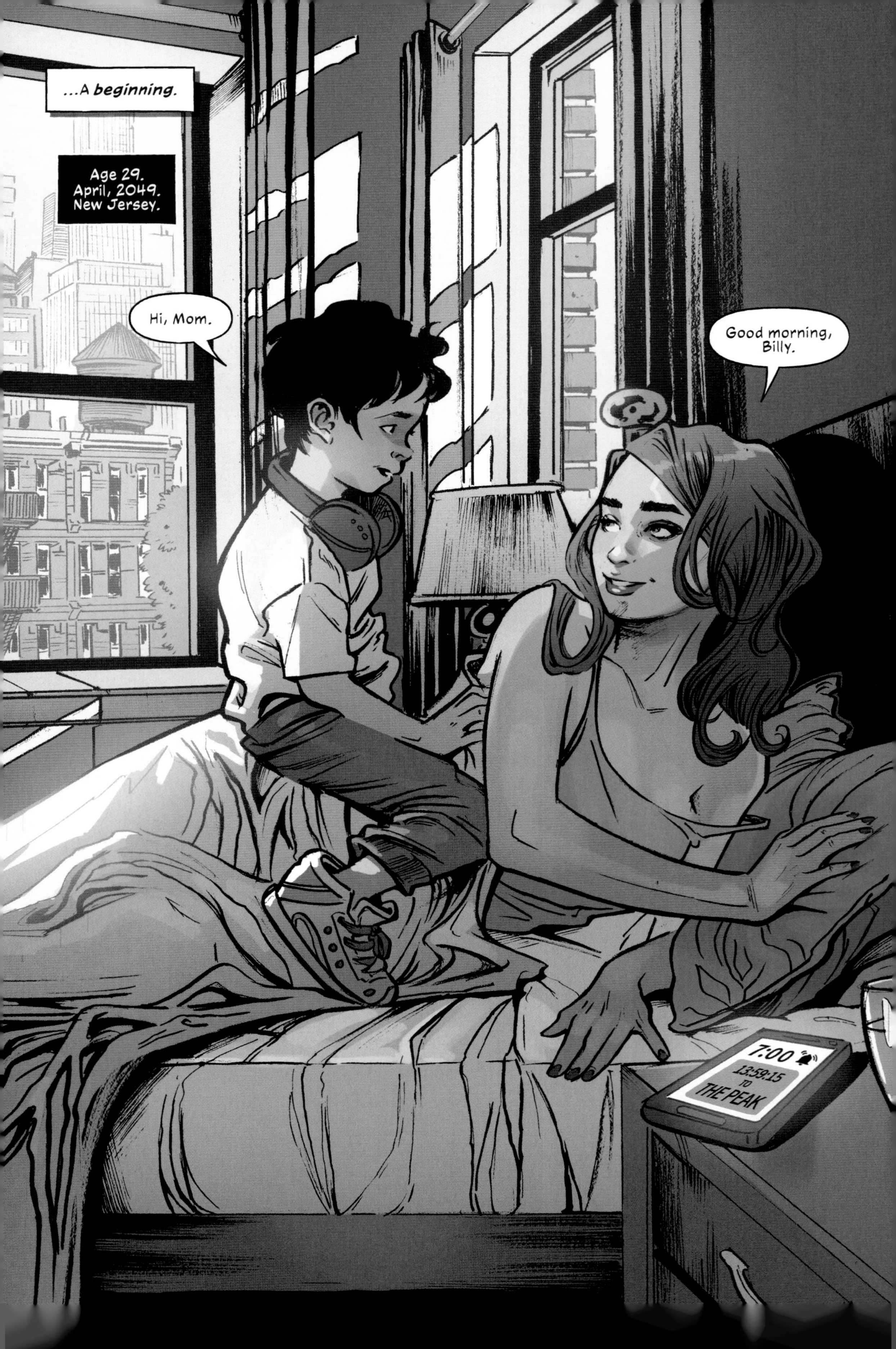
...A beginning.
Age 29.
April, 2049.
New Jersey.
Hi, Mom.
Good morning, Billy.
7:00
13:59:15
TO
THE PEAK

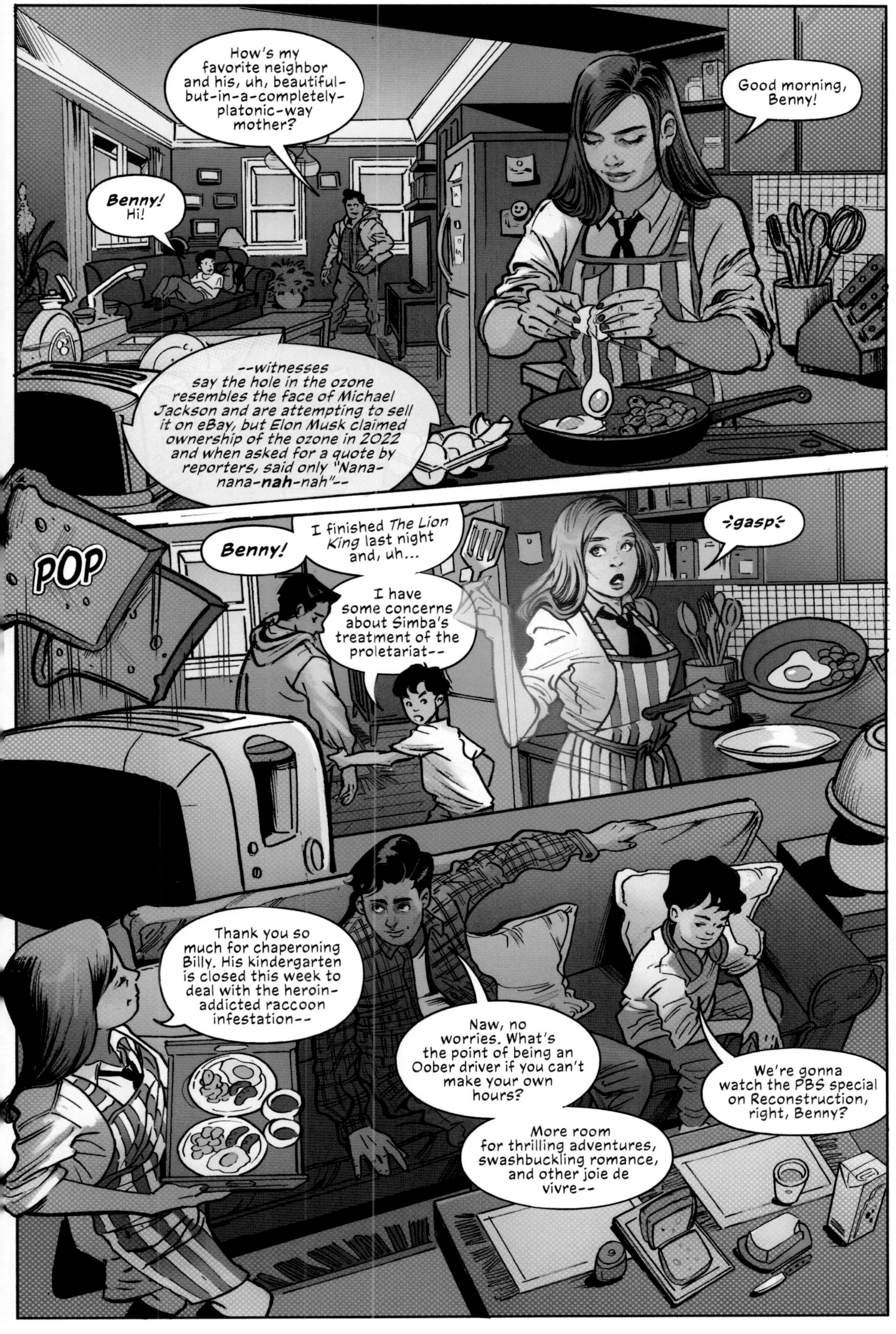
How's my favorite neighbor and his, uh, beautiful-but-in-a-completely-platonic-way mother?
Good morning, Benny!
Benny! Hi!
--witnesses say the hole in the ozone resembles the face of Michael Jackson and are attempting to sell it on eBay, but Elon Musk claimed ownership of the ozone in 2022 and when asked for a quote by reporters, said only "Nana-nana-**nah**-nah"--
POP
Benny!
I finished *The Lion King* last night and, uh...
I have some concerns about Simba's treatment of the proletariat--
gasp
Thank you so much for chaperoning Billy. His kindergarten is closed this week to deal with the heroin-addicted raccoon infestation--
Naw, no worries. What's the point of being an Ober driver if you can't make your own hours?
More room for thrilling adventures, swashbuckling romance, and other joie de vivre--
We're gonna watch the PBS special on Reconstruction, right, Benny?

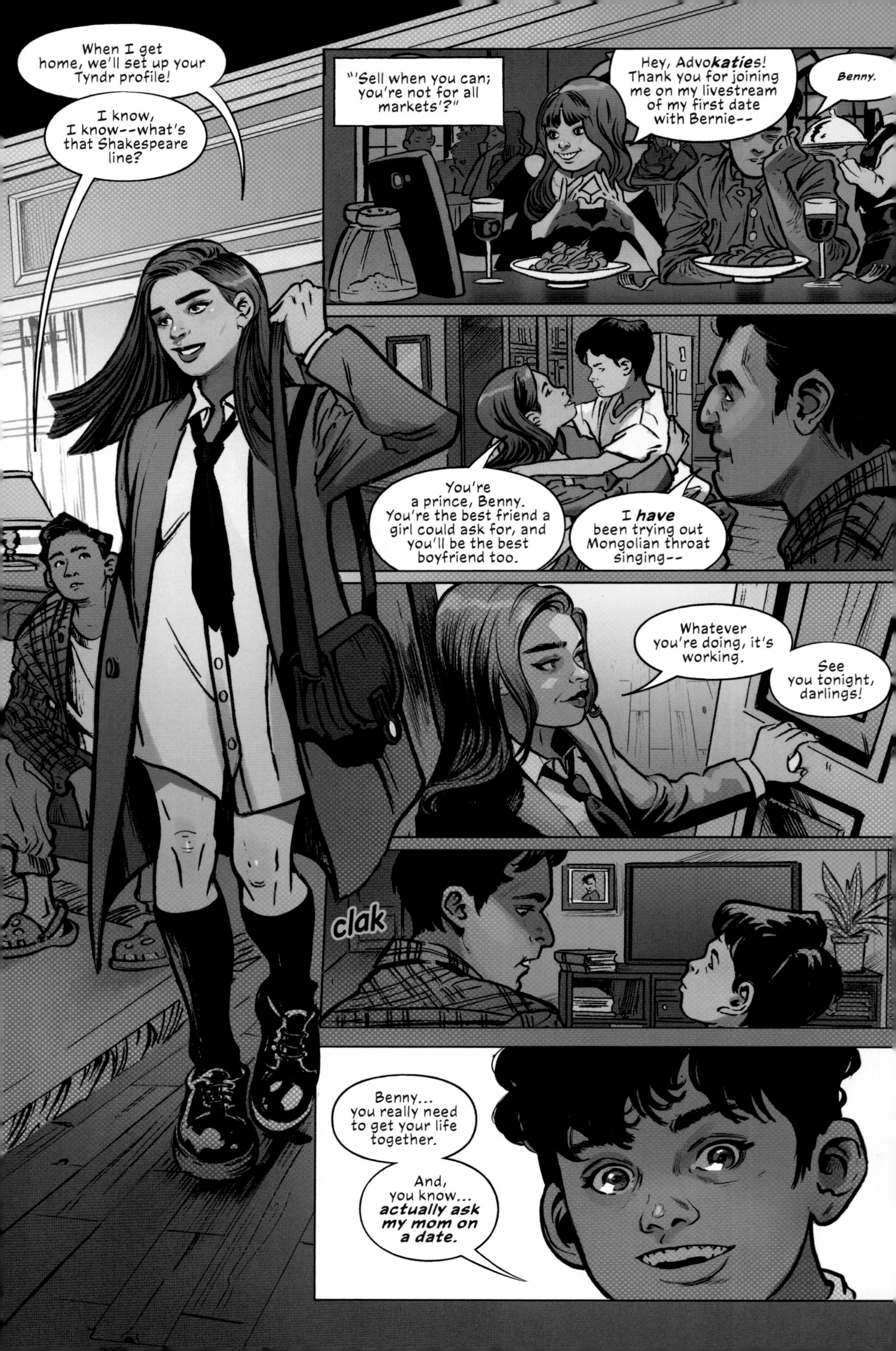

When I get home, we'll set up your Tyndr profile!
I know, I know--what's that Shakespeare line?
"'Sell when you can; you're not for all markets'?"
Hey, Advo**katies**! Thank you for joining me on my livestream of my first date with Bernie--
Benny.
You're a prince, Benny. You're the best friend a girl could ask for, and you'll be the best boyfriend too.
I **have** been trying out Mongolian throat singing--
Whatever you're doing, it's working.
See you tonight, darlings!
clak
Benny... you really need to get your life together.
And, you know... ***actually ask my mom on a date.***

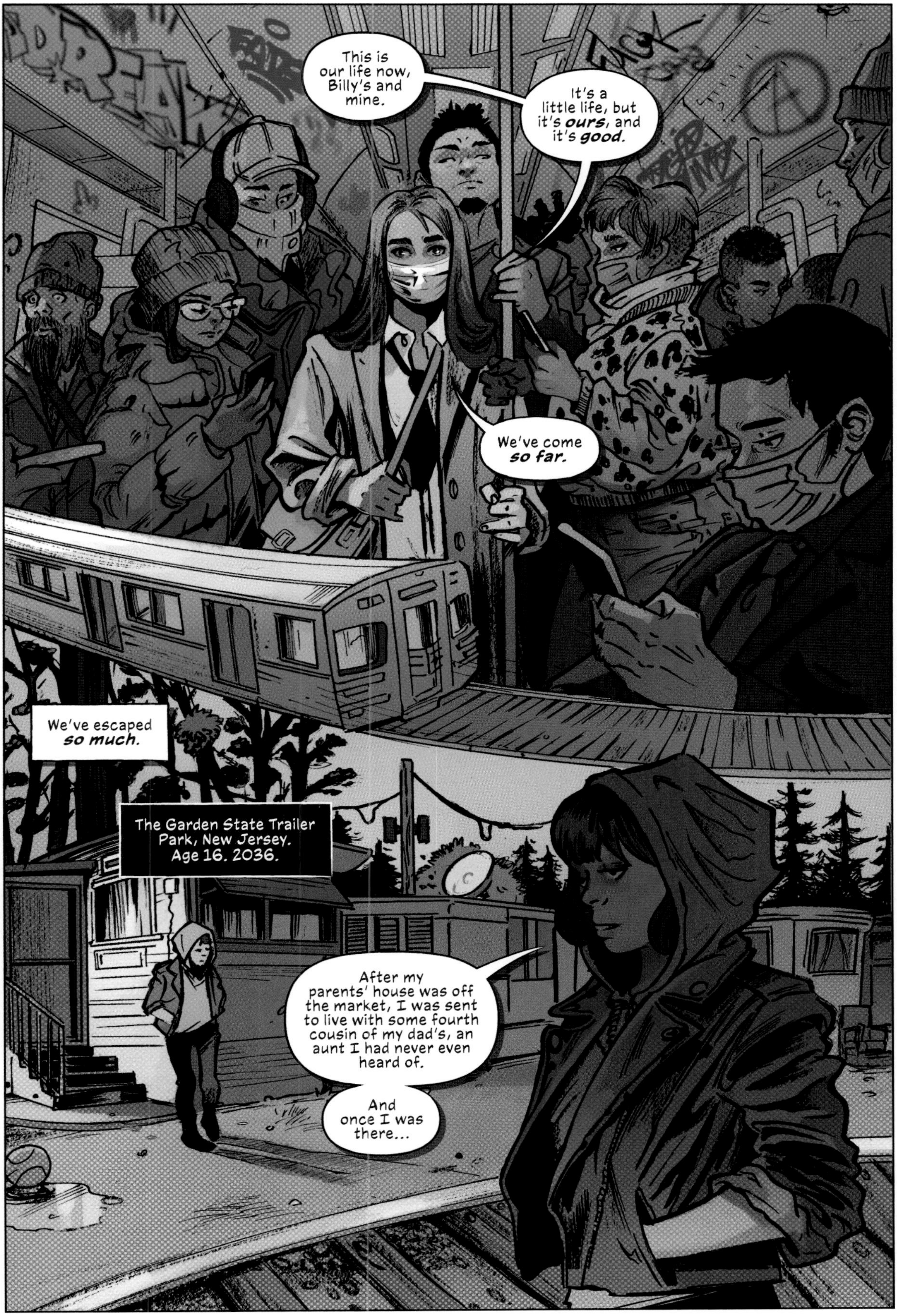
This is our life now, Billy's and mine.
It's a little life, but it's ***ours***, and it's ***good.***
We've come ***so far.***
We've escaped ***so much.***
The Garden State Trailer Park, New Jersey. Age 16. 2036.
After my parents' house was off the market, I was sent to live with some fourth cousin of my dad's, an aunt I had never even heard of.
And once I was there...

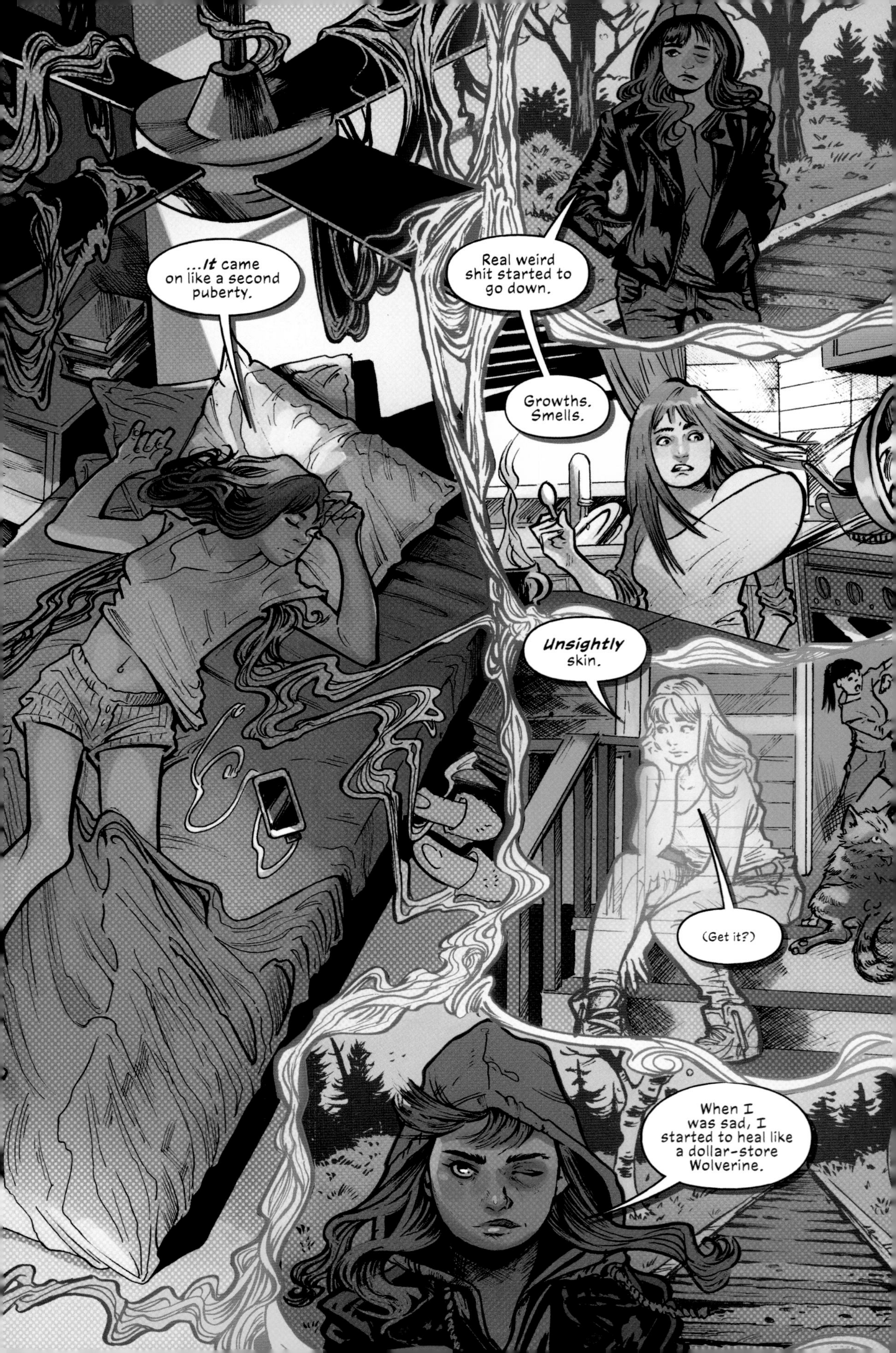

...*It* came on like a second puberty.
Real weird shit started to go down.
Growths. Smells.
Unsightly skin.
(Get it?)
When I was sad, I started to heal like a dollar-store Wolverine.

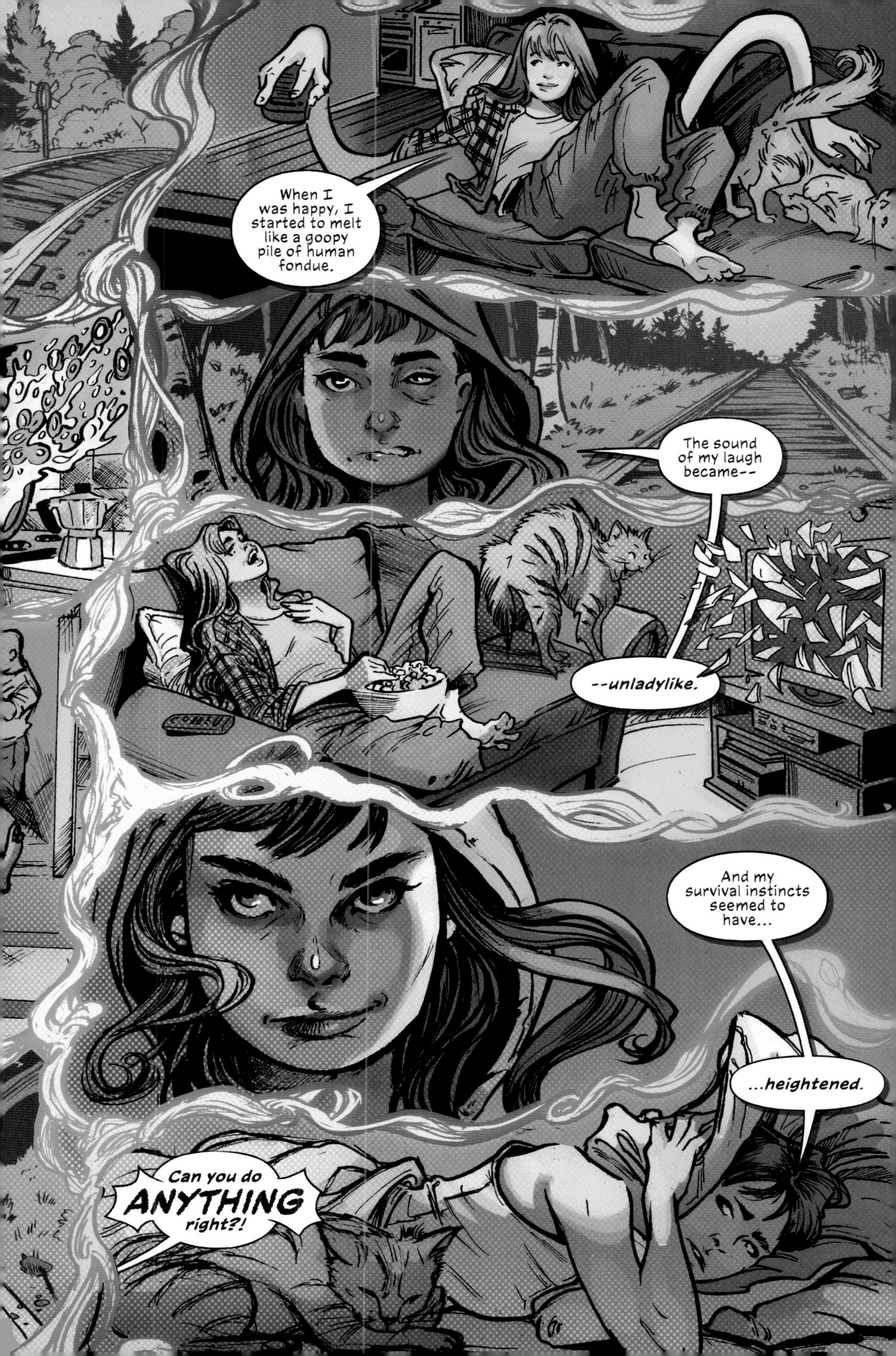
When I was happy, I started to melt like a goopy pile of human fondue.
The sound of my laugh became--
--unladylike.
And my survival instincts seemed to have...
...heightened.
Can you do ANYTHING right?!

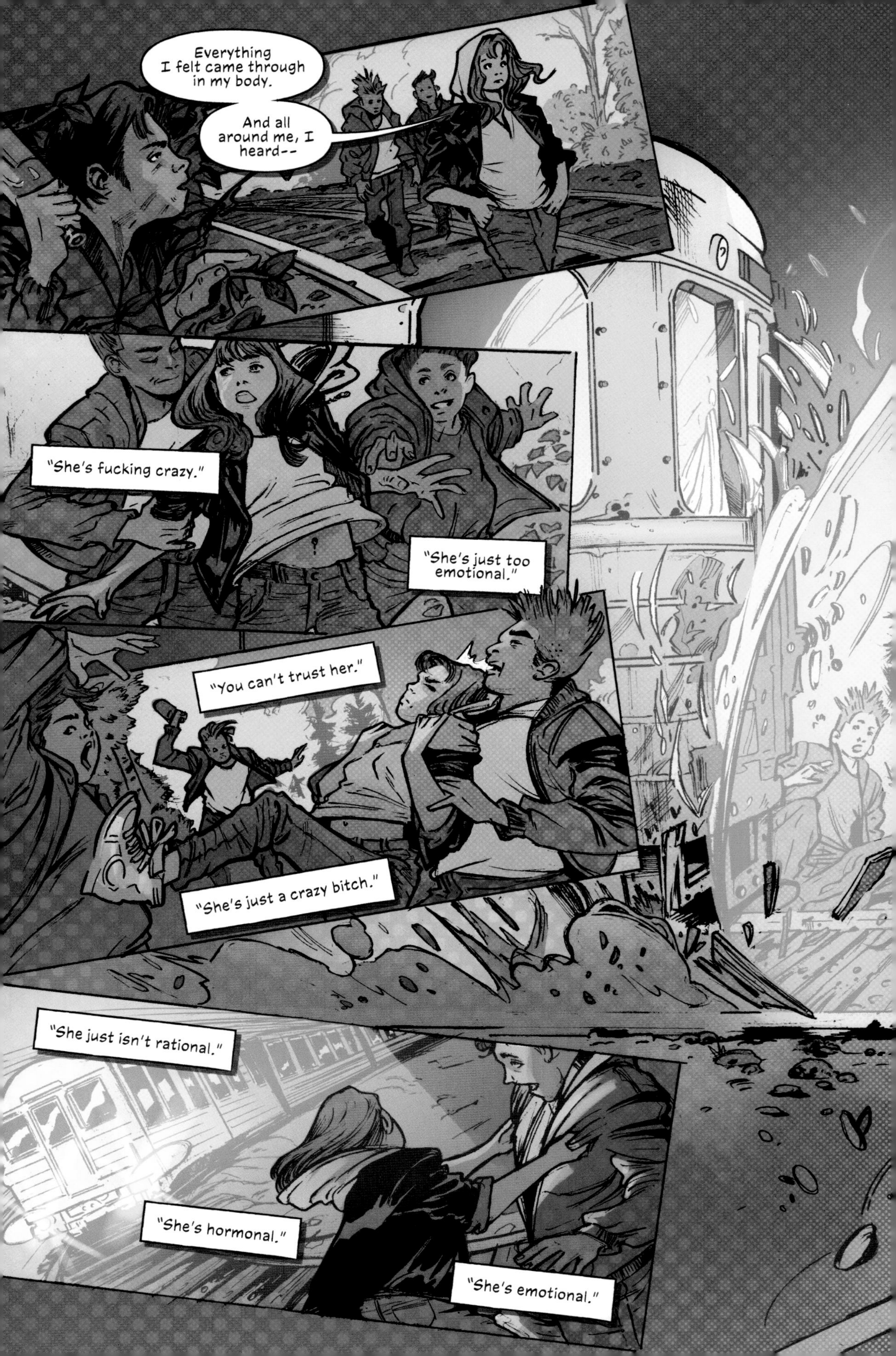
Everything I felt came through in my body.
And all around me, I heard--
"She's fucking crazy."
"She's just too emotional."
"You can't trust her."
"She's just a crazy bitch."
"She just isn't rational."
"She's hormonal."
"She's emotional."

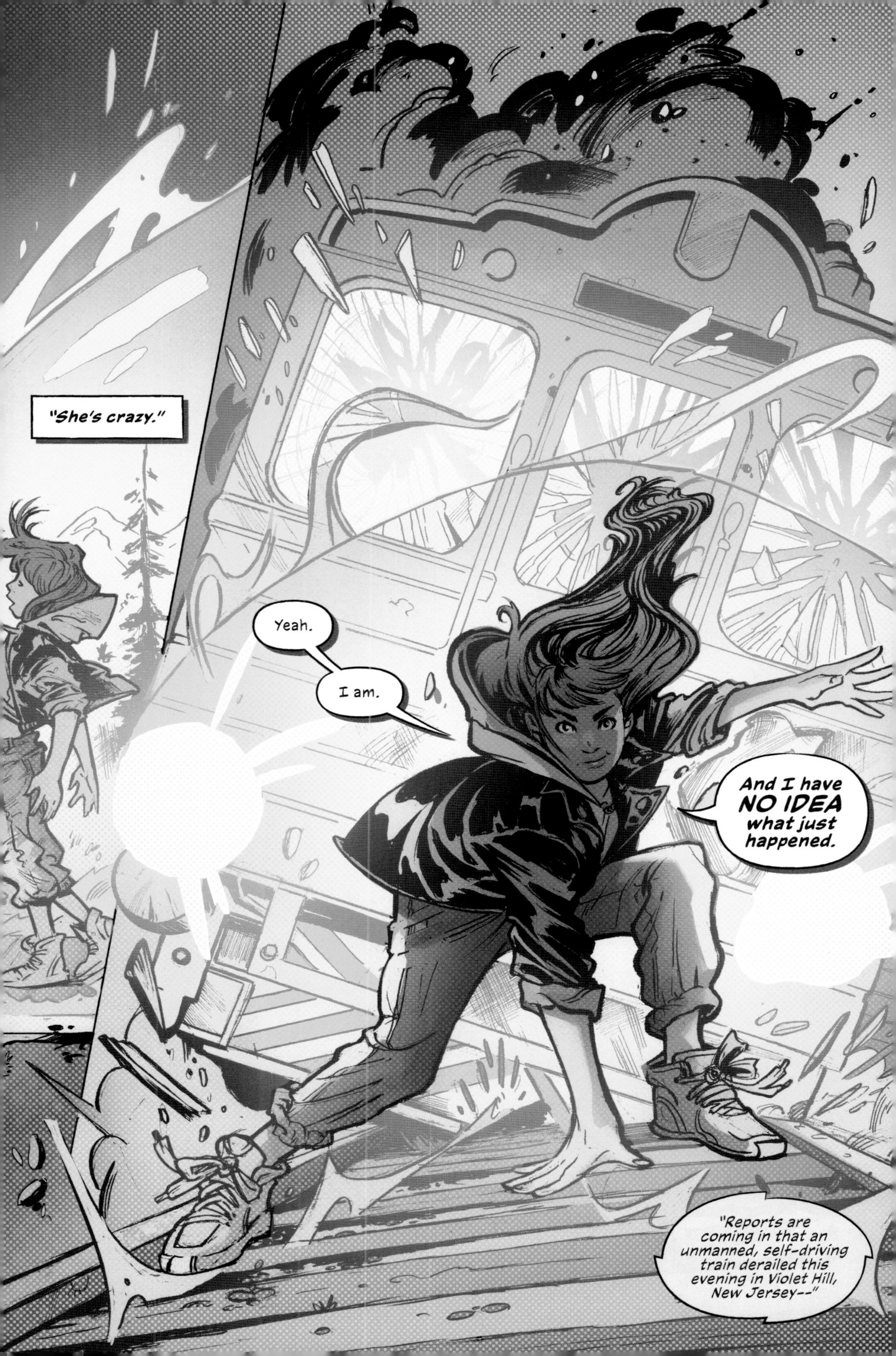
"She's crazy."
Yeah.
I am.
And I have NO IDEA what just happened.
"Reports are coming in that an unmanned, self-driving train derailed this evening in Violet Hill, New Jersey--"

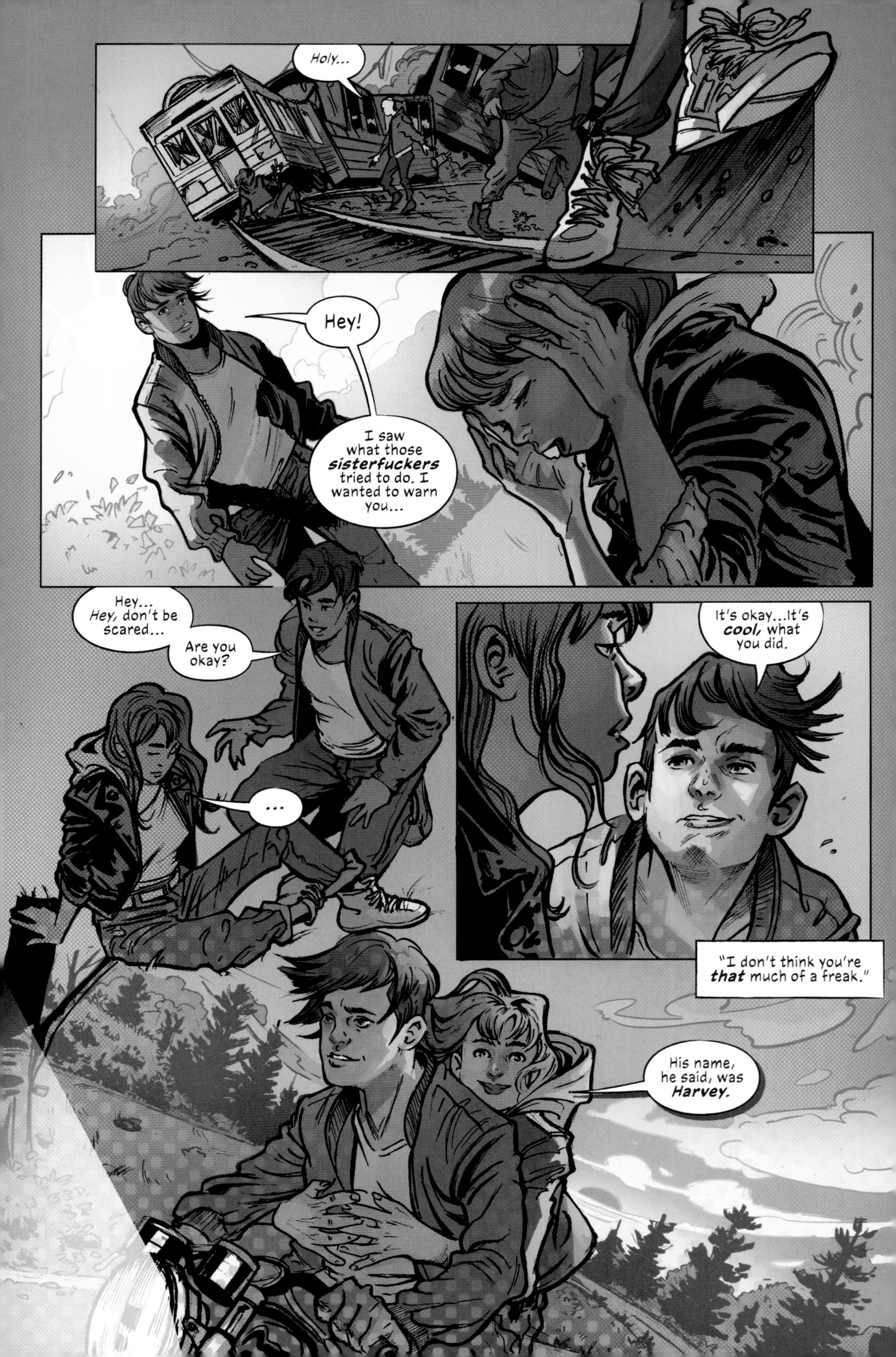
Holy...
Hey!
I saw what those *sisterfuckers* tried to do. I wanted to warn you...
Hey... *Hey,* don't be scared...
Are you okay?
...
It's okay...It's *cool,* what you did.
"I don't think you're *that* much of a freak."
His name, he said, was *Harvey.*

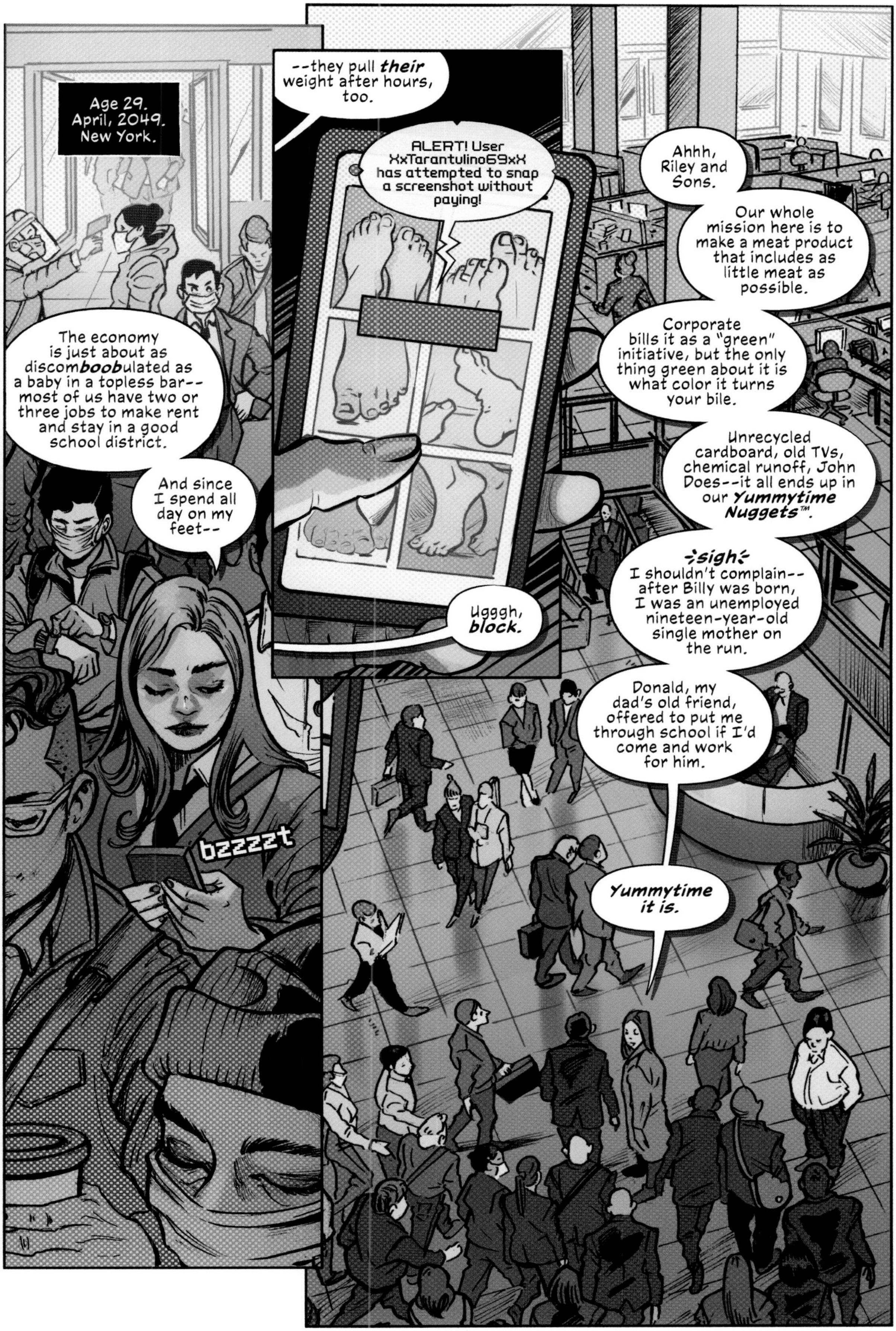
Age 29.
April, 2049.
New York.
The economy is just about as discom**boob**ulated as a baby in a topless bar--most of us have two or three jobs to make rent and stay in a good school district.
And since I spend all day on my feet--
bzzzzt
--they pull ***their*** weight after hours, too.
ALERT! User XxTarantulino69xX has attempted to snap a screenshot without paying!
Ugggh, ***block.***
Ahhh, Riley and Sons.
Our whole mission here is to make a meat product that includes as little meat as possible.
Corporate bills it as a "green" initiative, but the only thing green about it is what color it turns your bile.
Unrecycled cardboard, old TVs, chemical runoff, John Does--it all ends up in our ***Yummytime Nuggets™***.
sigh
I shouldn't complain--after Billy was born, I was an unemployed nineteen-year-old single mother on the run.
Donald, my dad's old friend, offered to put me through school if I'd come and work for him.
Yummytime it is.

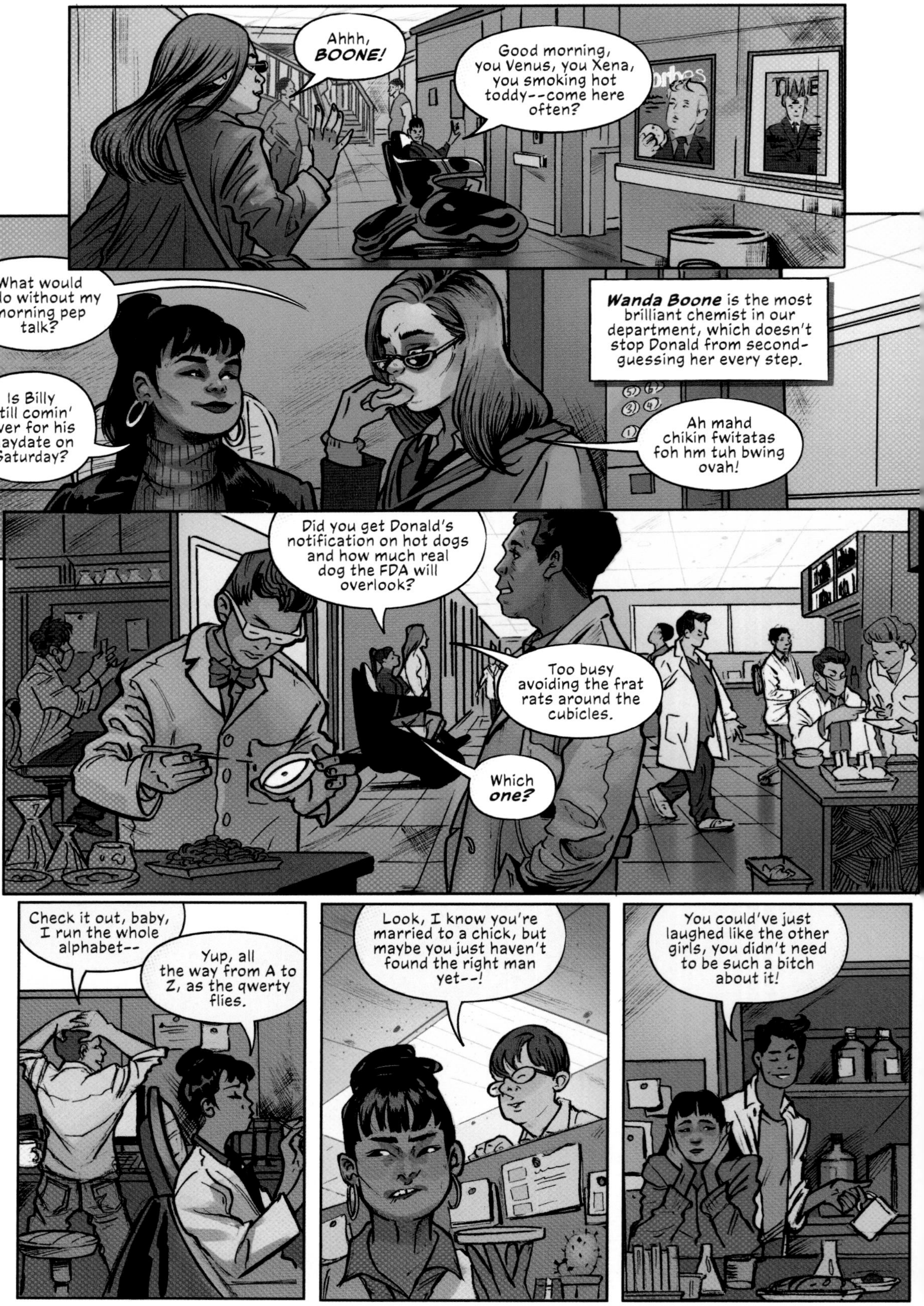
Ahhh, BOONE!
Good morning, you Venus, you Xena, you smoking hot toddy--come here often?
Forbes
TIME
What would I do without my morning pep talk?
Wanda Boone is the most brilliant chemist in our department, which doesn't stop Donald from second-guessing her every step.
Is Billy still comin' over for his playdate on Saturday?
Ah mahd chikin fwitatas foh hm tuh bwing ovah!
Did you get Donald's notification on hot dogs and how much real dog the FDA will overlook?
Too busy avoiding the frat rats around the cubicles.
Which one?
Check it out, baby, I run the whole alphabet--
Yup, all the way from A to Z, as the qwerty flies.
Look, I know you're married to a chick, but maybe you just haven't found the right man yet--!
You could've just laughed like the other girls, you didn't need to be such a bitch about it!

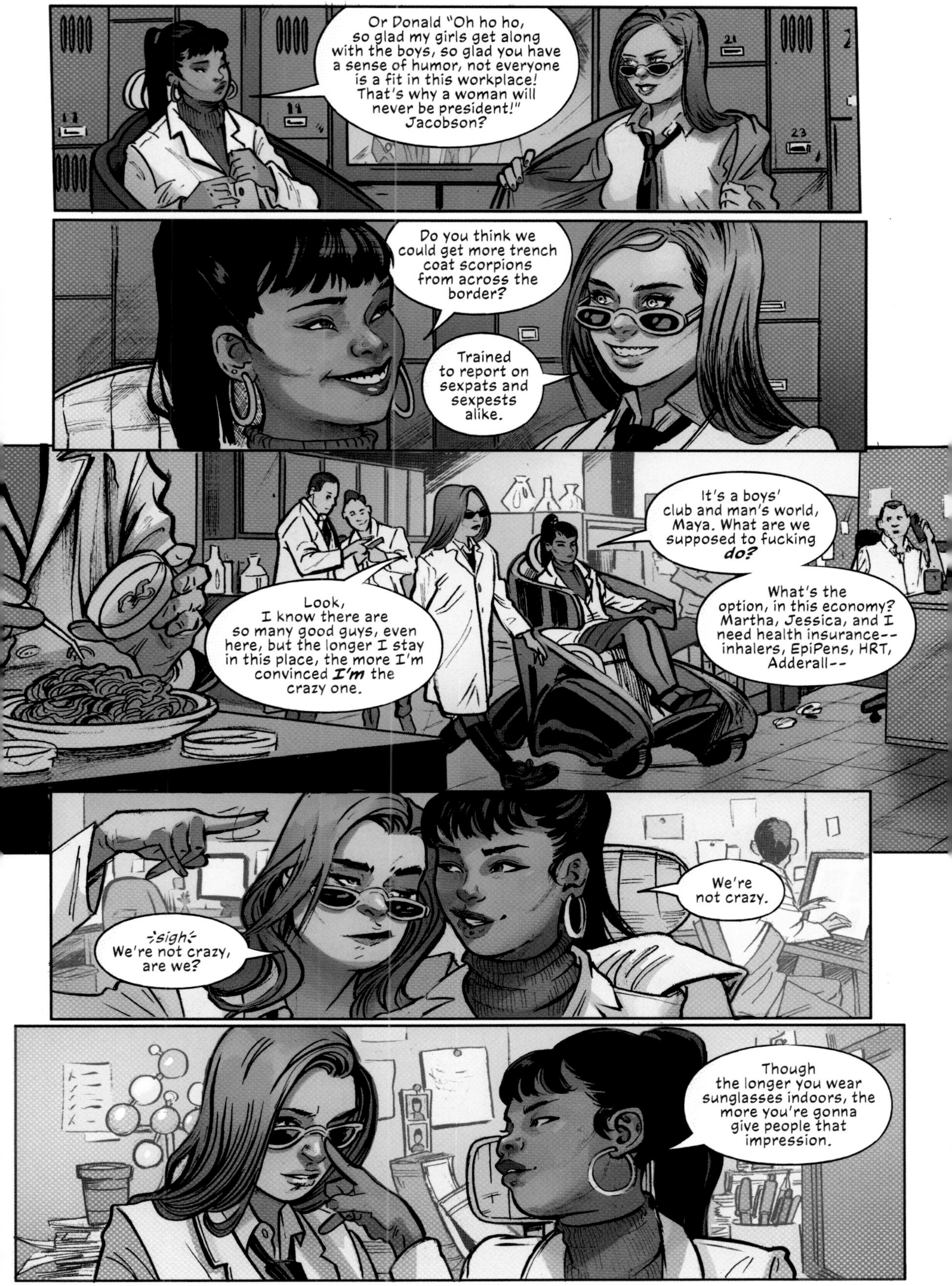
Or Donald "Oh ho ho, so glad my girls get along with the boys, so glad you have a sense of humor, not everyone is a fit in this workplace! That's why a woman will never be president!" Jacobson?
Do you think we could get more trench coat scorpions from across the border?
Trained to report on sexpats and sexpests alike.
It's a boys' club and man's world, Maya. What are we supposed to fucking ***do?***
What's the option, in this economy? Martha, Jessica, and I need health insurance-- inhalers, EpiPens, HRT, Adderall--
Look, I know there are so many good guys, even here, but the longer I stay in this place, the more I'm convinced ***I'm*** the crazy one.
We're not crazy.
-sigh- We're not crazy, are we?
Though the longer you wear sunglasses indoors, the more you're gonna give people that impression.

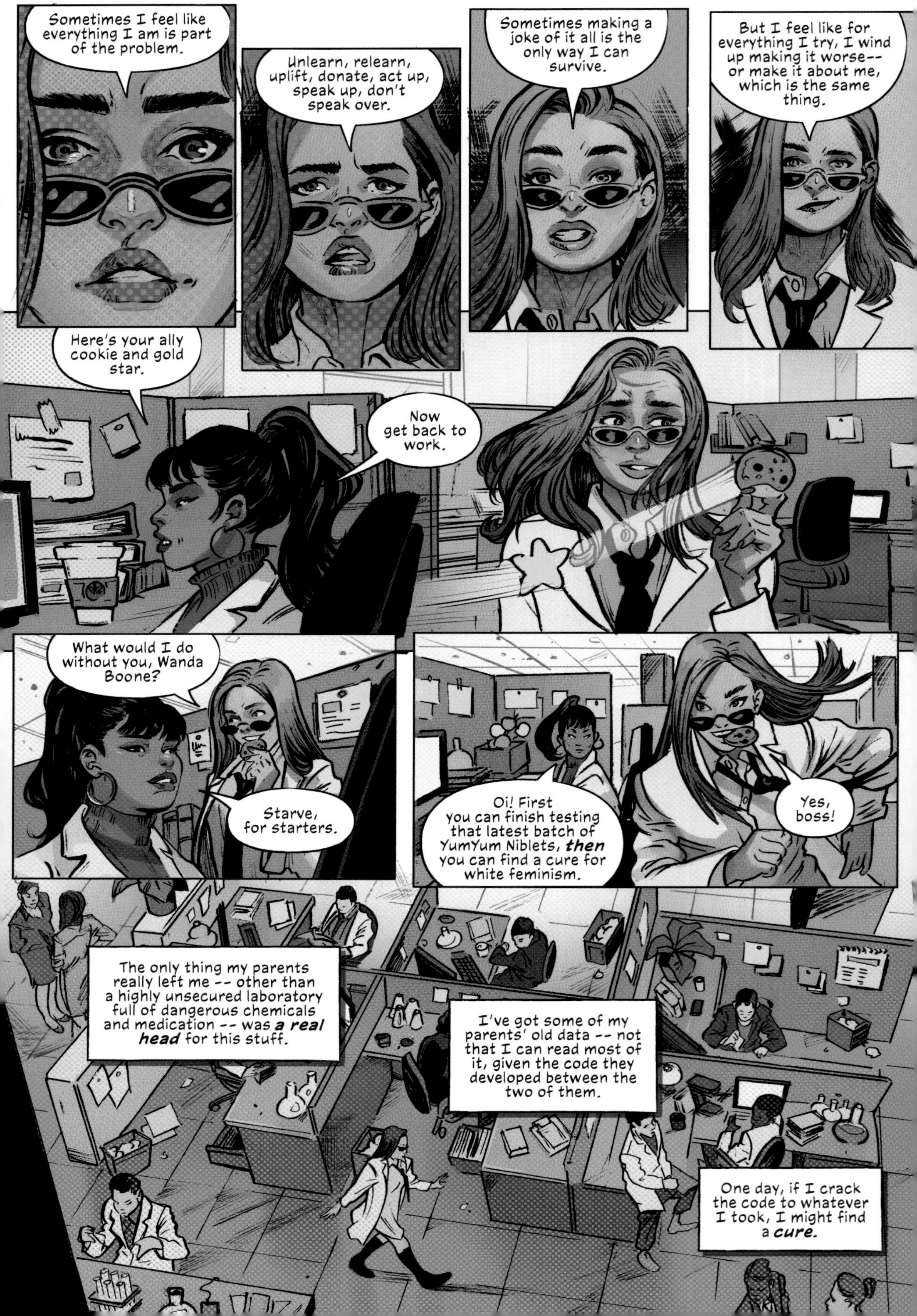
Sometimes I feel like everything I am is part of the problem.
Unlearn, relearn, uplift, donate, act up, speak up, don't speak over.
Sometimes making a joke of it all is the only way I can survive.
But I feel like for everything I try, I wind up making it worse-- or make it about me, which is the same thing.
Here's your ally cookie and gold star.
Now get back to work.
What would I do without you, Wanda Boone?
Starve, for starters.
Oi! First you can finish testing that latest batch of YumYum Niblets, **then** you can find a cure for white feminism.
Yes, boss!
The only thing my parents really left me -- other than a highly unsecured laboratory full of dangerous chemicals and medication -- was **a real head** for this stuff.
I've got some of my parents' old data -- not that I can read most of it, given the code they developed between the two of them.
One day, if I crack the code to whatever I took, I might find a **cure.**

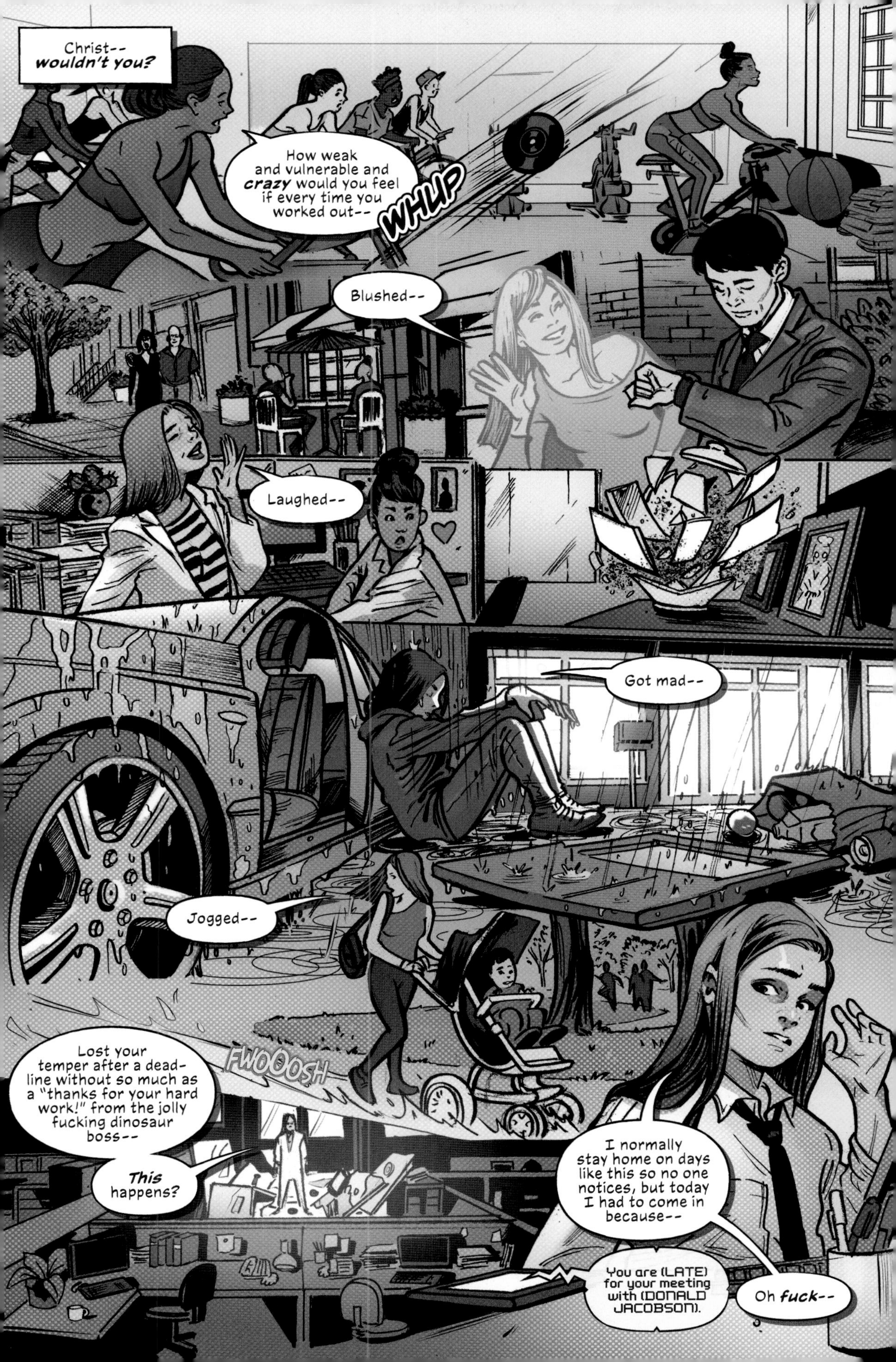
Christ-- *wouldn't you?*
How weak and vulnerable and *crazy* would you feel if every time you worked out--
WHLIP
Blushed--
Laughed--
Got mad--
Jogged--
FWOOOSH
Lost your temper after a deadline without so much as a "thanks for your hard work!" from the jolly fucking dinosaur boss--
This happens?
I normally stay home on days like this so no one notices, but today I had to come in because--
You are (LATE) for your meeting with (DONALD JACOBSON).
Oh *fuck*--

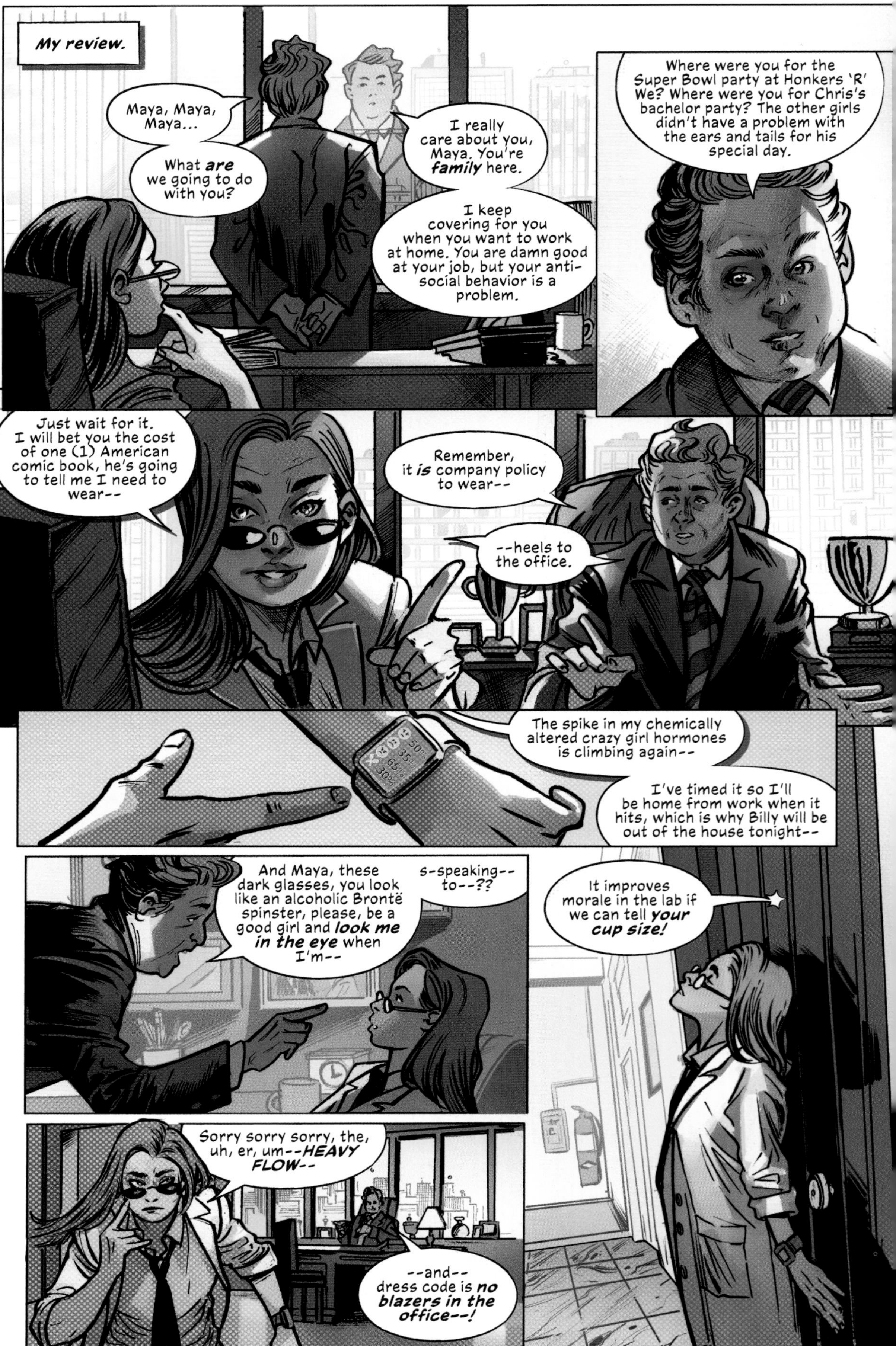

My review.
Maya, Maya, Maya...
What are we going to do with you?
I really care about you, Maya. You're family here.
I keep covering for you when you want to work at home. You are damn good at your job, but your anti-social behavior is a problem.
Where were you for the Super Bowl party at Honkers 'R' We? Where were you for Chris's bachelor party? The other girls didn't have a problem with the ears and tails for his special day.
Just wait for it. I will bet you the cost of one (1) American comic book, he's going to tell me I need to wear--
Remember, it is company policy to wear--
--heels to the office.
50%
35%
65%
30%
The spike in my chemically altered crazy girl hormones is climbing again--
I've timed it so I'll be home from work when it hits, which is why Billy will be out of the house tonight--
And Maya, these dark glasses, you look like an alcoholic Brontë spinster, please, be a good girl and look me in the eye when I'm--
s-speaking-- to--??
It improves morale in the lab if we can tell your cup size!
Sorry sorry sorry, the, uh, er, um--HEAVY FLOW--
--and-- dress code is no blazers in the office--!

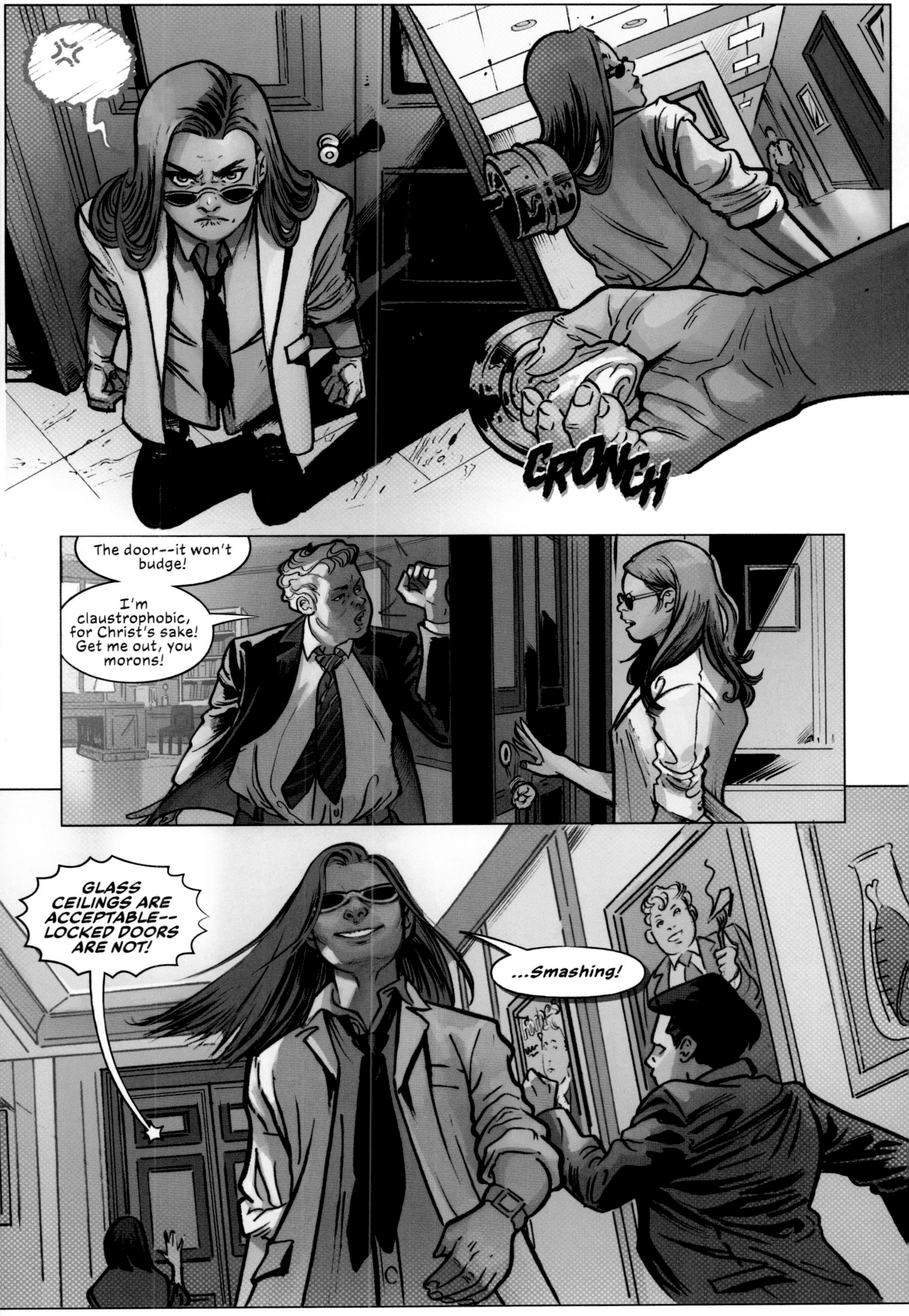
CRONCH
The door--it won't budge!
I'm claustrophobic, for Christ's sake! Get me out, you morons!
GLASS CEILINGS ARE ACCEPTABLE-- LOCKED DOORS ARE NOT!
...Smashing!

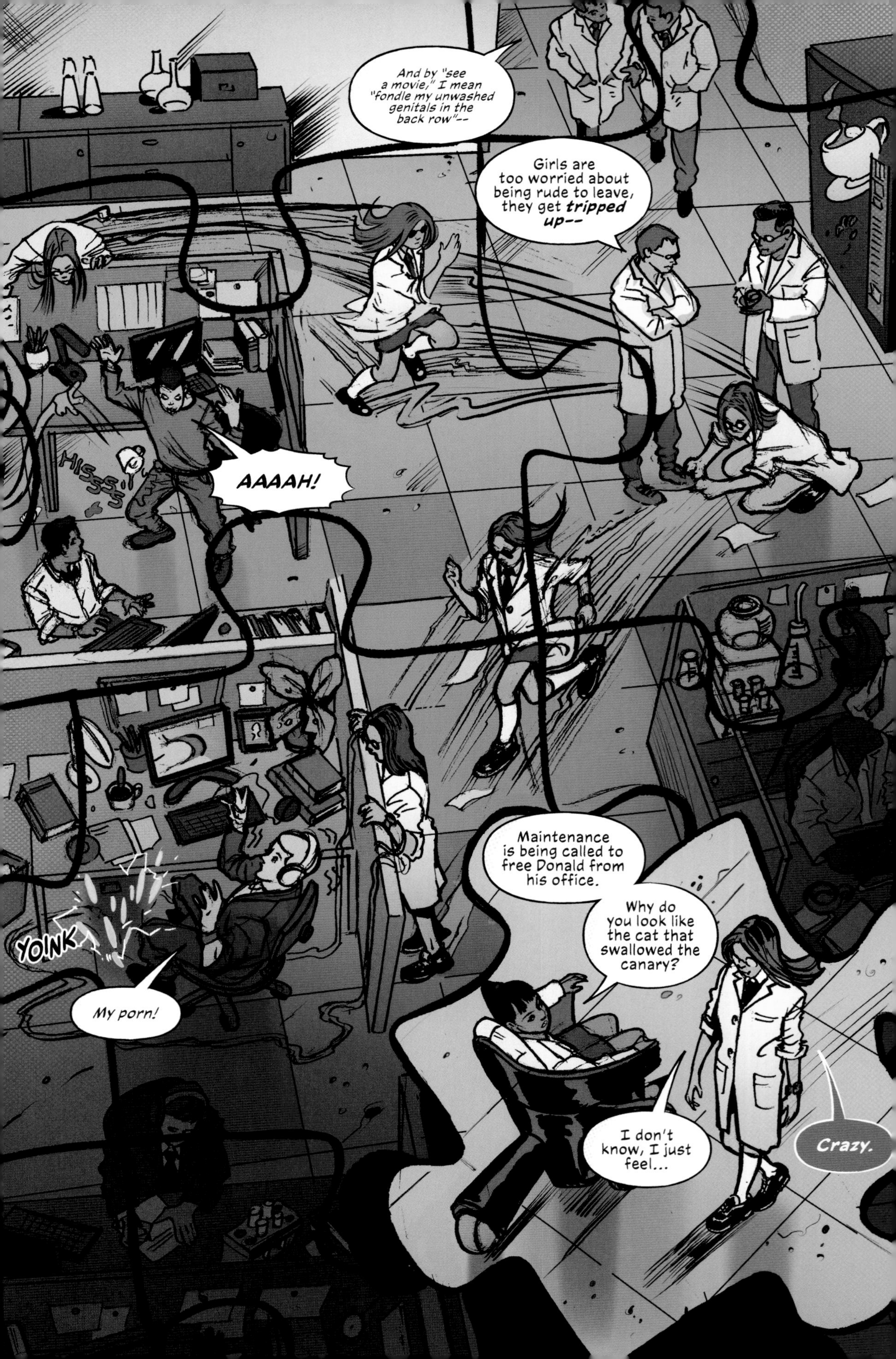
And by "see a movie," I mean "fondle my unwashed genitals in the back row"--
Girls are too worried about being rude to leave, they get *tripped up*--
HISSSS
AAAAH!
YOINK
My porn!
Maintenance is being called to free Donald from his office.
Why do you look like the cat that swallowed the canary?
I don't know, I just feel...
Crazy.

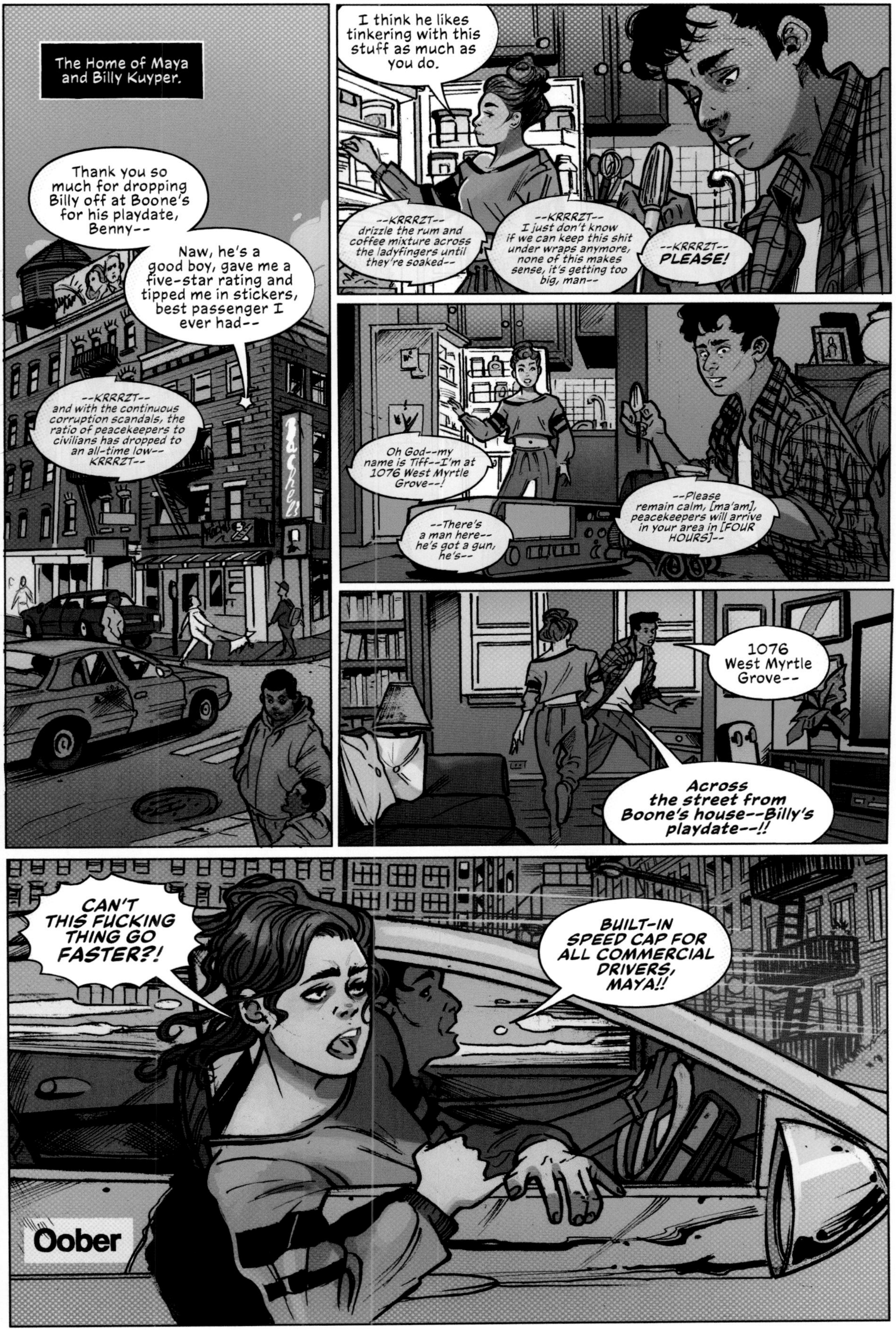

The Home of Maya and Billy Kuyper.
Thank you so much for dropping Billy off at Boone's for his playdate, Benny--
Naw, he's a good boy, gave me a five-star rating and tipped me in stickers, best passenger I ever had--
--KRRRZT-- and with the continuous corruption scandals, the ratio of peacekeepers to civilians has dropped to an all-time low-- KRRRZT--
I think he likes tinkering with this stuff as much as you do.
--KRRRZT-- drizzle the rum and coffee mixture across the ladyfingers until they're soaked--
--KRRRZT-- I just don't know if we can keep this shit under wraps anymore, none of this makes sense, it's getting too big, man--
--KRRRZT-- PLEASE!
Oh God--my name is Tiff--I'm at 1076 West Myrtle Grove--!
--There's a man here-- he's got a gun, he's--
--Please remain calm, [ma'am], peacekeepers will arrive in your area in [FOUR HOURS]--
1076 West Myrtle Grove--
Across the street from Boone's house--Billy's playdate--!!
CAN'T THIS FUCKING THING GO FASTER?!
BUILT-IN SPEED CAP FOR ALL COMMERCIAL DRIVERS, MAYA!!
Oober

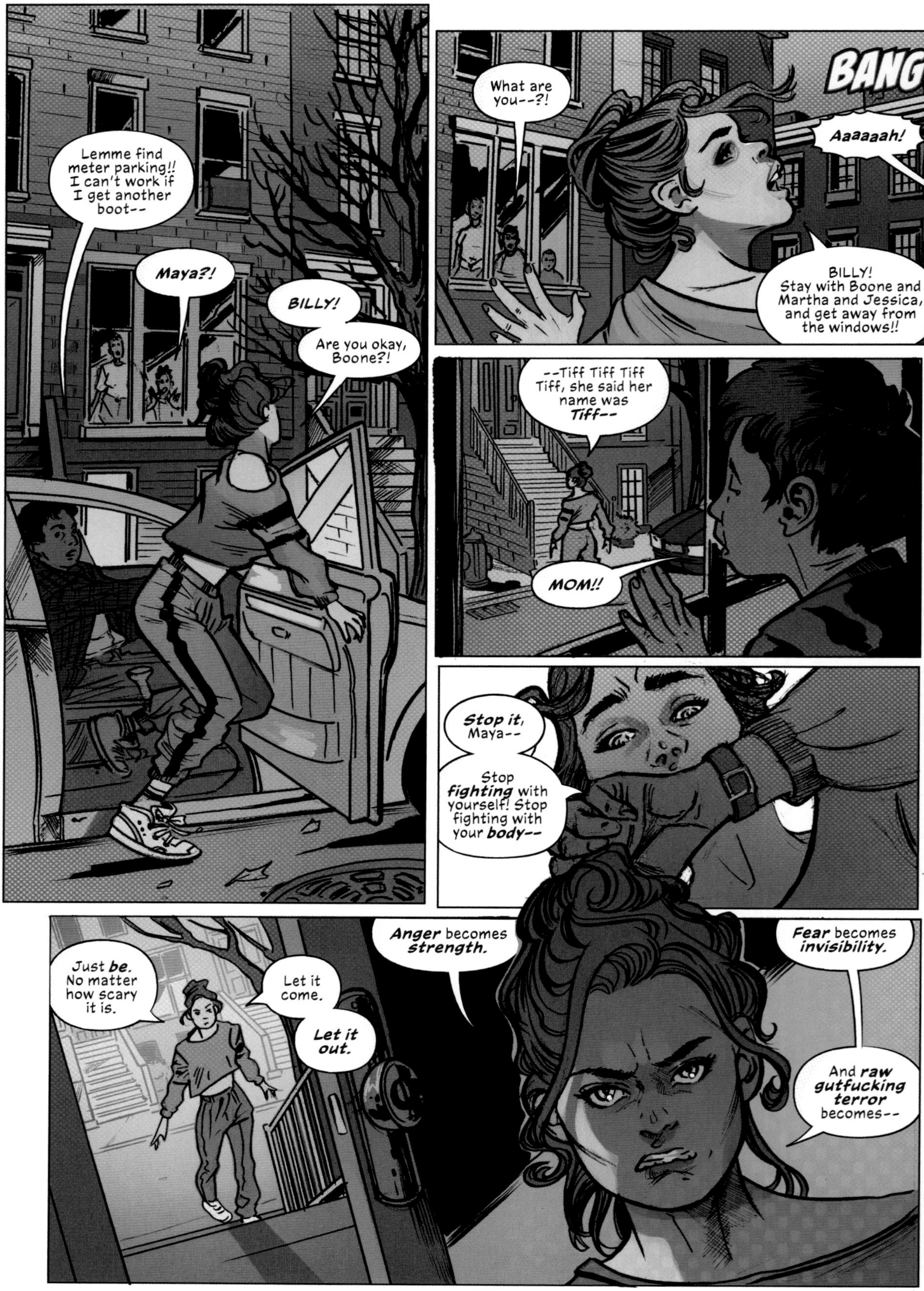
Lemme find meter parking!! I can't work if I get another boot--
Maya?!
BILLY!
Are you okay, Boone?!
What are you--?!
BANG
Aaaaaah!
BILLY! Stay with Boone and Martha and Jessica, and get away from the windows!!
--Tiff Tiff Tiff Tiff, she said her name was Tiff--
MOM!!
Stop it, Maya--
Stop fighting with yourself! Stop fighting with your body--
Just be. No matter how scary it is.
Let it come.
Let it out.
Anger becomes strength.
Fear becomes invisibility.
And raw gutfucking terror becomes--

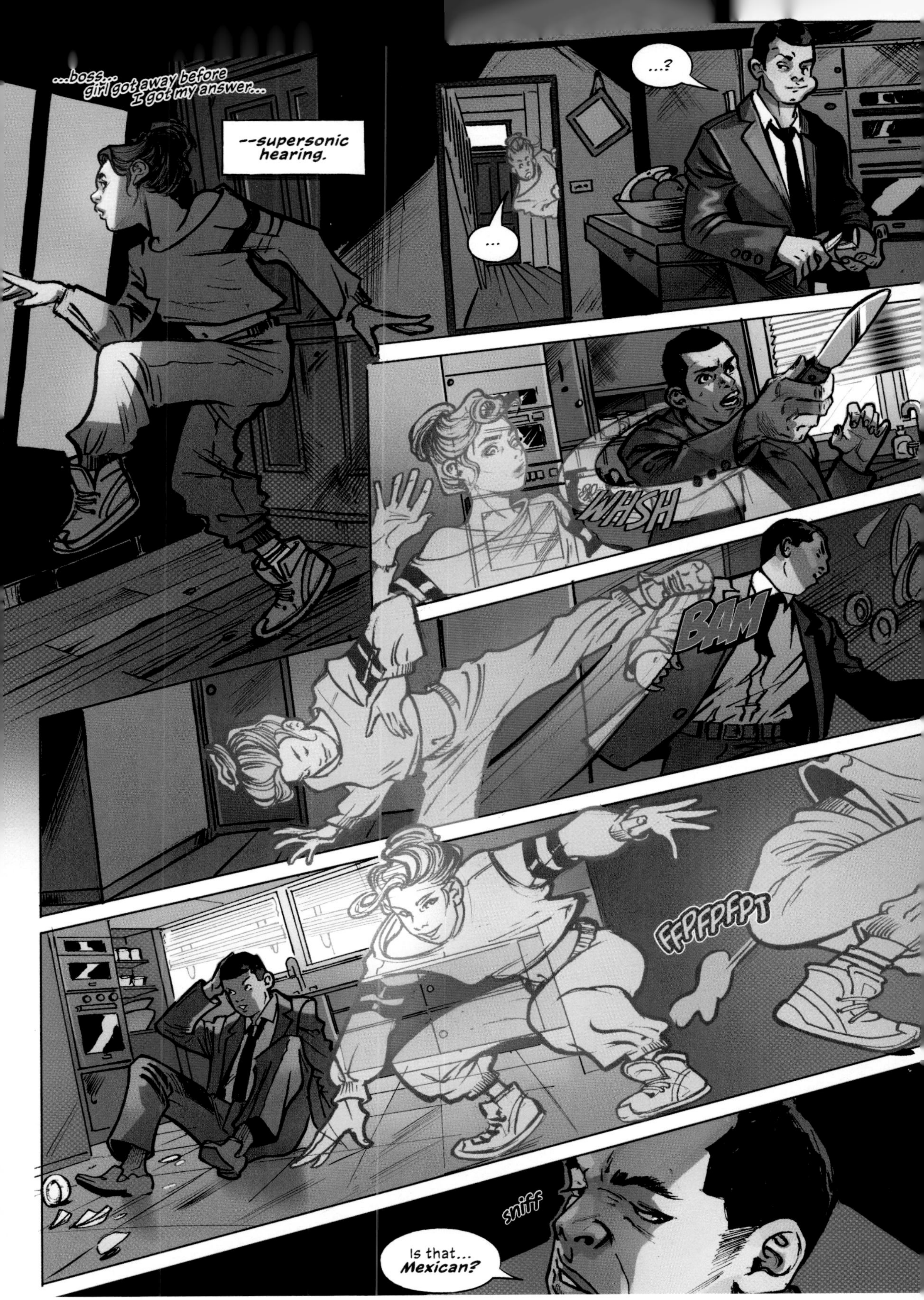
...boss... girl got away before I got my answer...
--supersonic hearing.
...?
...
WHSH
BAM
FFPFPFPT
sniff
Is that... Mexican?

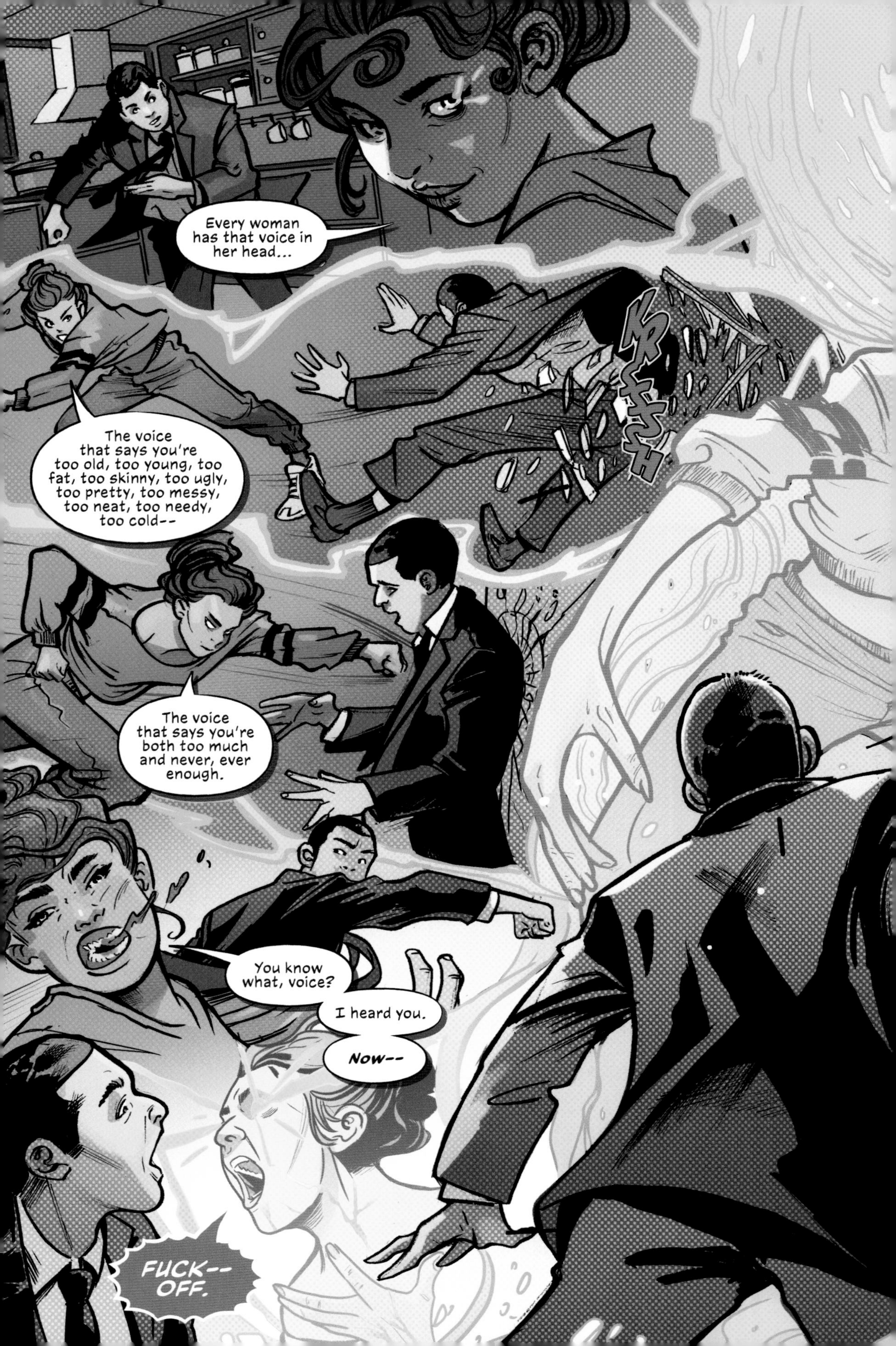

Every woman has that voice in her head...
KRSHHH
The voice that says you're too old, too young, too fat, too skinny, too ugly, too pretty, too messy, too neat, too needy, too cold--
The voice that says you're both too much and never, ever enough.
You know what, voice?
I heard you.
Now--
FUCK-- OFF.

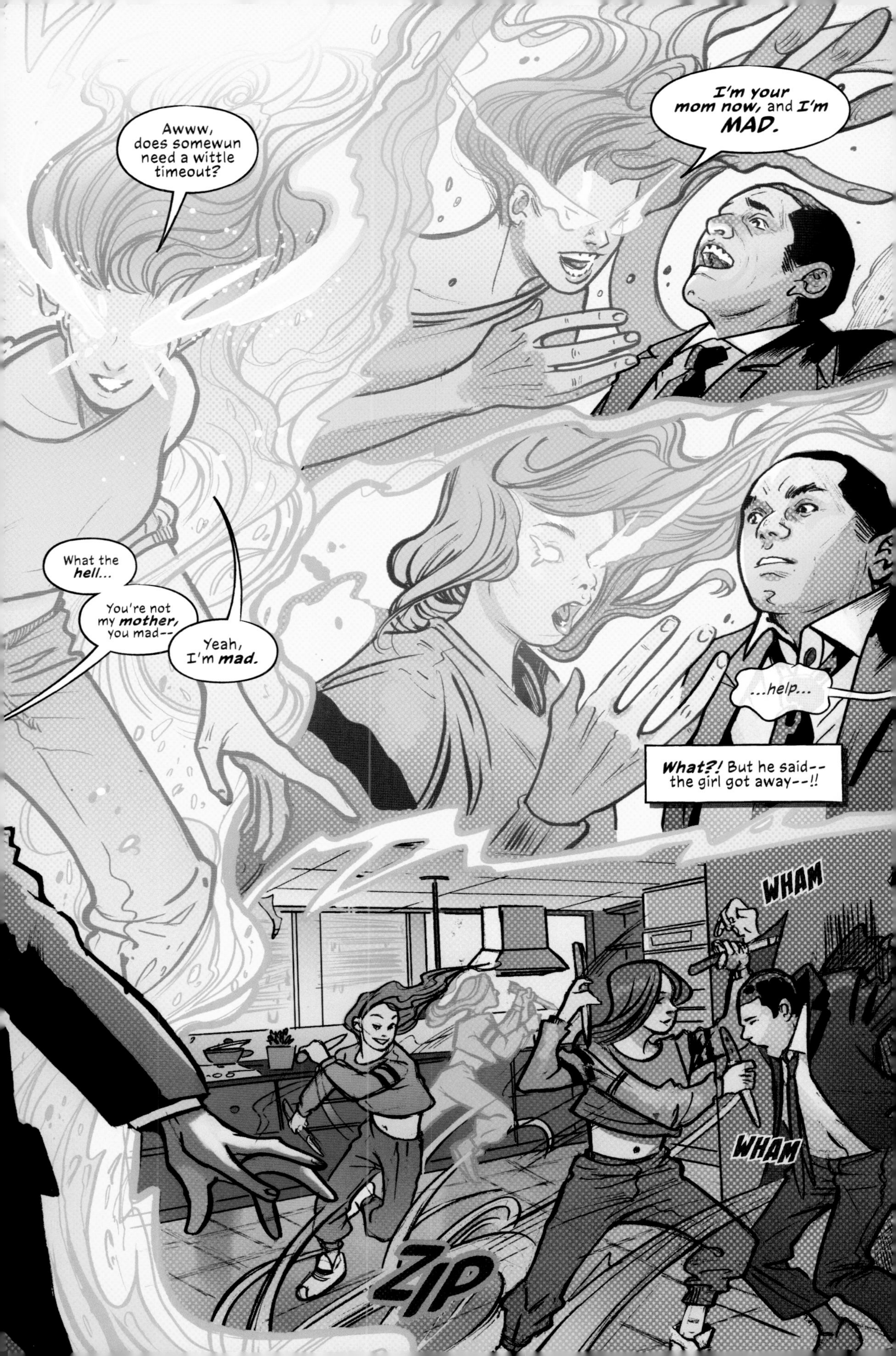

Awww, does somewun need a wittle timeout?
I'm your mom now, and I'm MAD.
What the hell...
You're not my mother, you mad--
Yeah, I'm mad.
...help...
What?! But he said-- the girl got away--!!
WHAM
WHAM
ZIP

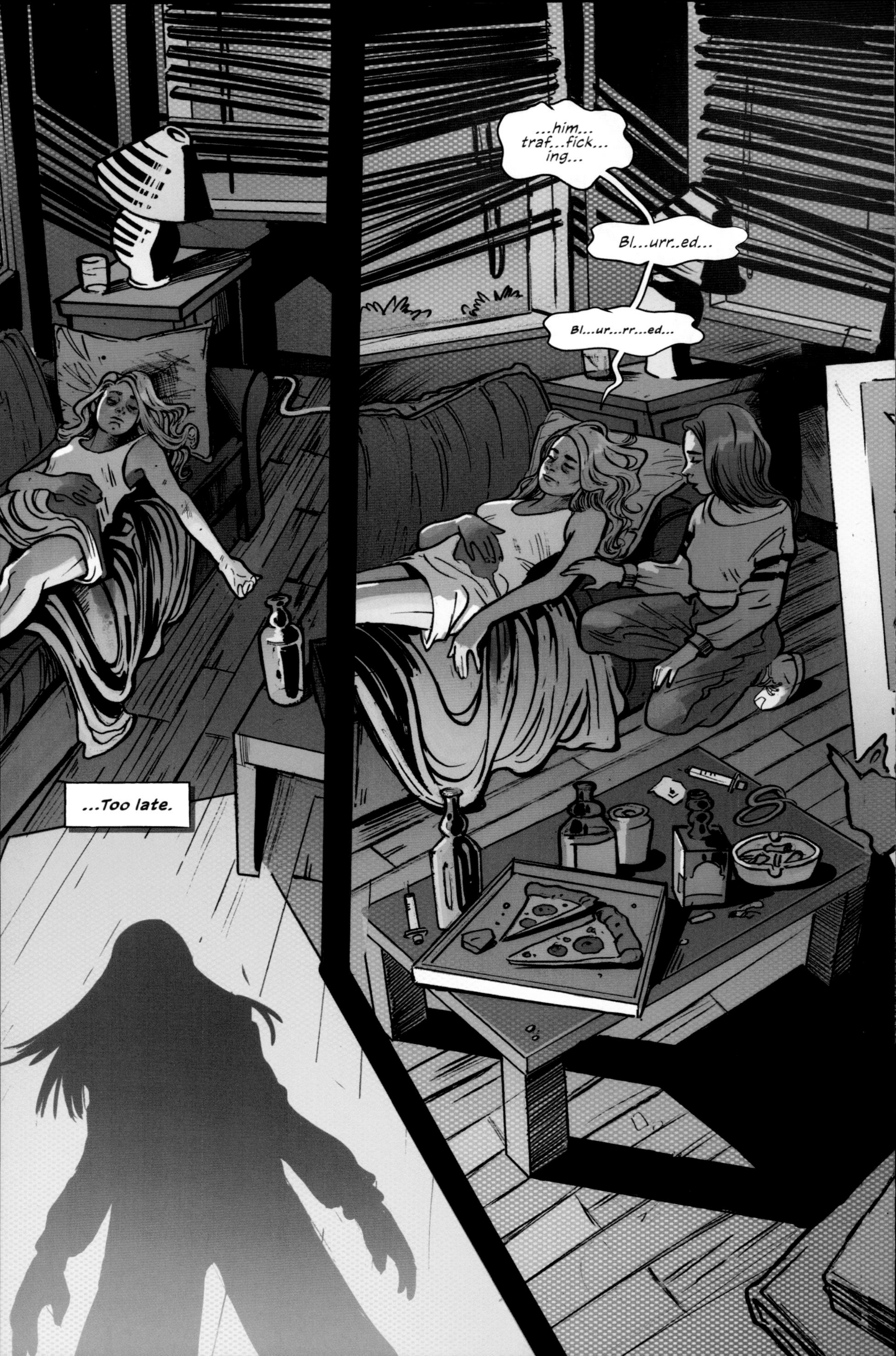
...Too late.
...him... traf...fick... ing...
Bl...urr..ed...
Bl...ur...rr...ed...

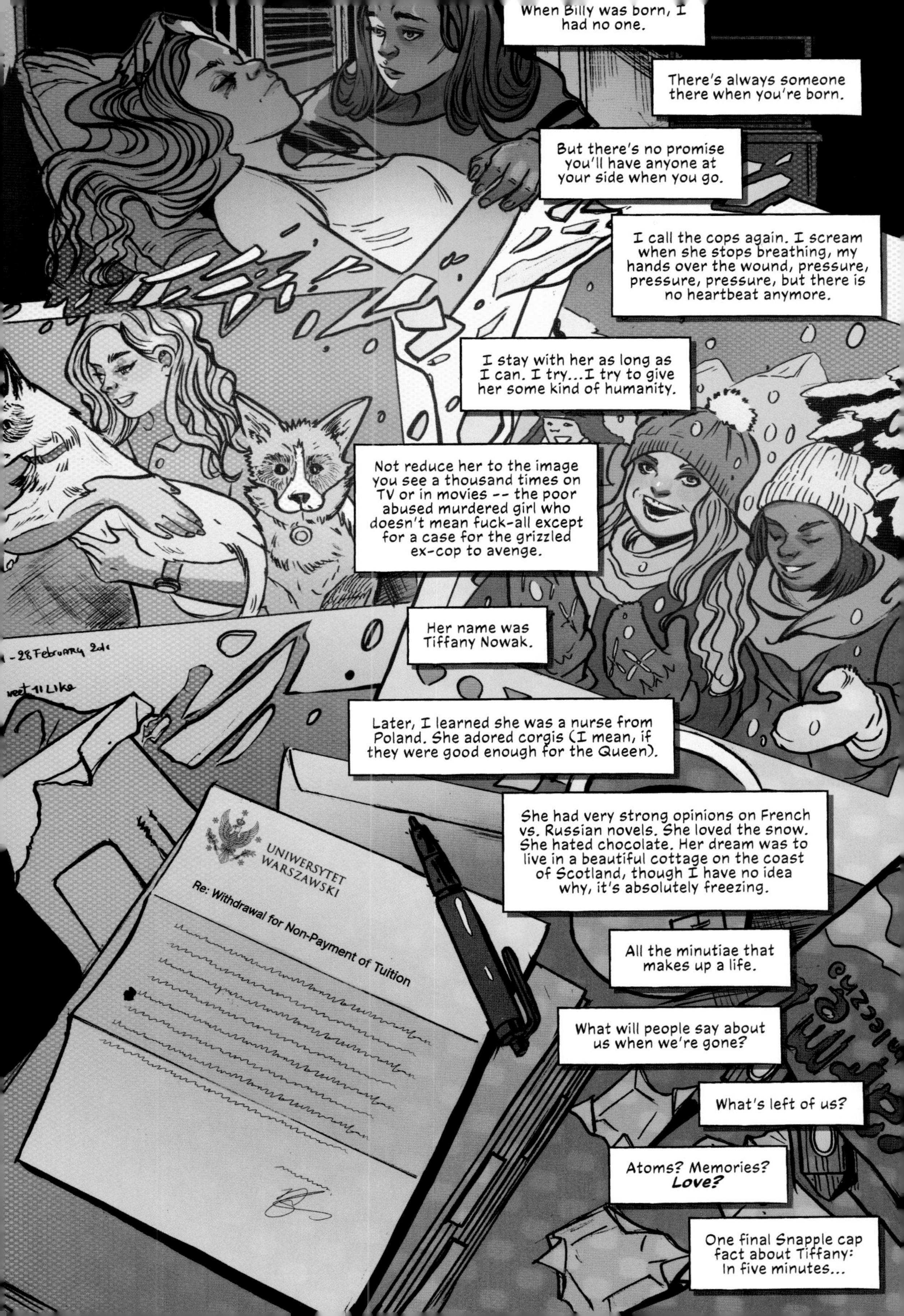
When Billy was born, I had no one.
There's always someone there when you're born.
But there's no promise you'll have anyone at your side when you go.
I call the cops again. I scream when she stops breathing, my hands over the wound, pressure, pressure, pressure, but there is no heartbeat anymore.
I stay with her as long as I can. I try...I try to give her some kind of humanity.
Not reduce her to the image you see a thousand times on TV or in movies -- the poor abused murdered girl who doesn't mean fuck-all except for a case for the grizzled ex-cop to avenge.
Her name was Tiffany Nowak.
Later, I learned she was a nurse from Poland. She adored corgis (I mean, if they were good enough for the Queen).
UNIWERSYTET WARSZAWSKI
Re: Withdrawal for Non-Payment of Tuition
She had very strong opinions on French vs. Russian novels. She loved the snow. She hated chocolate. Her dream was to live in a beautiful cottage on the coast of Scotland, though I have no idea why, it's absolutely freezing.
All the minutiae that makes up a life.
What will people say about us when we're gone?
What's left of us?
Atoms? Memories? *Love?*
One final Snapple cap fact about Tiffany: In five minutes...

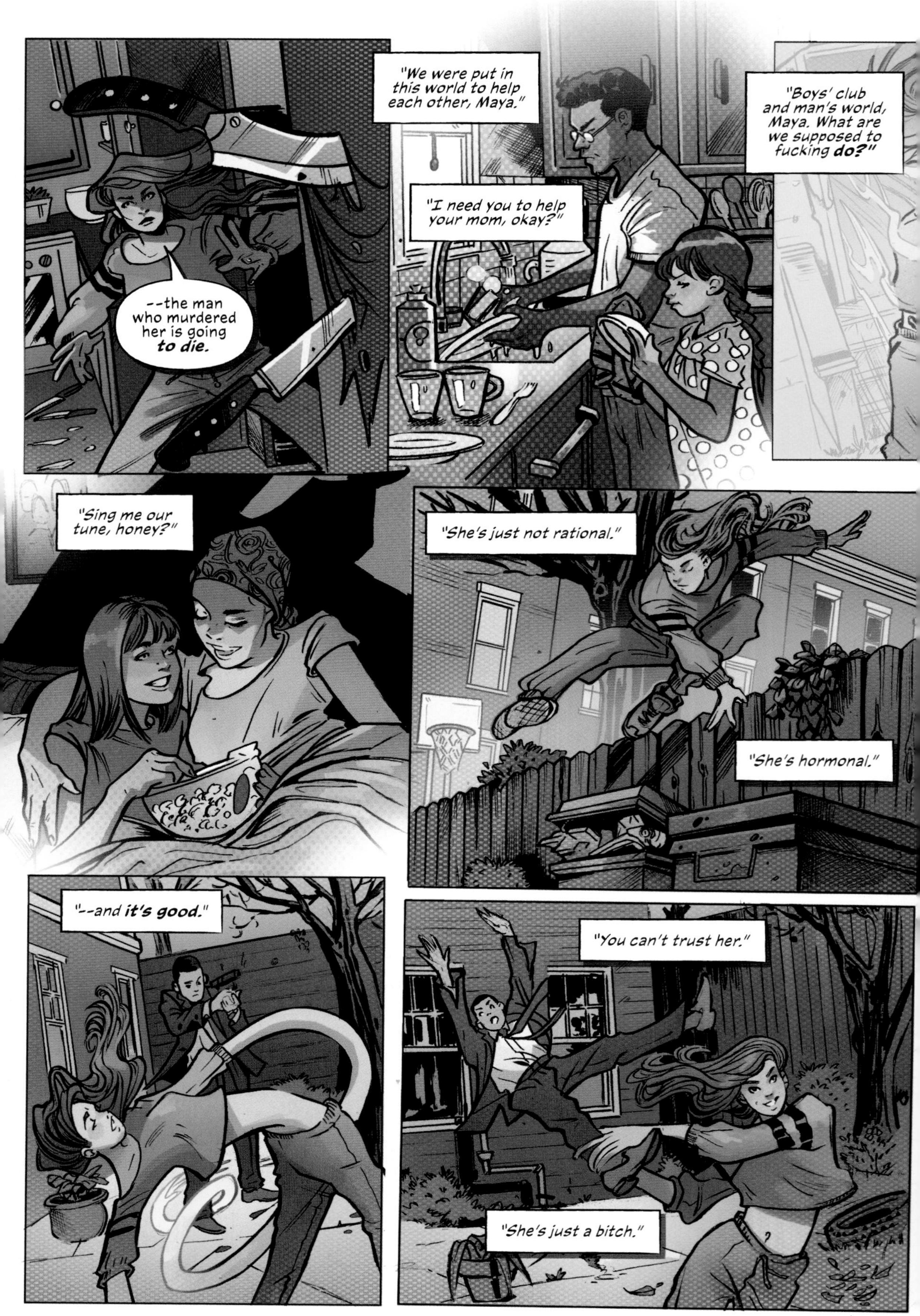

--the man who murdered her is going **to die.**
"We were put in this world to help each other, Maya."
"I need you to help your mom, okay?"
"Boys' club and man's world, Maya. What are we supposed to fucking **do?**"
"Sing me our tune, honey?"
"She's just not rational."
"She's hormonal."
"--and **it's good.**"
"You can't trust her."
"She's just a bitch."

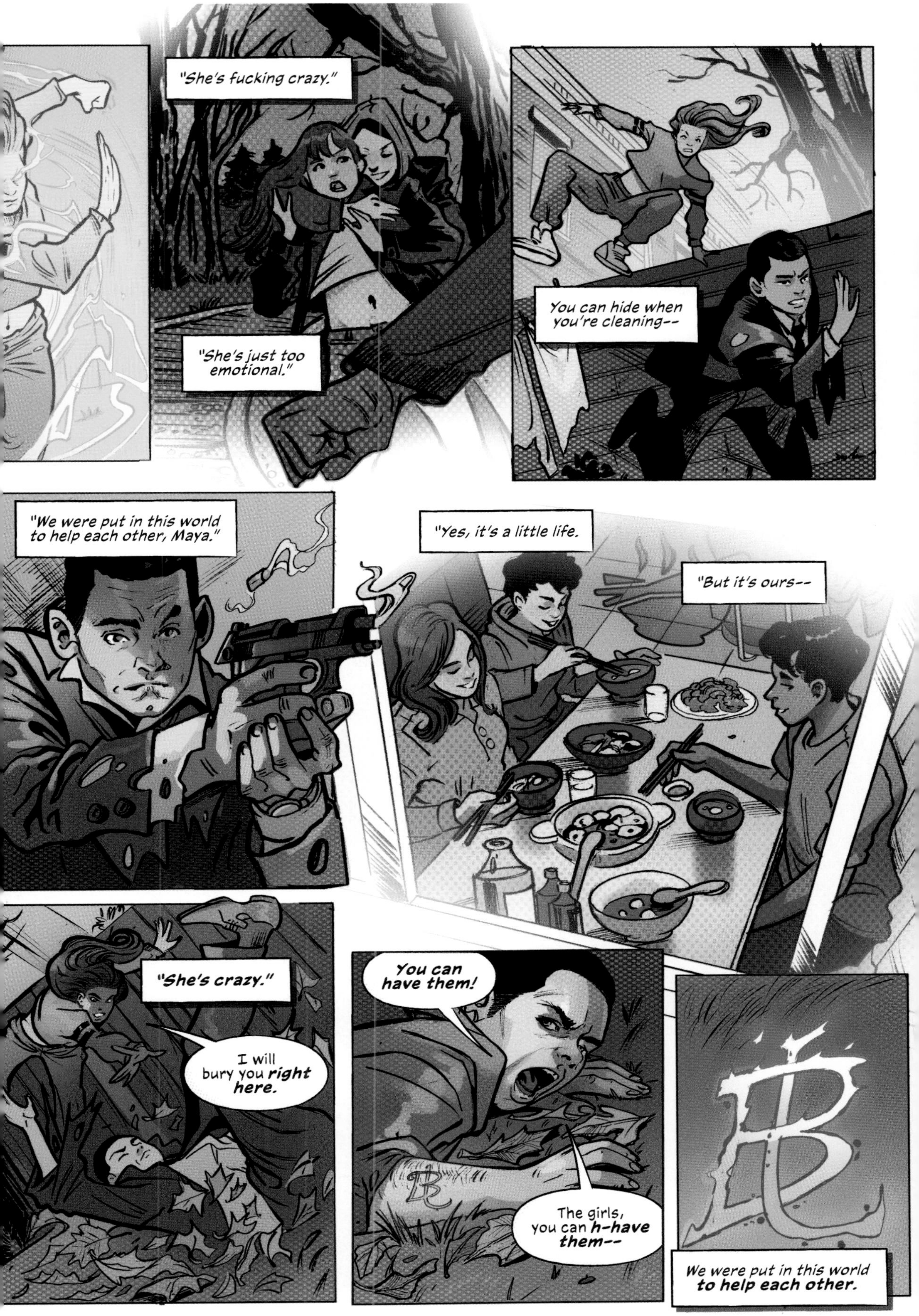
"She's fucking crazy."
"She's just too emotional."
You can hide when you're cleaning--
"We were put in this world to help each other, Maya."
"Yes, it's a little life.
"But it's ours--
"She's crazy."
I will bury you right here.
You can have them!
The girls, you can h-have them--
We were put in this world to help each other.

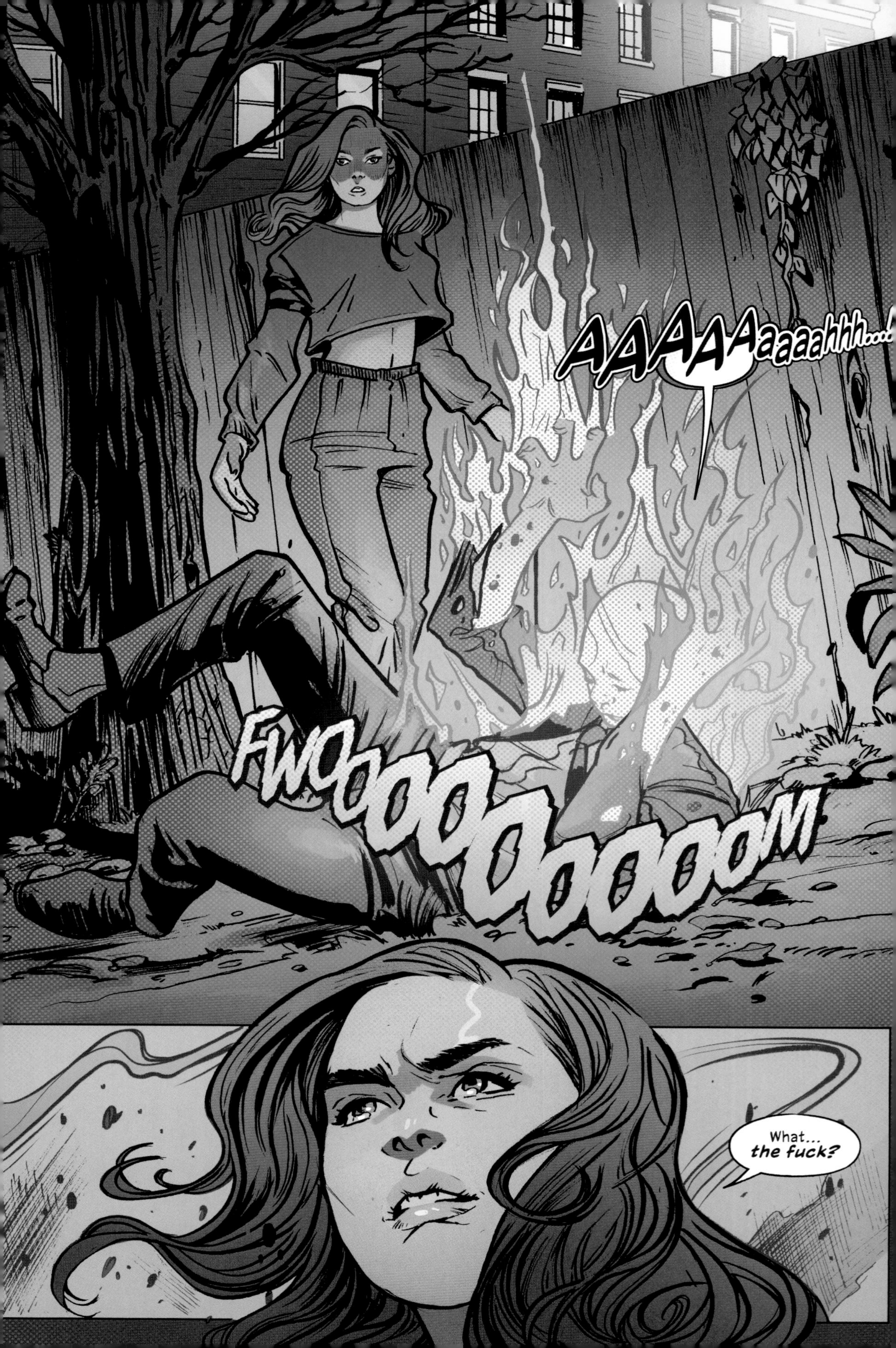
AAAAAaaaahhh...!
FWOOOOOOOOOOOM
What... the fuck?

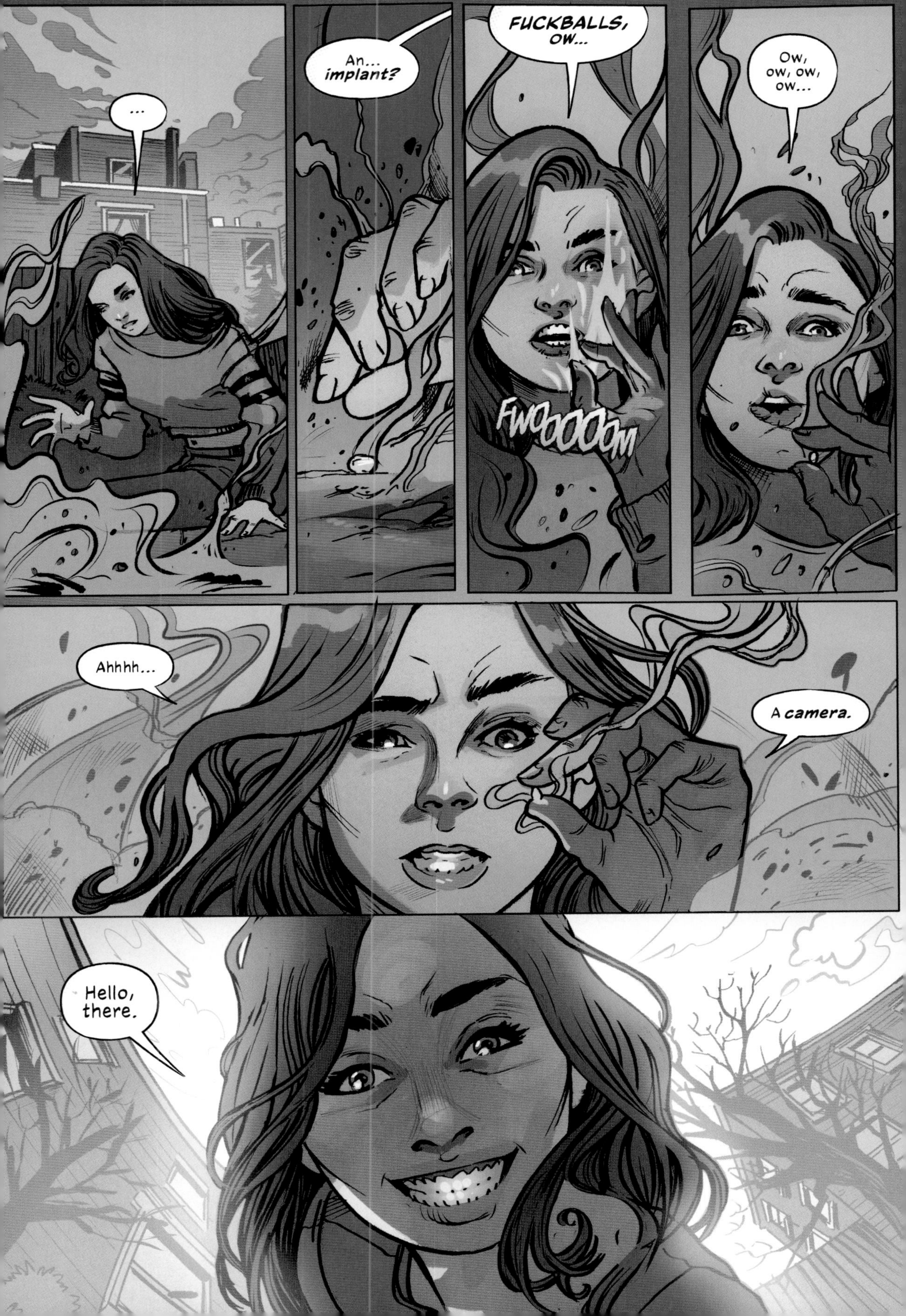
...
An... *implant?*
FUCKBALLS, OW...
FWOOOOOM
Ow, ow, ow, ow...
Ahhhh...
A *camera.*
Hello, there.

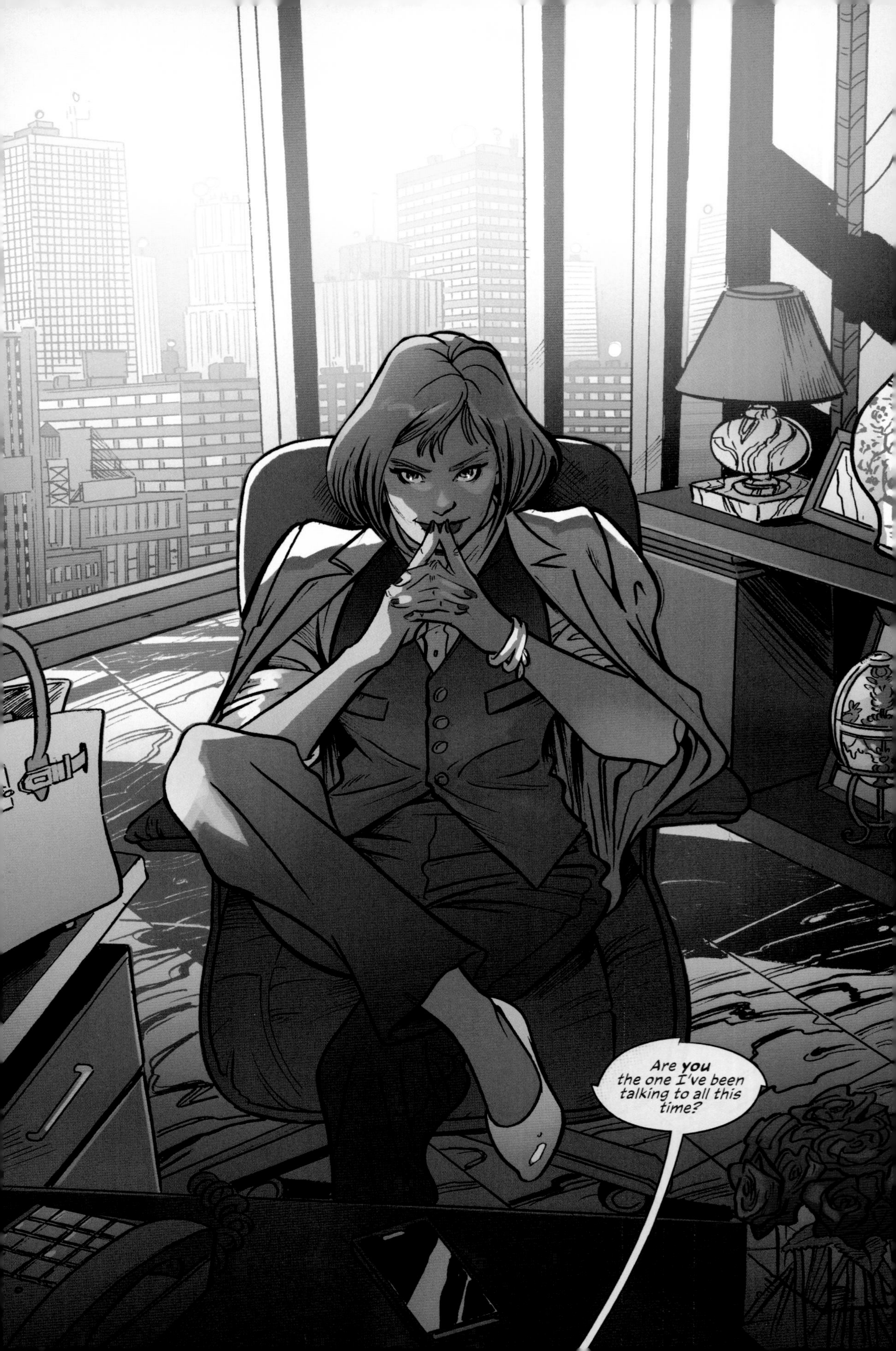
Are **you** the one I've been talking to all this time?

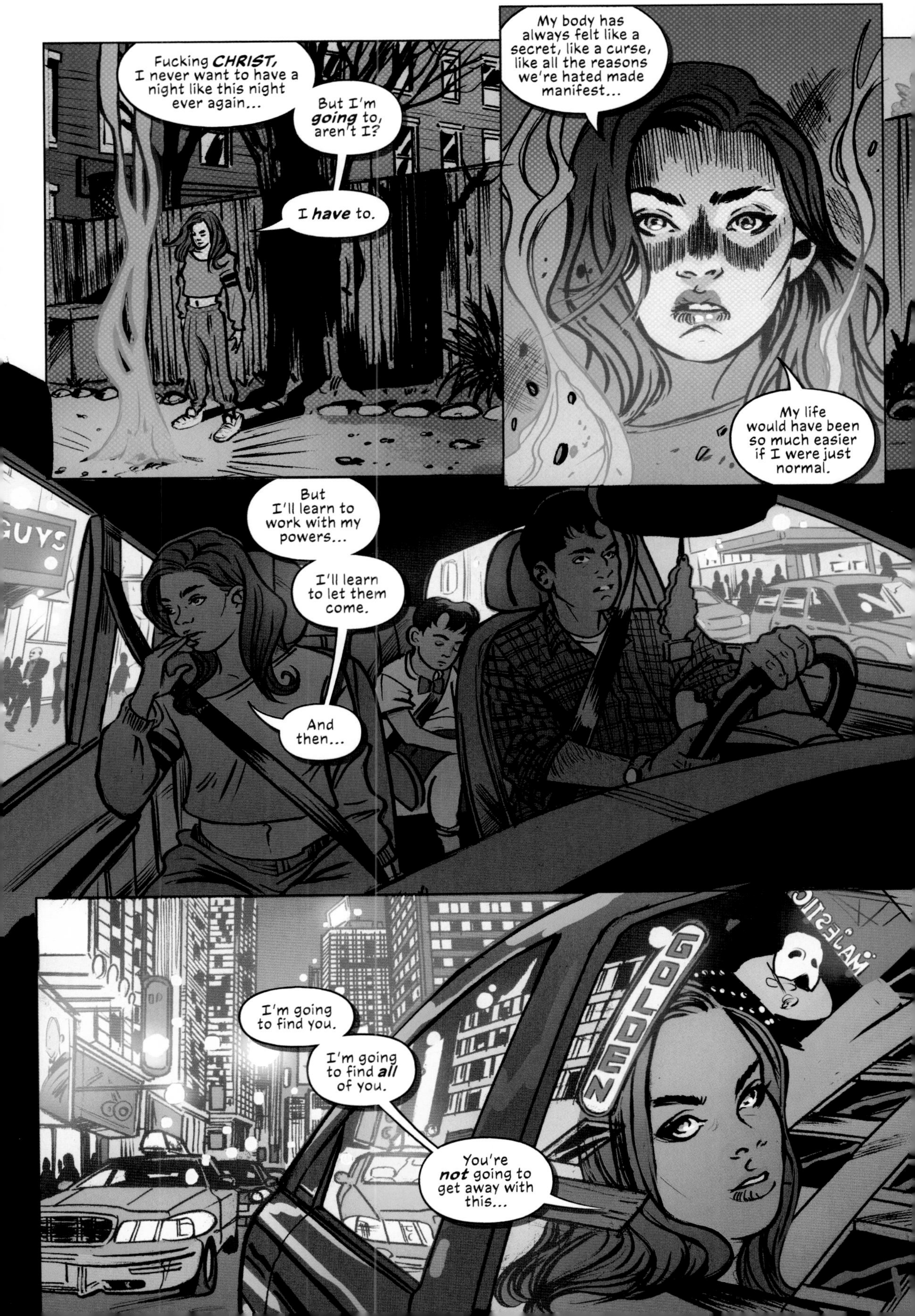
Fucking **CHRIST,** I never want to have a night like this night ever again...
But I'm ***going*** to, aren't I?
I ***have*** to.
My body has always felt like a secret, like a curse, like all the reasons we're hated made manifest...
My life would have been so much easier if I were just normal.
GUYS
But I'll learn to work with my powers...
I'll learn to let them come.
And then...
GOLDEN
I'm going to find you.
I'm going to find ***all*** of you.
You're ***not*** going to get away with this...

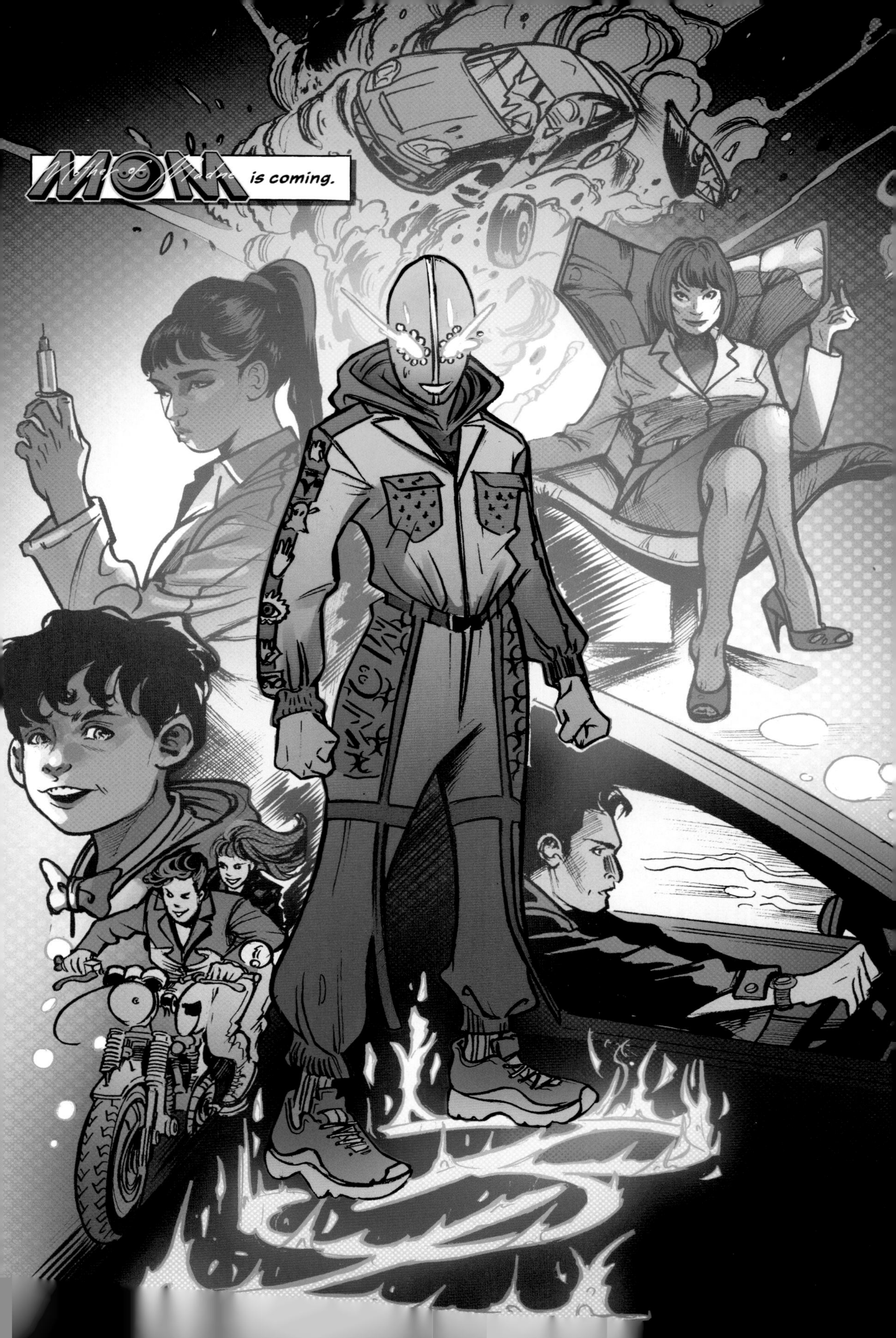
MOM is coming.

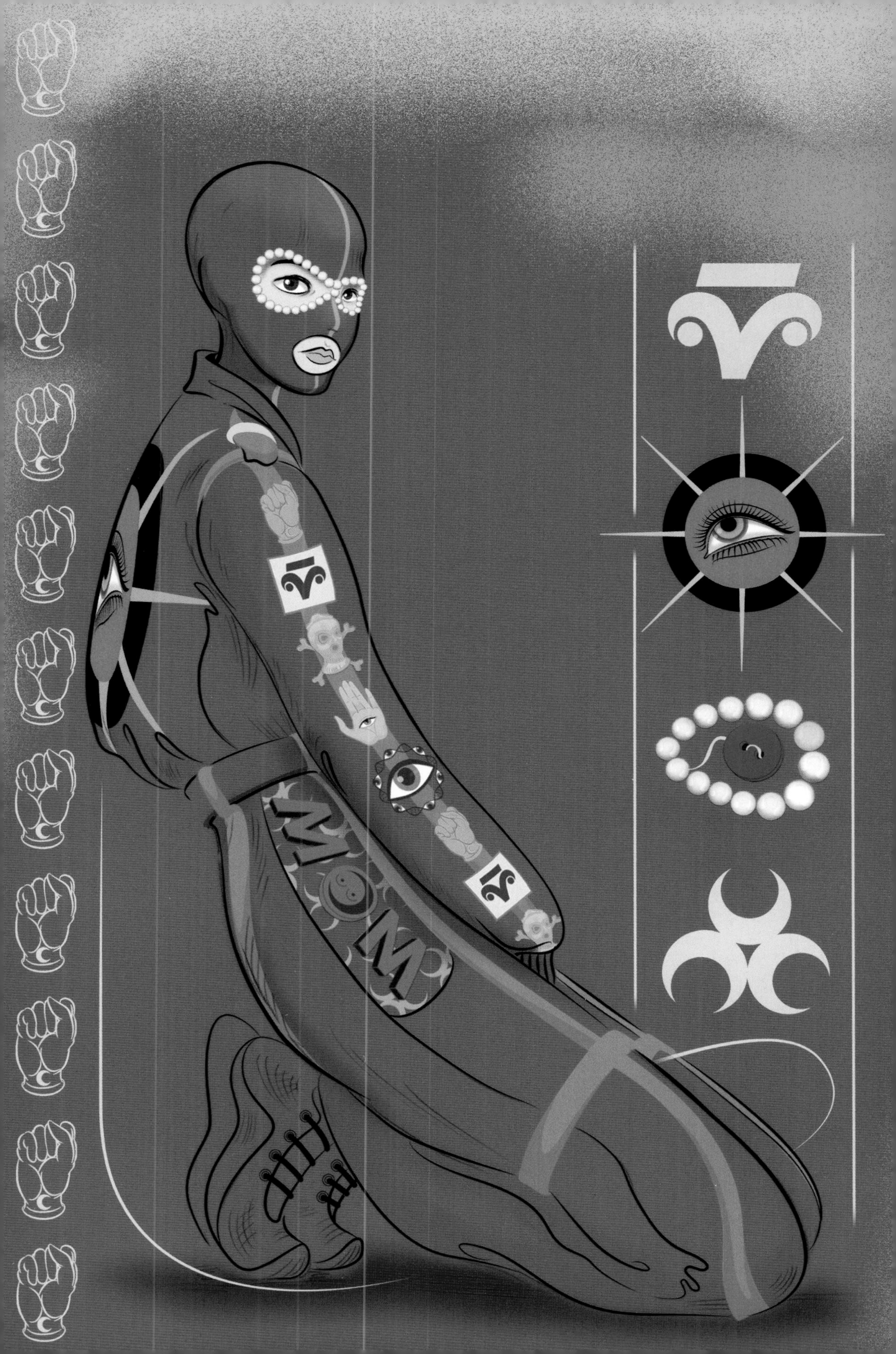
MOM

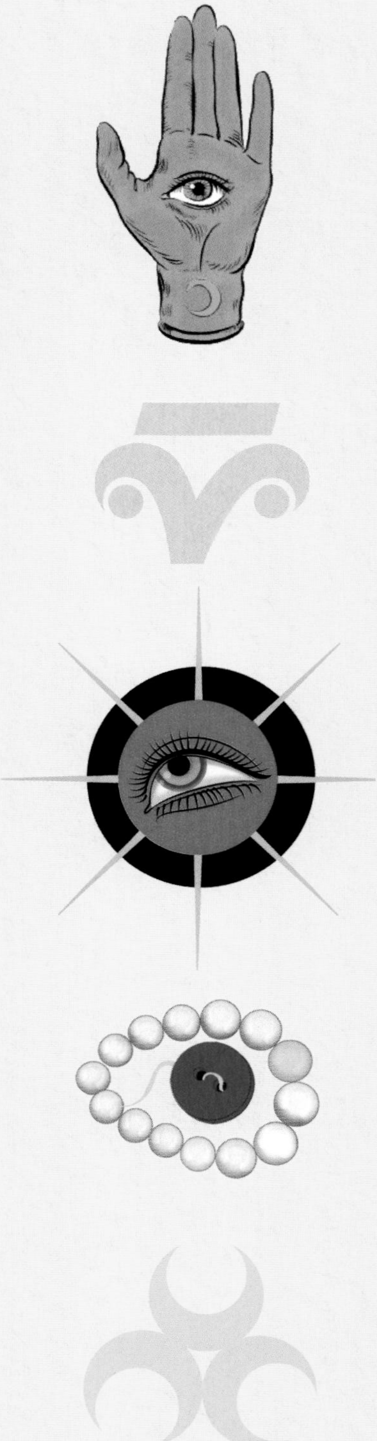
MOM

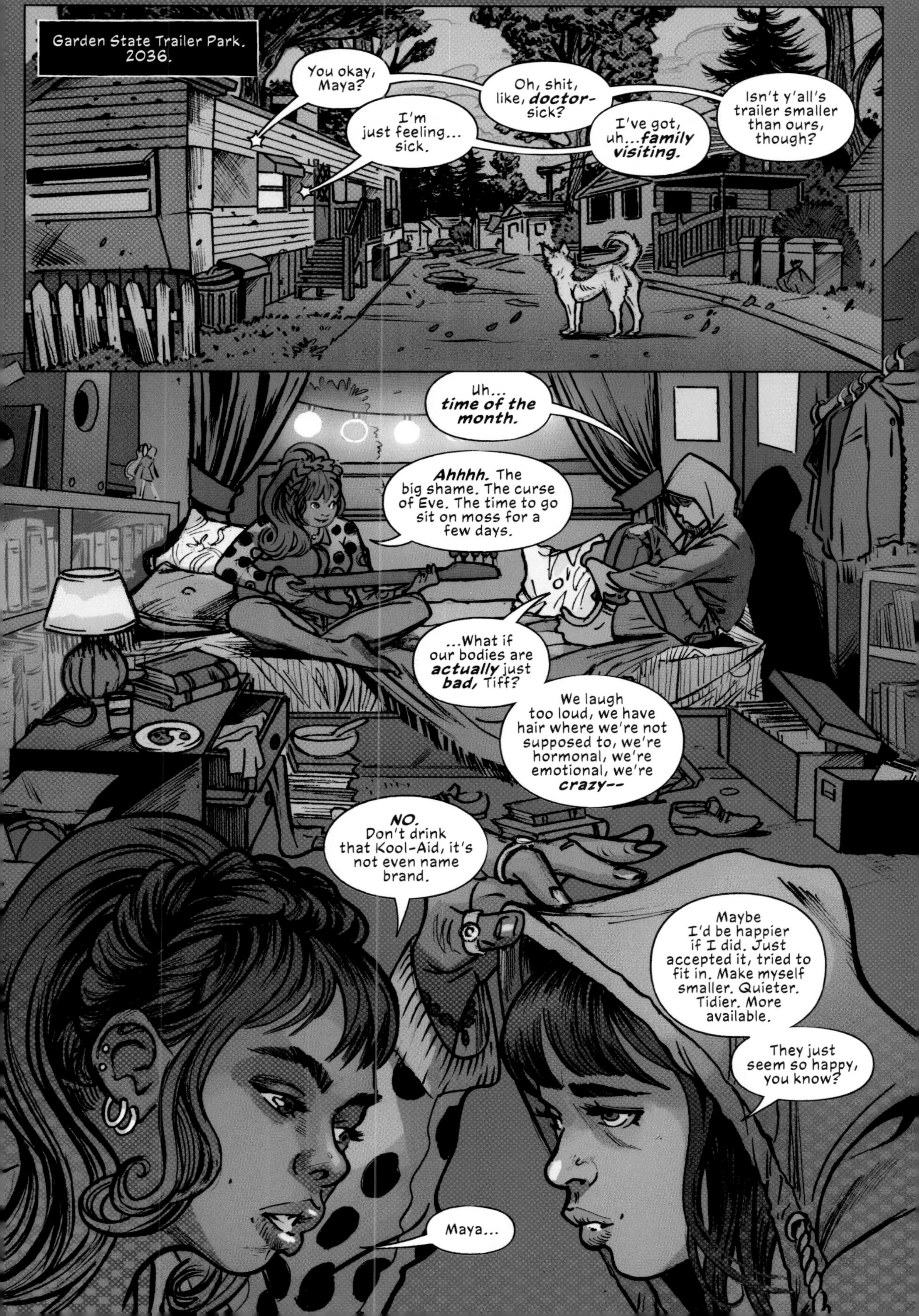

Garden State Trailer Park. 2036.
You okay, Maya?
I'm just feeling... sick.
Oh, shit, like, doctor-sick?
I've got, uh...family visiting.
Isn't y'all's trailer smaller than ours, though?
Uh... time of the month.
Ahhhh. The big shame. The curse of Eve. The time to go sit on moss for a few days.
...What if our bodies are actually just bad, Tiff?
We laugh too loud, we have hair where we're not supposed to, we're hormonal, we're emotional, we're crazy--
NO. Don't drink that Kool-Aid, it's not even name brand.
Maybe I'd be happier if I did. Just accepted it, tried to fit in. Make myself smaller. Quieter. Tidier. More available.
They just seem so happy, you know?
Maya...

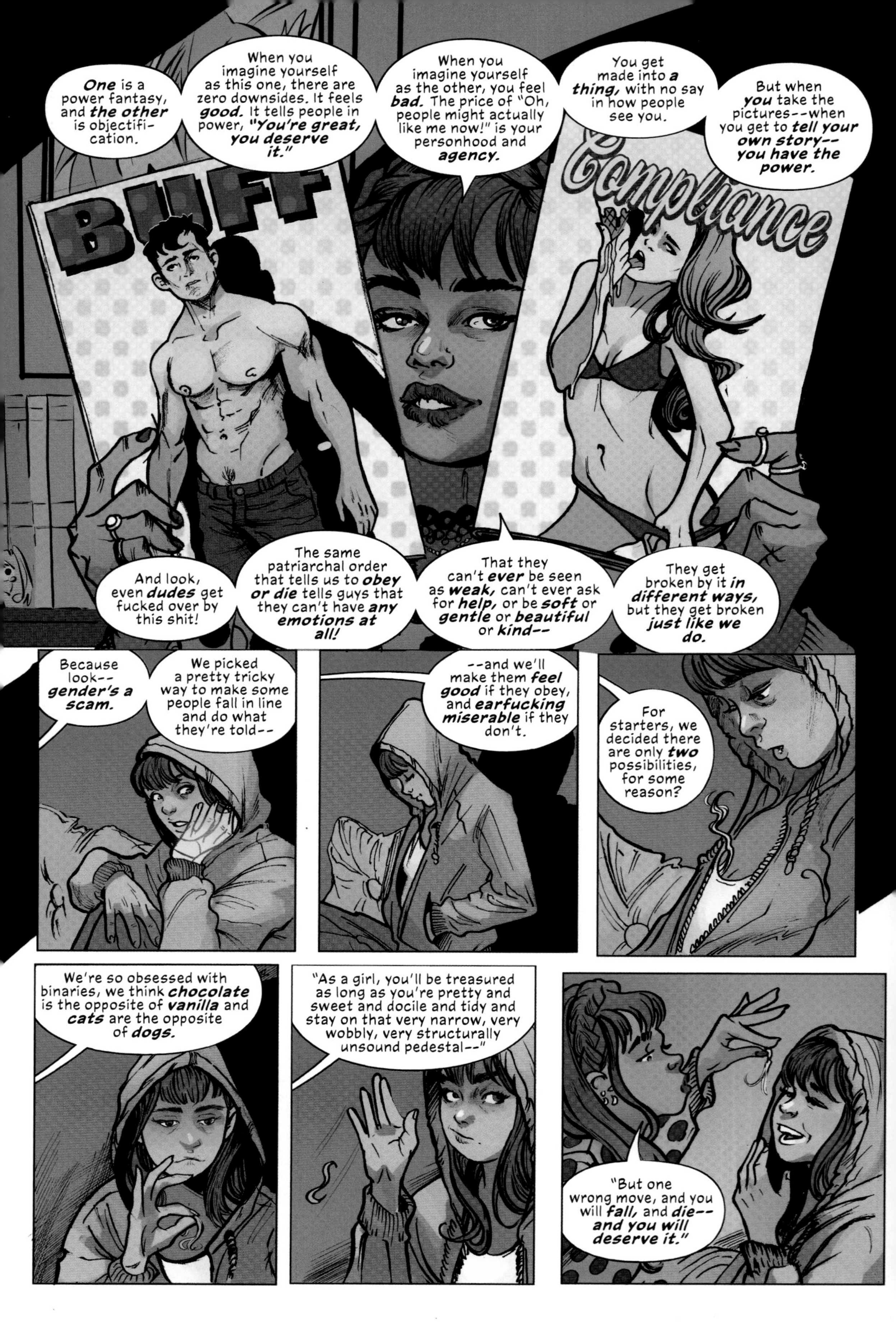

One is a power fantasy, and the other is objectifi-cation.
When you imagine yourself as this one, there are zero downsides. It feels good. It tells people in power, "You're great, you deserve it."
When you imagine yourself as the other, you feel bad. The price of "Oh, people might actually like me now!" is your personhood and agency.
You get made into a thing, with no say in how people see you.
But when you take the pictures--when you get to tell your own story--you have the power.
BUFF
Compliance
And look, even dudes get fucked over by this shit!
The same patriarchal order that tells us to obey or die tells guys that they can't have any emotions at all!
That they can't ever be seen as weak, can't ever ask for help, or be soft or gentle or beautiful or kind--
They get broken by it in different ways, but they get broken just like we do.
Because look--gender's a scam.
We picked a pretty tricky way to make some people fall in line and do what they're told--
--and we'll make them feel good if they obey, and earfucking miserable if they don't.
For starters, we decided there are only two possibilities, for some reason?
We're so obsessed with binaries, we think chocolate is the opposite of vanilla and cats are the opposite of dogs.
"As a girl, you'll be treasured as long as you're pretty and sweet and docile and tidy and stay on that very narrow, very wobbly, very structurally unsound pedestal--"
"But one wrong move, and you will fall, and die--and you will deserve it."

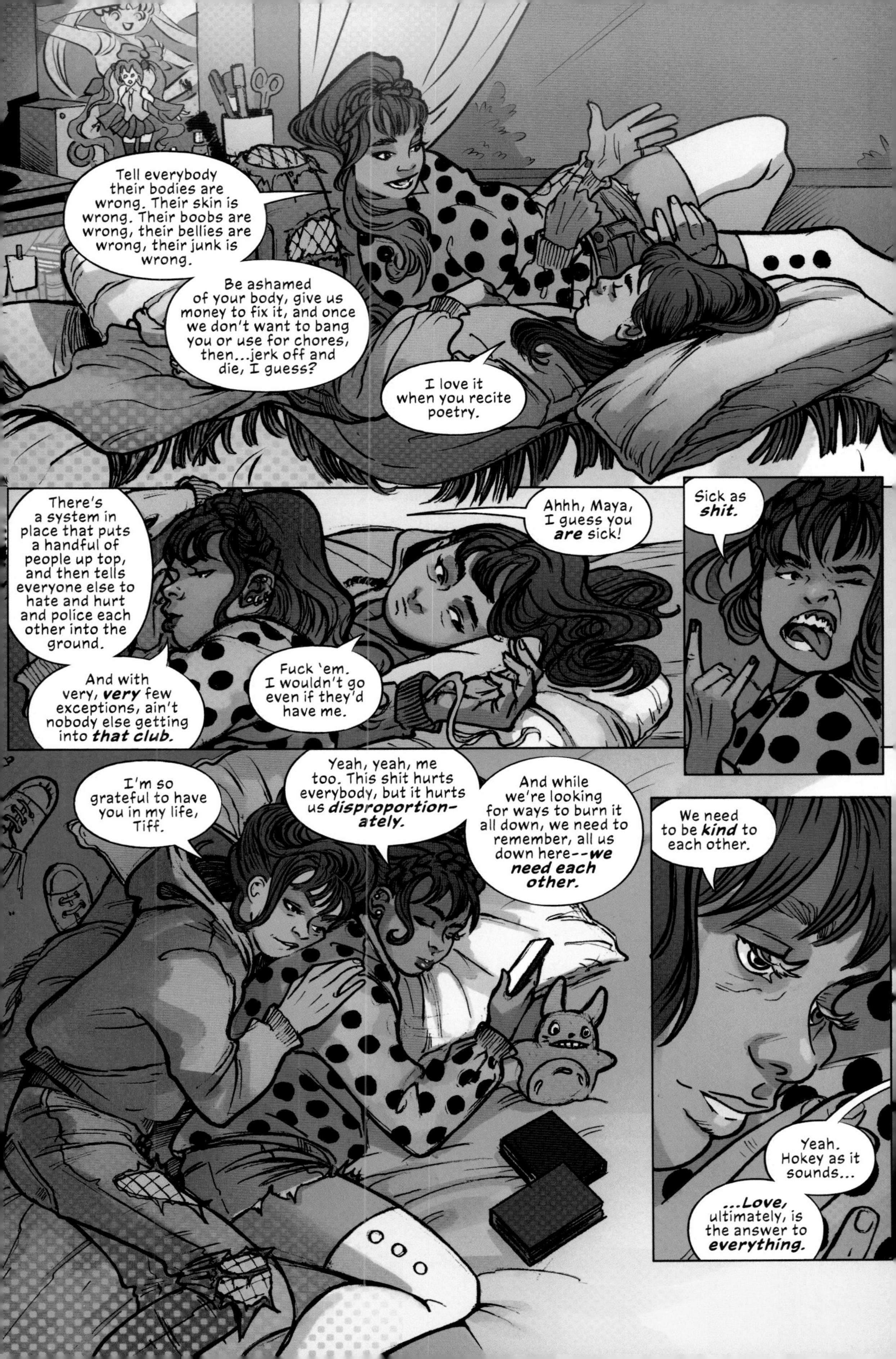
Tell everybody their bodies are wrong. Their skin is wrong. Their boobs are wrong, their bellies are wrong, their junk is wrong.
Be ashamed of your body, give us money to fix it, and once we don't want to bang you or use for chores, then...jerk off and die, I guess?
I love it when you recite poetry.
There's a system in place that puts a handful of people up top, and then tells everyone else to hate and hurt and police each other into the ground.
Ahhh, Maya, I guess you are sick!
And with very, very few exceptions, ain't nobody else getting into that club.
Fuck 'em. I wouldn't go even if they'd have me.
Sick as shit.
I'm so grateful to have you in my life, Tiff.
Yeah, yeah, me too. This shit hurts everybody, but it hurts us disproportion-ately.
And while we're looking for ways to burn it all down, we need to remember, all us down here--we need each other.
We need to be kind to each other.
Yeah. Hokey as it sounds...
...Love, ultimately, is the answer to everything.

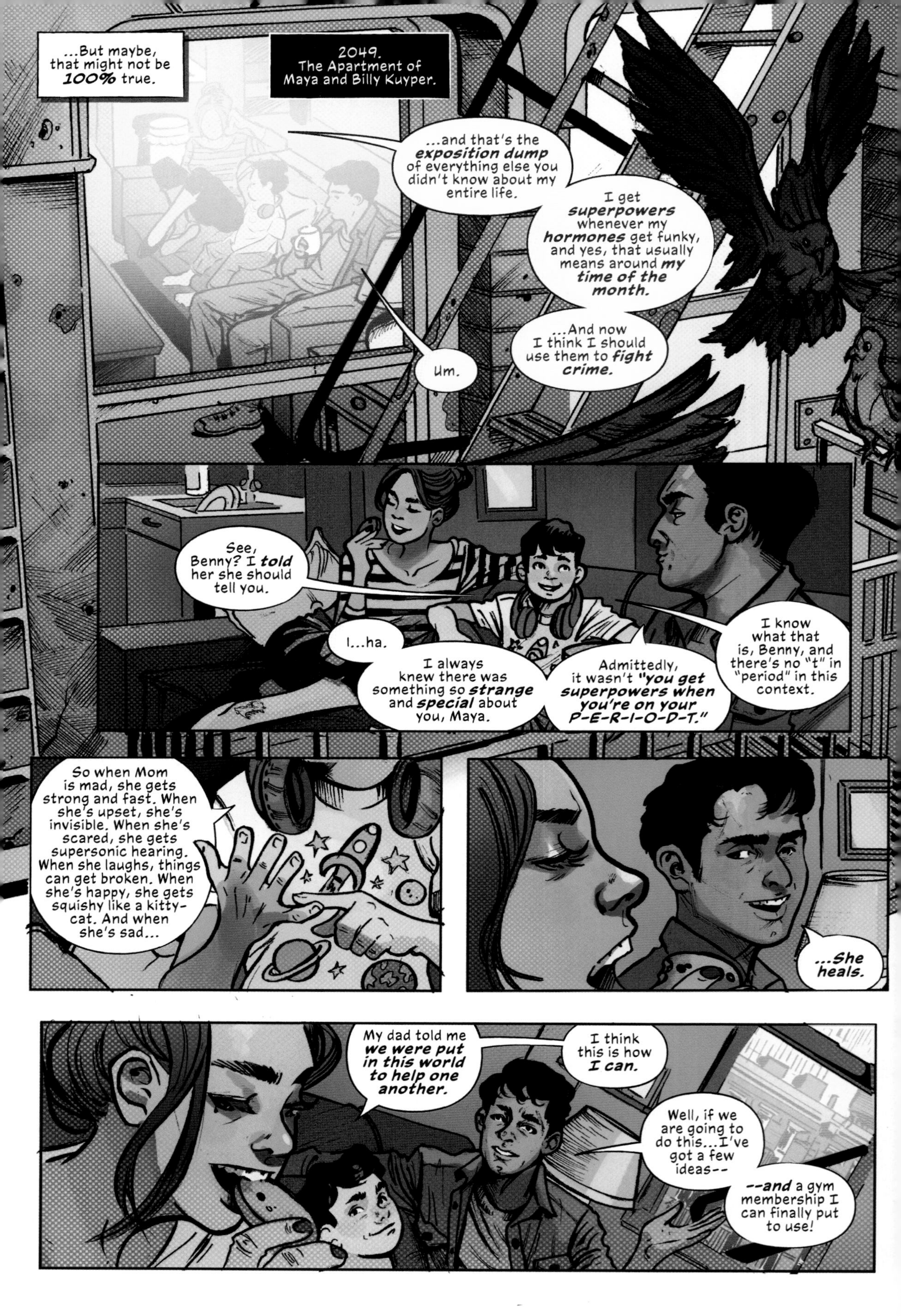
...But maybe, that might not be 100% true.
2049. The Apartment of Maya and Billy Kuyper.
...and that's the exposition dump of everything else you didn't know about my entire life.
I get superpowers whenever my hormones get funky, and yes, that usually means around my time of the month.
...And now I think I should use them to fight crime.
Um.
See, Benny? I told her she should tell you.
I...ha.
I always knew there was something so strange and special about you, Maya.
Admittedly, it wasn't "you get superpowers when you're on your P-E-R-I-O-D-T."
I know what that is, Benny, and there's no "t" in "period" in this context.
So when Mom is mad, she gets strong and fast. When she's upset, she's invisible. When she's scared, she gets supersonic hearing. When she laughs, things can get broken. When she's happy, she gets squishy like a kitty-cat. And when she's sad...
...She heals.
My dad told me we were put in this world to help one another.
I think this is how I can.
Well, if we are going to do this...I've got a few ideas--
--and a gym membership I can finally put to use!

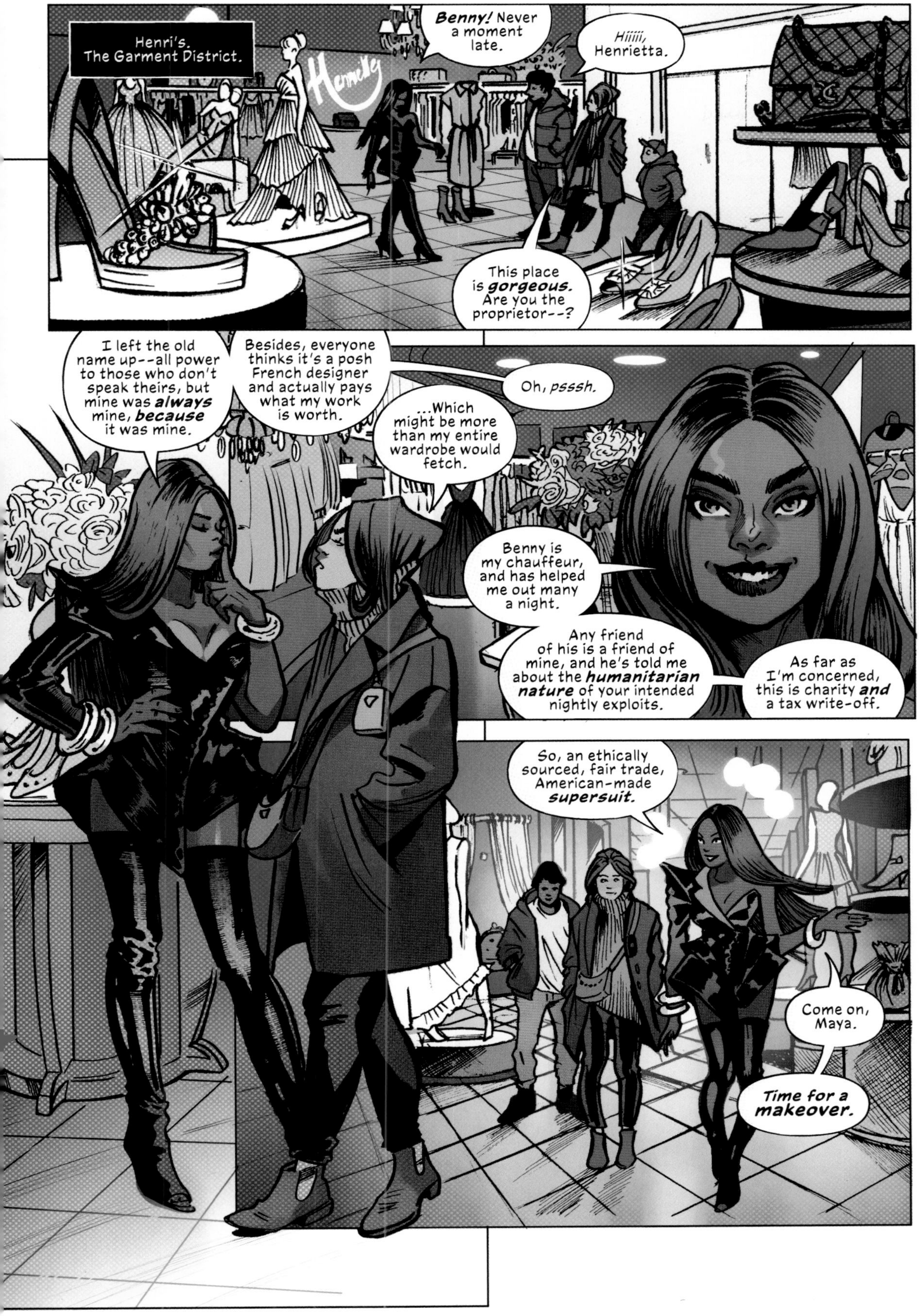

Henri's. The Garment District.
Benny! Never a moment late.
Hiiiii, Henrietta.
This place is gorgeous. Are you the proprietor--?
I left the old name up--all power to those who don't speak theirs, but mine was always mine, because it was mine.
Besides, everyone thinks it's a posh French designer and actually pays what my work is worth.
Oh, psssh.
...Which might be more than my entire wardrobe would fetch.
Benny is my chauffeur, and has helped me out many a night.
Any friend of his is a friend of mine, and he's told me about the humanitarian nature of your intended nightly exploits.
As far as I'm concerned, this is charity and a tax write-off.
So, an ethically sourced, fair trade, American-made supersuit.
Come on, Maya.
Time for a makeover.

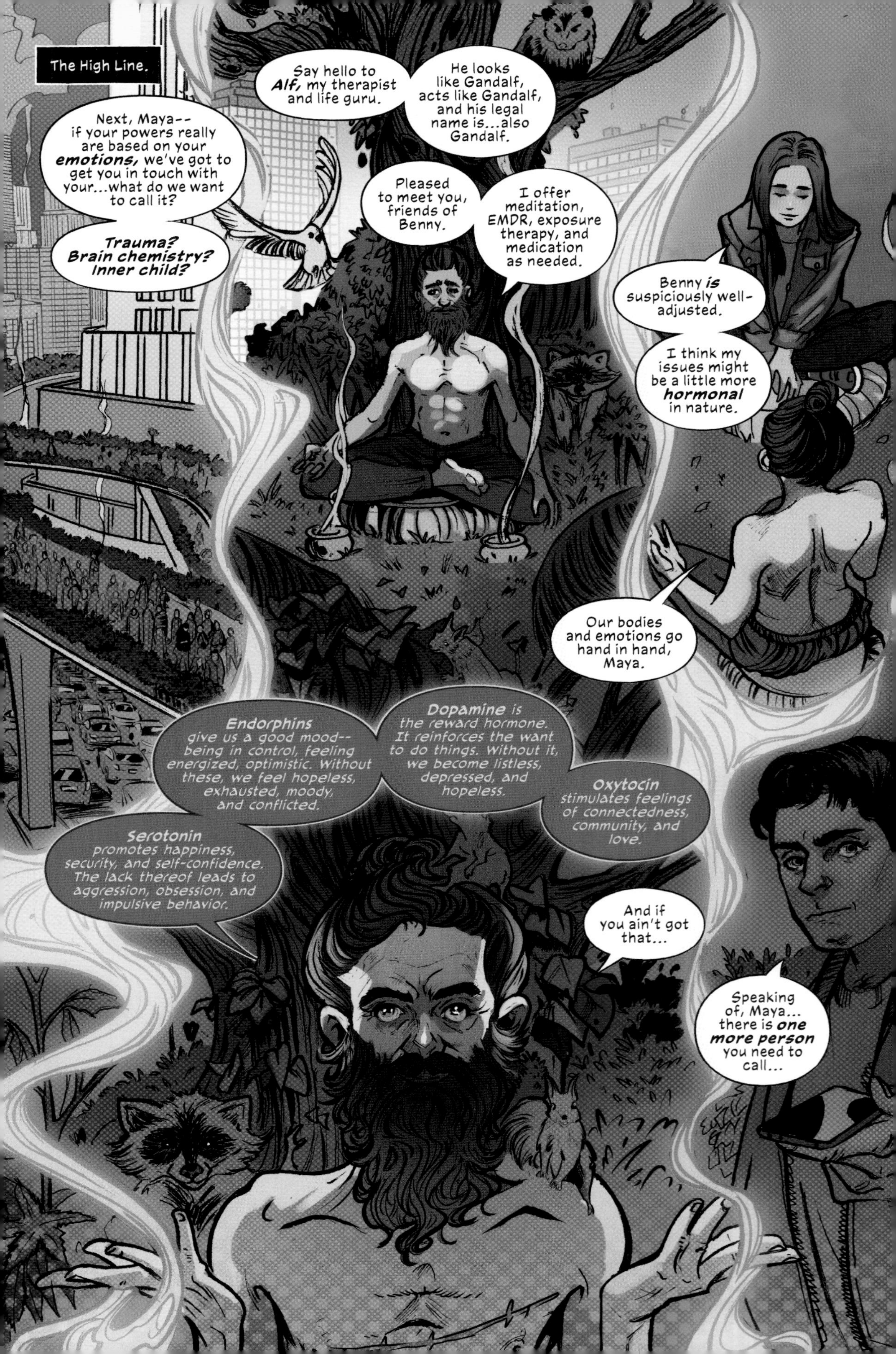
The High Line.
Next, Maya-- if your powers really are based on your **emotions,** we've got to get you in touch with your...what do we want to call it?
Trauma? Brain chemistry? Inner child?
Say hello to ***Alf,*** my therapist and life guru.
He looks like Gandalf, acts like Gandalf, and his legal name is...also Gandalf.
Pleased to meet you, friends of Benny.
I offer meditation, EMDR, exposure therapy, and medication as needed.
Benny ***is*** suspiciously well-adjusted.
I think my issues might be a little more ***hormonal*** in nature.
Our bodies and emotions go hand in hand, Maya.
Endorphins *give us a good mood--being in control, feeling energized, optimistic. Without these, we feel hopeless, exhausted, moody, and conflicted.*
Dopamine *is the reward hormone. It reinforces the want to do things. Without it, we become listless, depressed, and hopeless.*
Oxytocin *stimulates feelings of connectedness, community, and love.*
Serotonin *promotes happiness, security, and self-confidence. The lack thereof leads to aggression, obsession, and impulsive behavior.*
And if you ain't got that...
Speaking of, Maya... there is ***one more person*** you need to call...

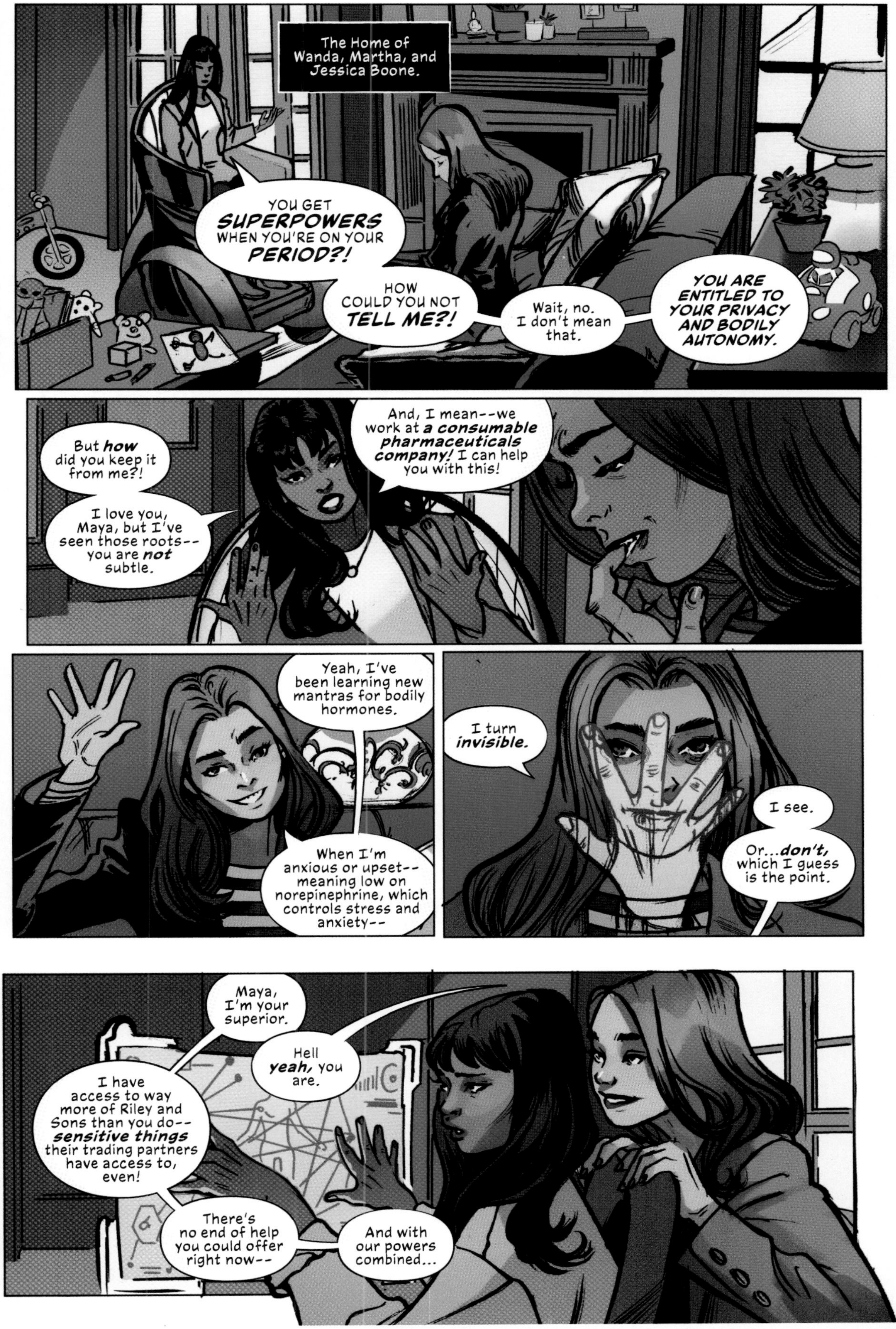

The Home of Wanda, Martha, and Jessica Boone.
YOU GET SUPERPOWERS WHEN YOU'RE ON YOUR PERIOD?!
HOW COULD YOU NOT TELL ME?!
Wait, no. I don't mean that.
YOU ARE ENTITLED TO YOUR PRIVACY AND BODILY AUTONOMY.
But how did you keep it from me?!
I love you, Maya, but I've seen those roots--you are not subtle.
And, I mean--we work at a consumable pharmaceuticals company! I can help you with this!
Yeah, I've been learning new mantras for bodily hormones.
When I'm anxious or upset--meaning low on norepinephrine, which controls stress and anxiety--
I turn invisible.
I see.
Or...don't, which I guess is the point.
Maya, I'm your superior.
Hell yeah, you are.
I have access to way more of Riley and Sons than you do--sensitive things their trading partners have access to, even!
There's no end of help you could offer right now--
And with our powers combined...

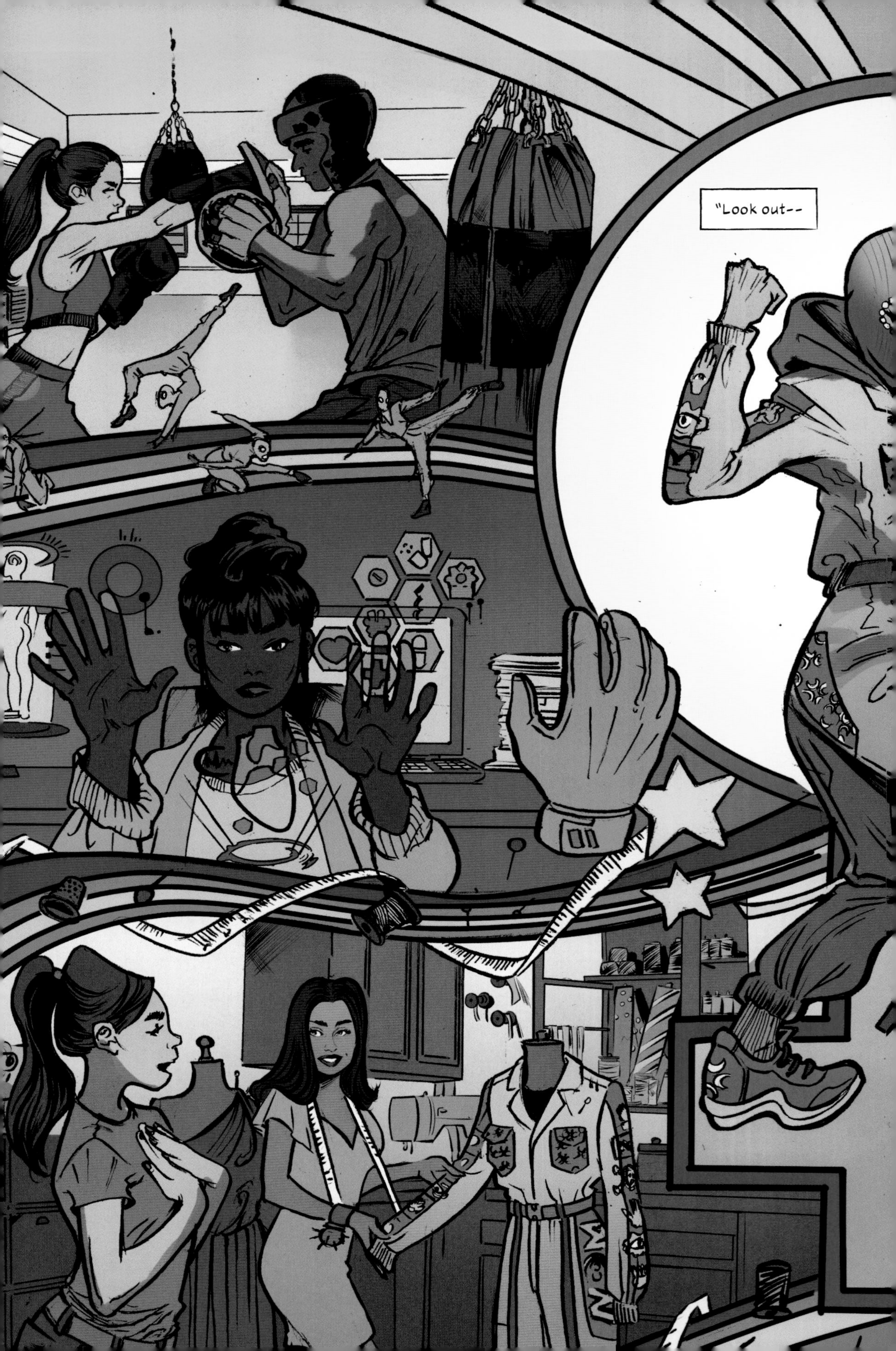
"Look out--

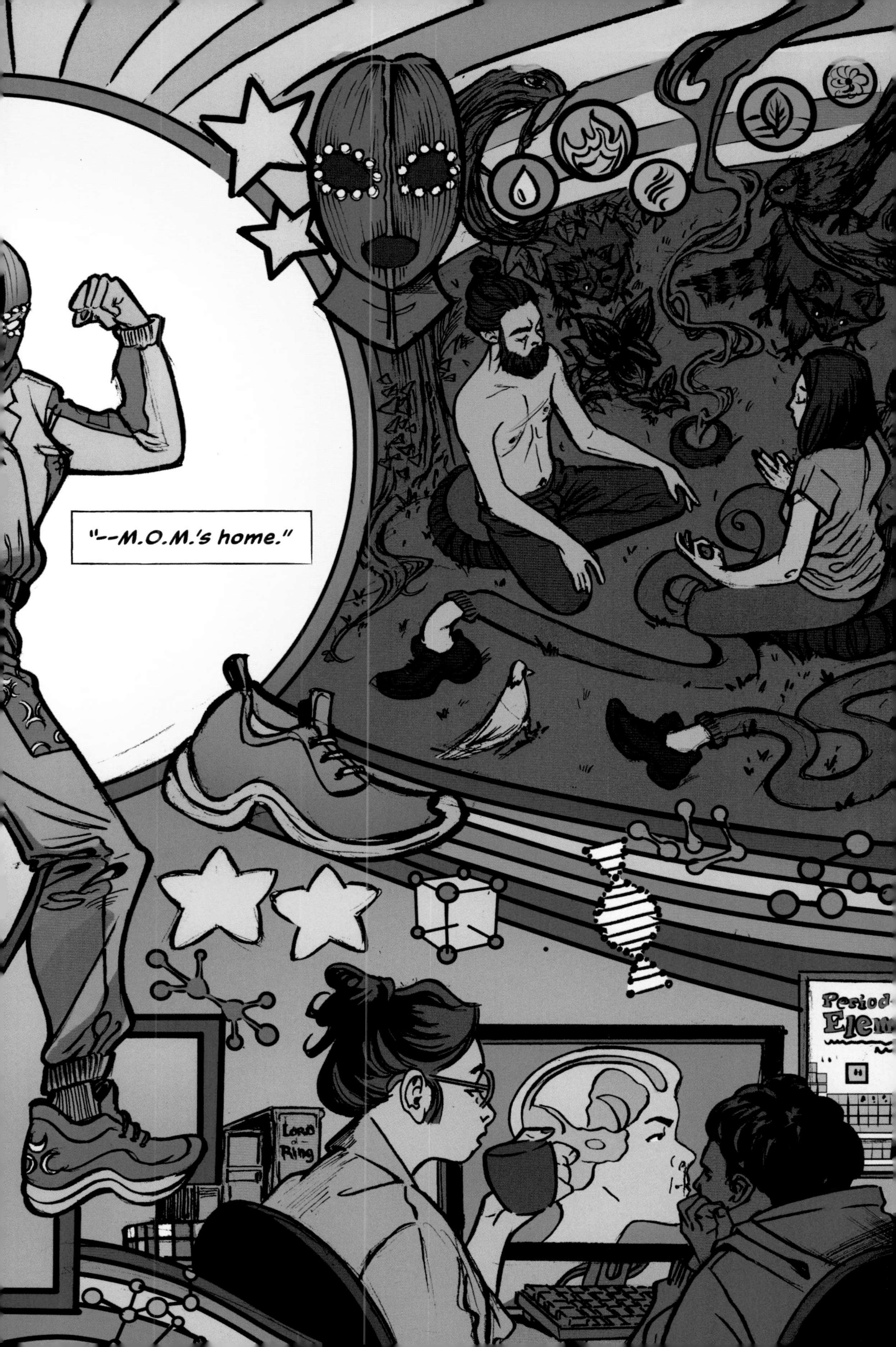
"--M.O.M.'s home."
Period
Elem
Lord
of
Ring

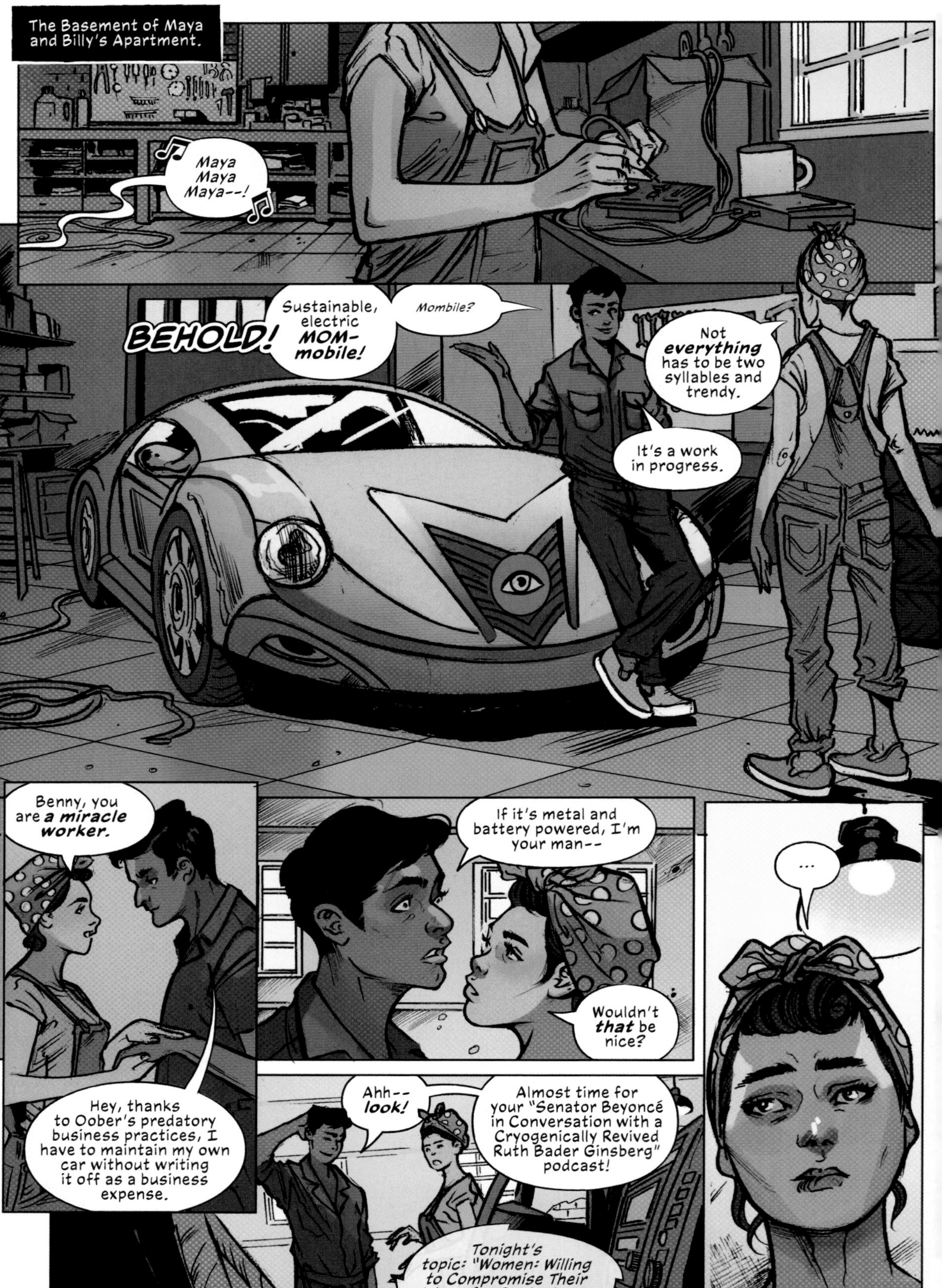
The Basement of Maya and Billy's Apartment.
Maya Maya Maya--!
BEHOLD!
Sustainable, electric MOM-mobile!
Mombile?
Not everything has to be two syllables and trendy.
It's a work in progress.
Benny, you are a miracle worker.
Hey, thanks to Oober's predatory business practices, I have to maintain my own car without writing it off as a business expense.
If it's metal and battery powered, I'm your man--
Wouldn't that be nice?
...
Ahh-- look!
Almost time for your "Senator Beyoncé in Conversation with a Cryogenically Revived Ruth Bader Ginsberg" podcast!
Tonight's topic: "Women: Willing to Compromise Their Values for Basic Human Affection?"

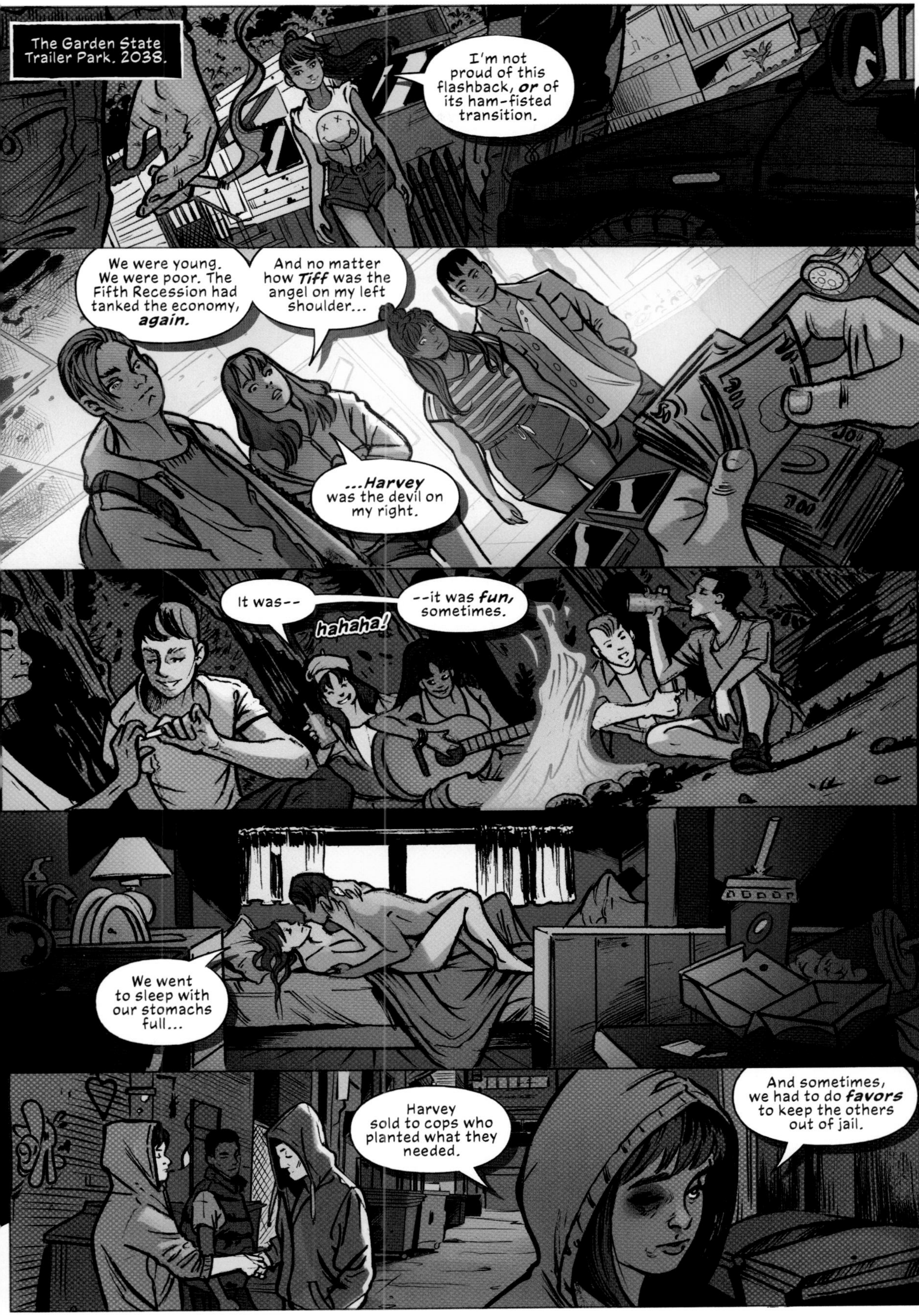
The Garden State Trailer Park. 2038.
I'm not proud of this flashback, *or* of its ham-fisted transition.
We were young. We were poor. The Fifth Recession had tanked the economy, *again.*
And no matter how *Tiff* was the angel on my left shoulder...
...Harvey was the devil on my right.
It was--
--it was *fun,* sometimes.
hahaha!
We went to sleep with our stomachs full...
Harvey sold to cops who planted what they needed.
And sometimes, we had to do *favors* to keep the others out of jail.

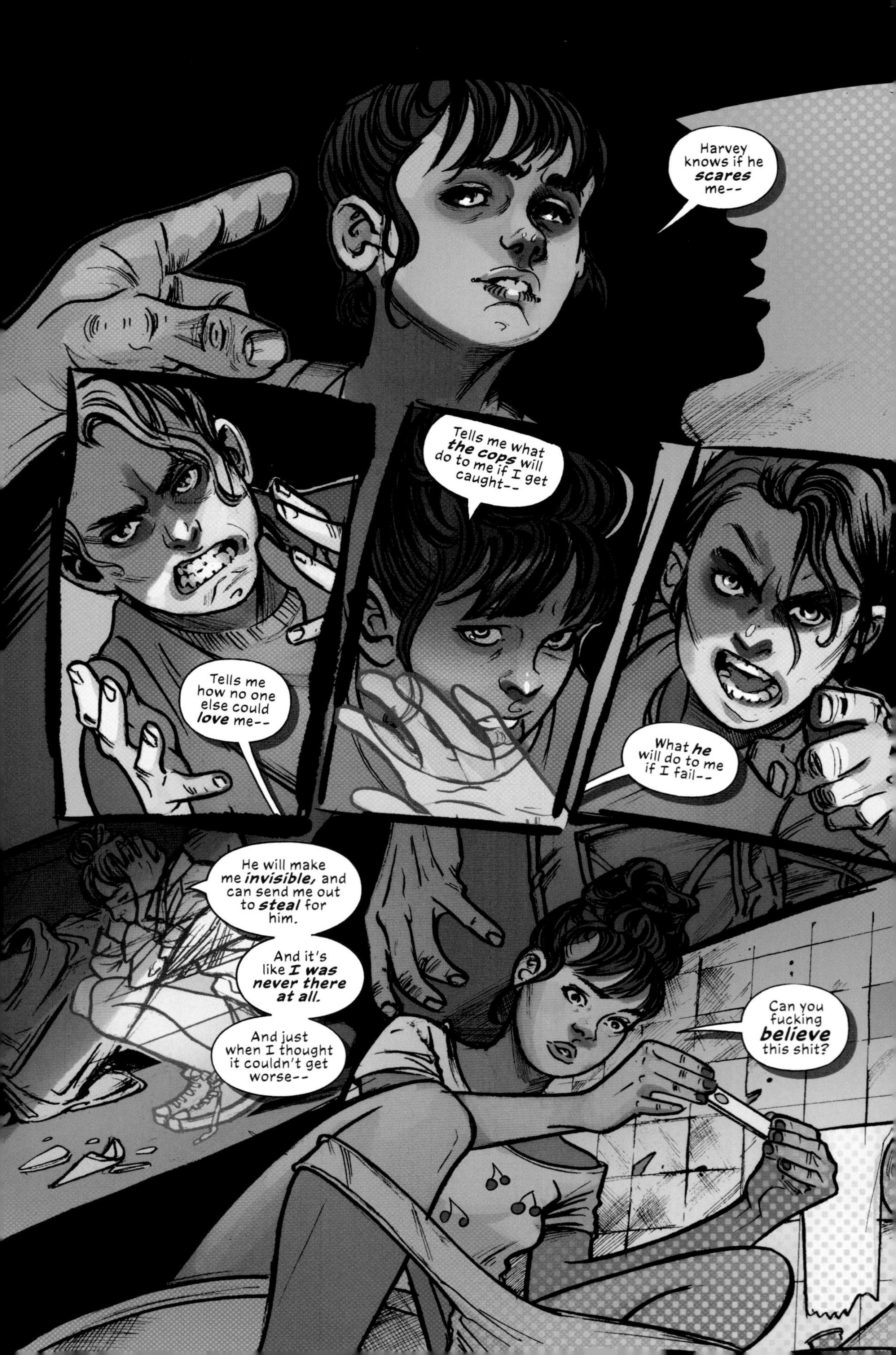
Harvey knows if he scares me--
Tells me how no one else could love me--
Tells me what the cops will do to me if I get caught--
What he will do to me if I fail--
He will make me invisible, and can send me out to steal for him.
And it's like I was never there at all.
And just when I thought it couldn't get worse--
Can you fucking believe this shit?

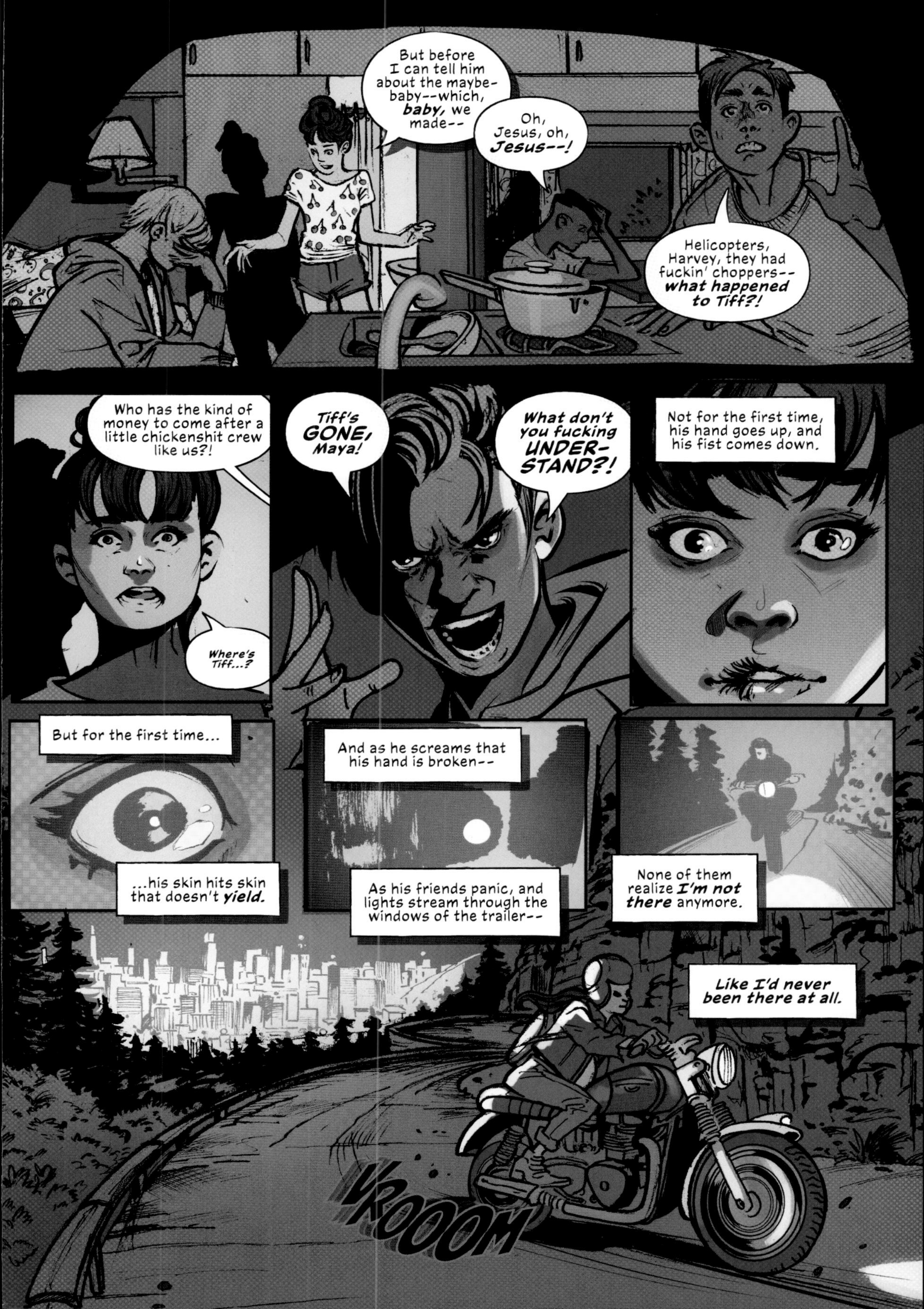
But before I can tell him about the maybe-baby--which, ***baby,*** we made--
Oh, Jesus, oh, ***Jesus--!***
Helicopters, Harvey, they had fuckin' choppers-- ***what happened to Tiff?!***
Who has the kind of money to come after a little chickenshit crew like us?!
Where's Tiff...?
Tiff's GONE, Maya!
What don't you fucking UNDER-STAND?!
Not for the first time, his hand goes up, and his fist comes down.
But for the first time...
...his skin hits skin that doesn't ***yield.***
And as he screams that his hand is broken--
As his friends panic, and lights stream through the windows of the trailer--
None of them realize ***I'm not there*** anymore.
Like I'd never been there at all.
VROOOM

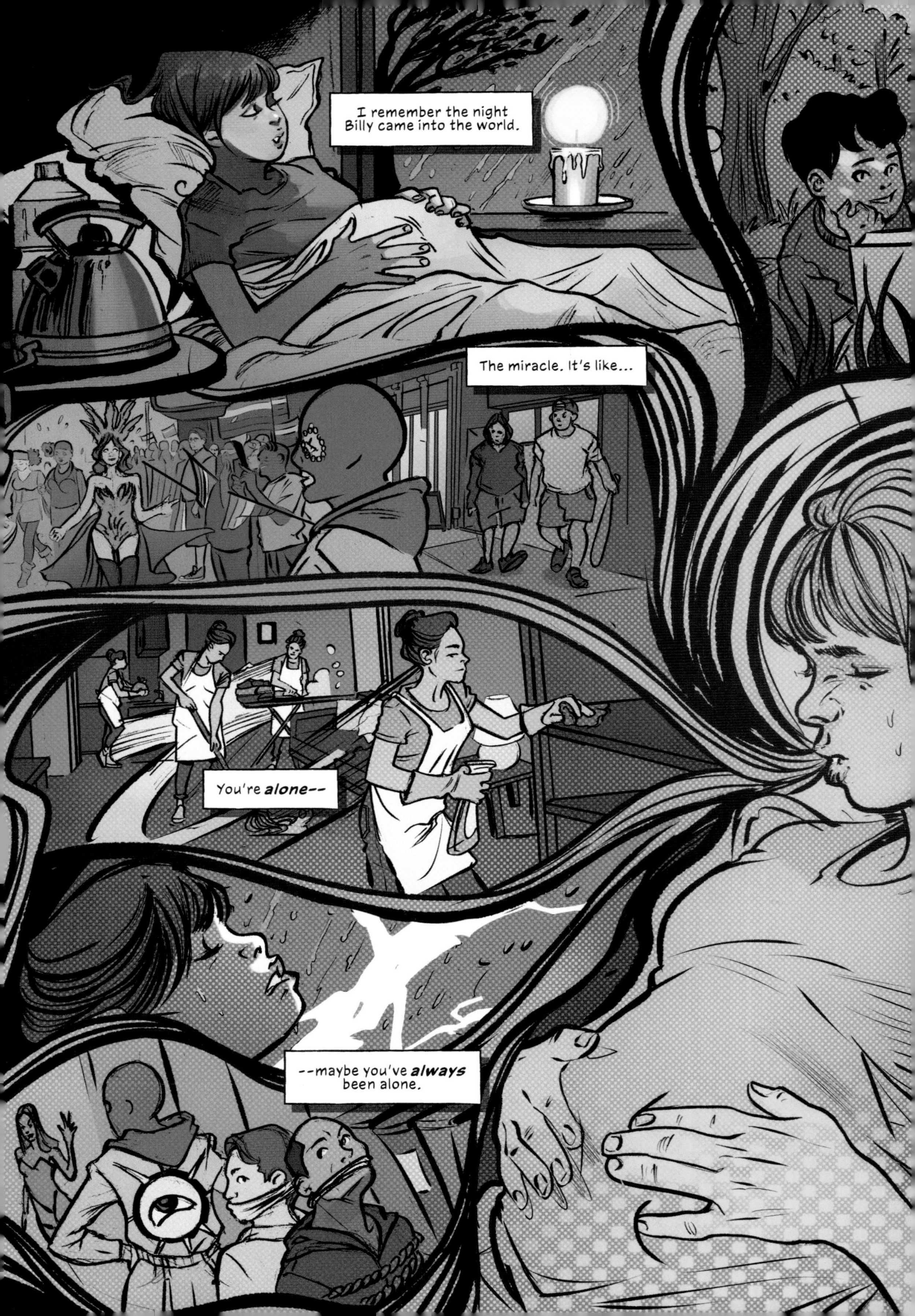
I remember the night
Billy came into the world.
The miracle. It's like...
You're **alone--**
--maybe you've **always**
been alone.

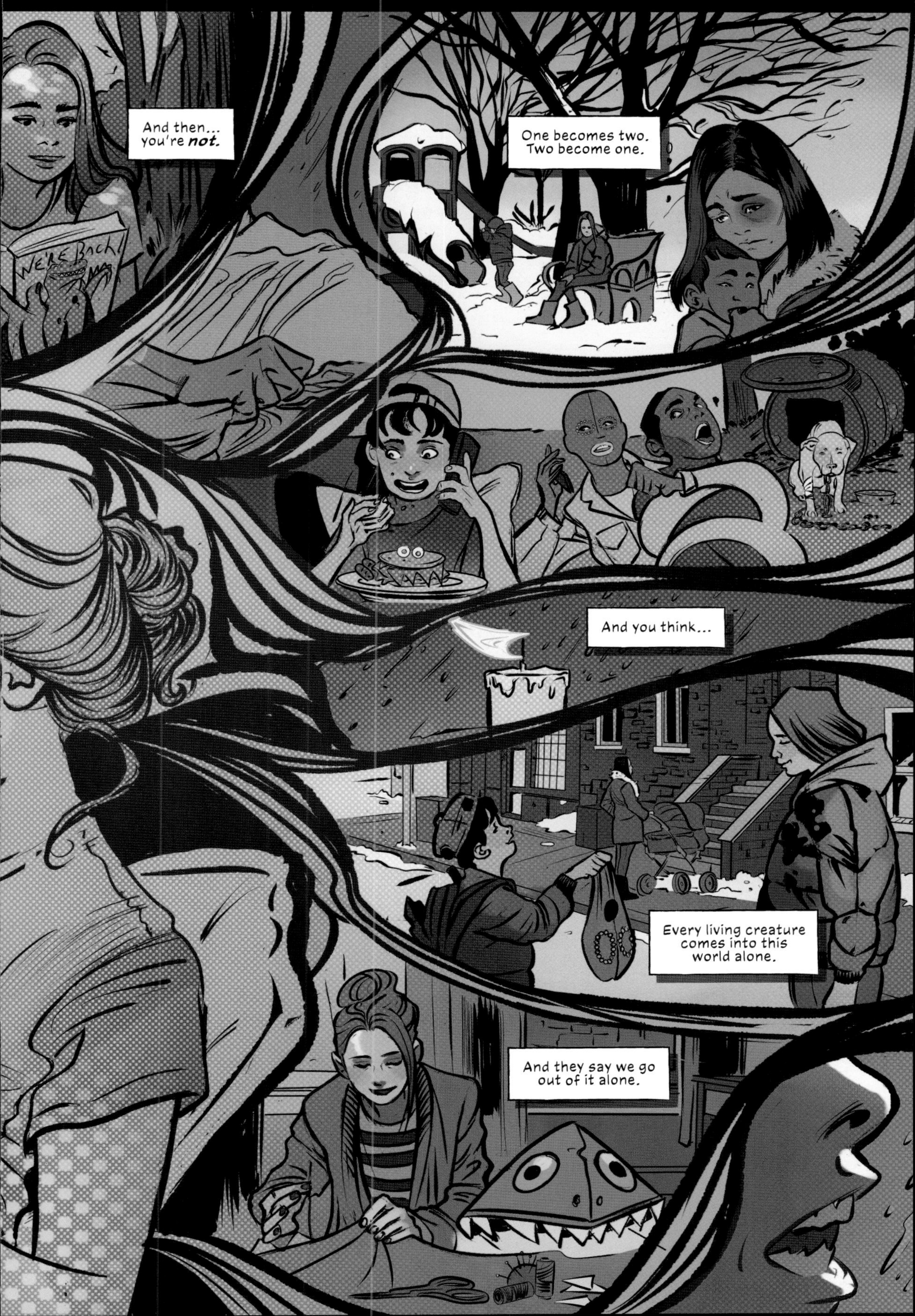
WE'RE BACK!
And then... you're **not.**
One becomes two. Two become one.
And you think...
Every living creature comes into this world alone.
And they say we go out of it alone.

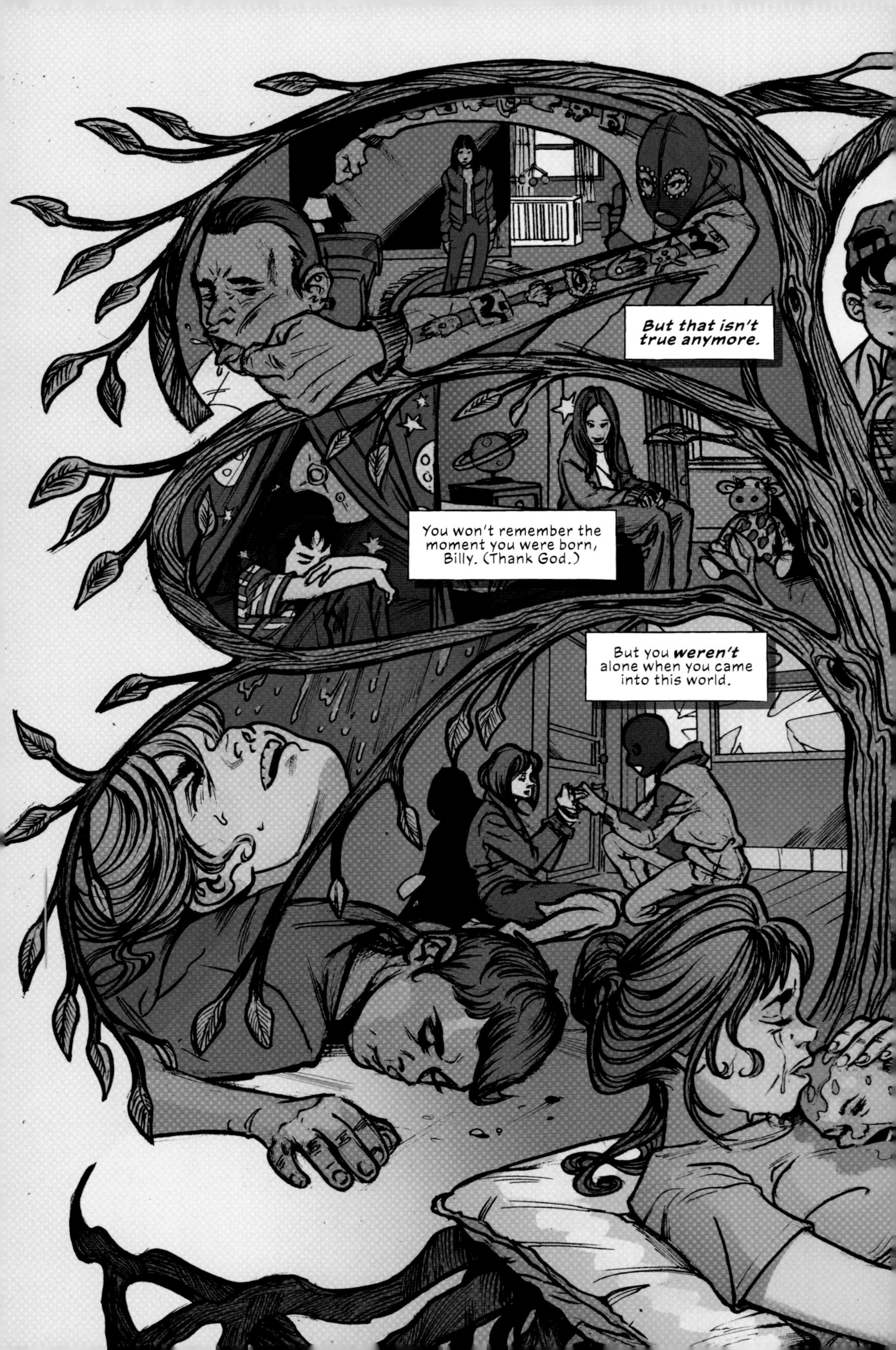
But that isn't true anymore.
You won't remember the moment you were born, Billy. (Thank God.)
But you weren't alone when you came into this world.

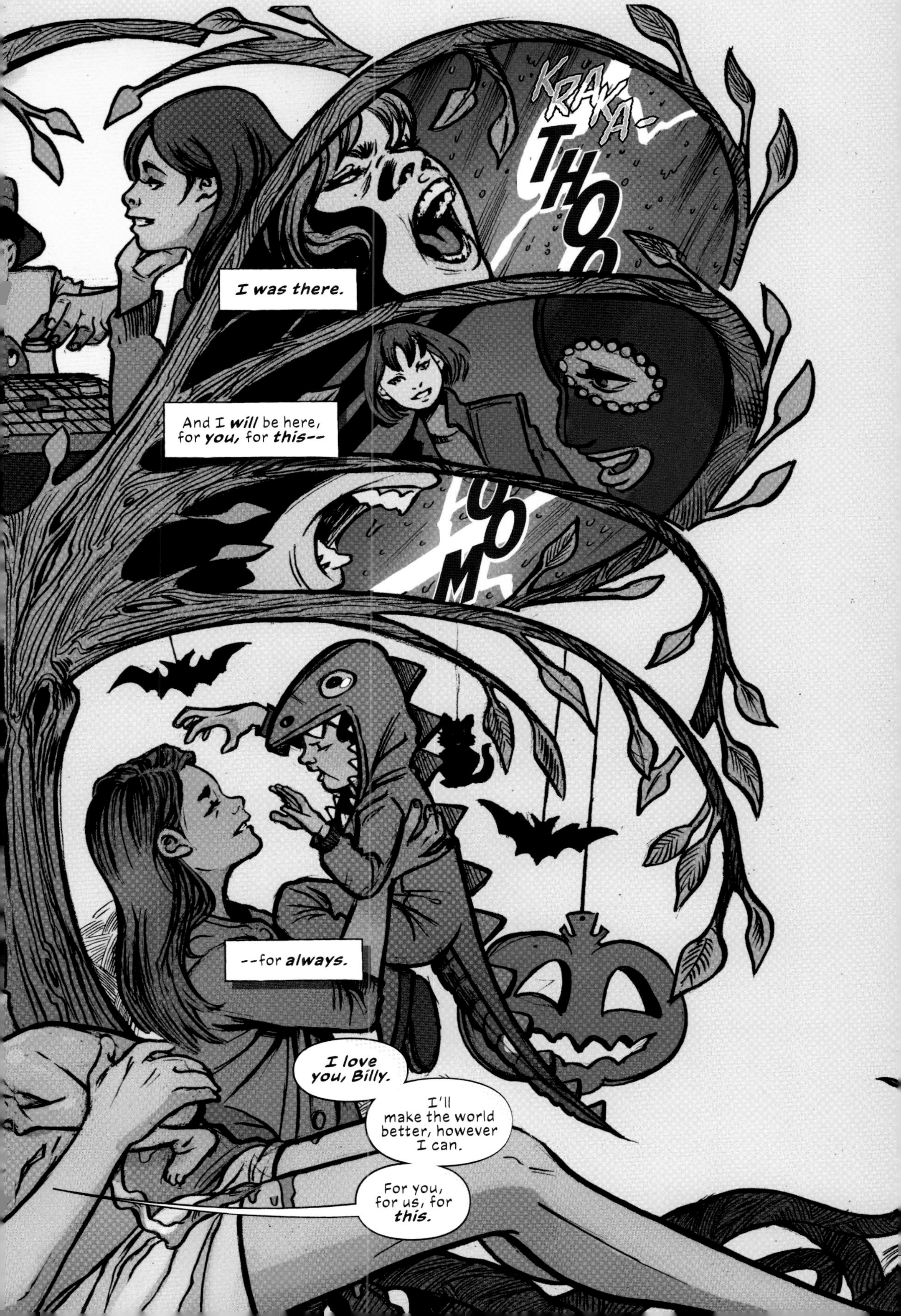
KRAKA-
THOO
I was there.
And I *will* be here, for *you,* for *this--*
OOOM
--for *always.*
I love you, Billy.
I'll make the world better, however I can.
For you, for us, for *this.*

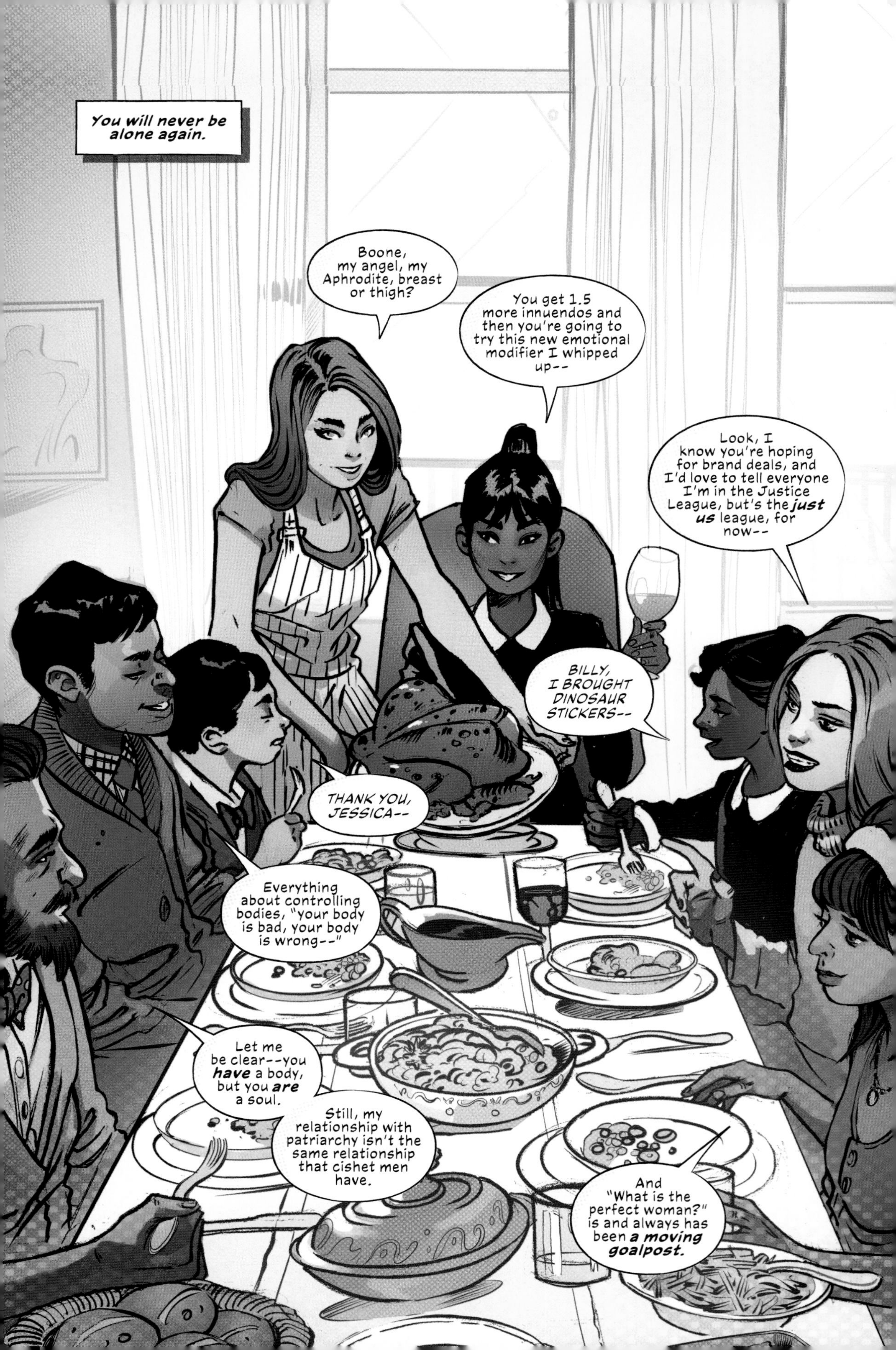
You will never be alone again.
Boone, my angel, my Aphrodite, breast or thigh?
You get 1.5 more innuendos and then you're going to try this new emotional modifier I whipped up--
Look, I know you're hoping for brand deals, and I'd love to tell everyone I'm in the Justice League, but's the just us league, for now--
BILLY, I BROUGHT DINOSAUR STICKERS--
THANK YOU, JESSICA--
Everything about controlling bodies, "your body is bad, your body is wrong--"
Let me be clear--you have a body, but you are a soul.
Still, my relationship with patriarchy isn't the same relationship that cishet men have.
And "What is the perfect woman?" is and always has been a moving goalpost.

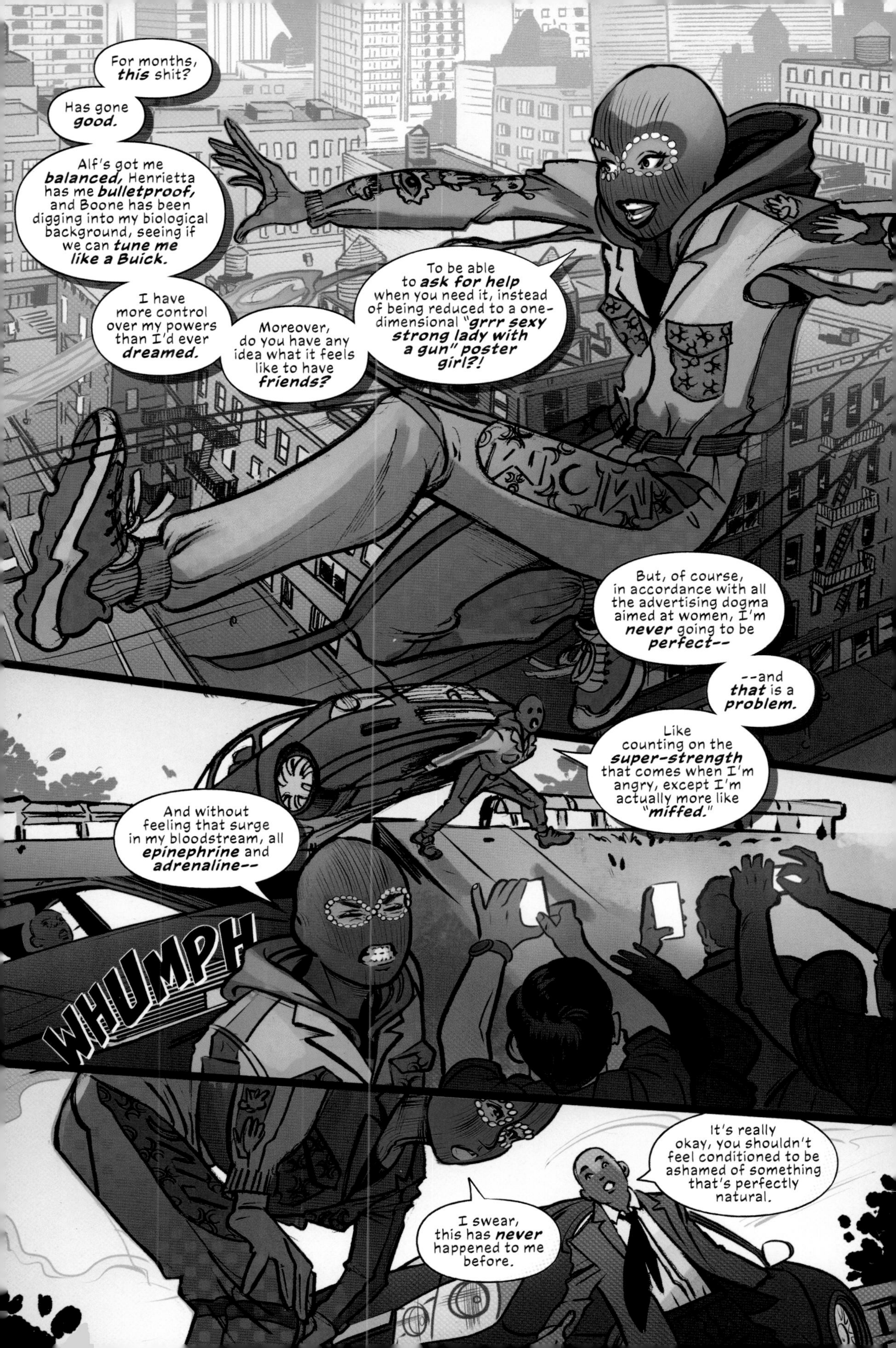
For months, this shit?
Has gone good.
Alf's got me balanced, Henrietta has me bulletproof, and Boone has been digging into my biological background, seeing if we can tune me like a Buick.
I have more control over my powers than I'd ever dreamed.
Moreover, do you have any idea what it feels like to have friends?
To be able to ask for help when you need it, instead of being reduced to a one-dimensional "grrr sexy strong lady with a gun" poster girl?!
But, of course, in accordance with all the advertising dogma aimed at women, I'm never going to be perfect--
--and that is a problem.
Like counting on the super-strength that comes when I'm angry, except I'm actually more like "miffed."
And without feeling that surge in my bloodstream, all epinephrine and adrenaline--
WHUMPH
It's really okay, you shouldn't feel conditioned to be ashamed of something that's perfectly natural.
I swear, this has never happened to me before.

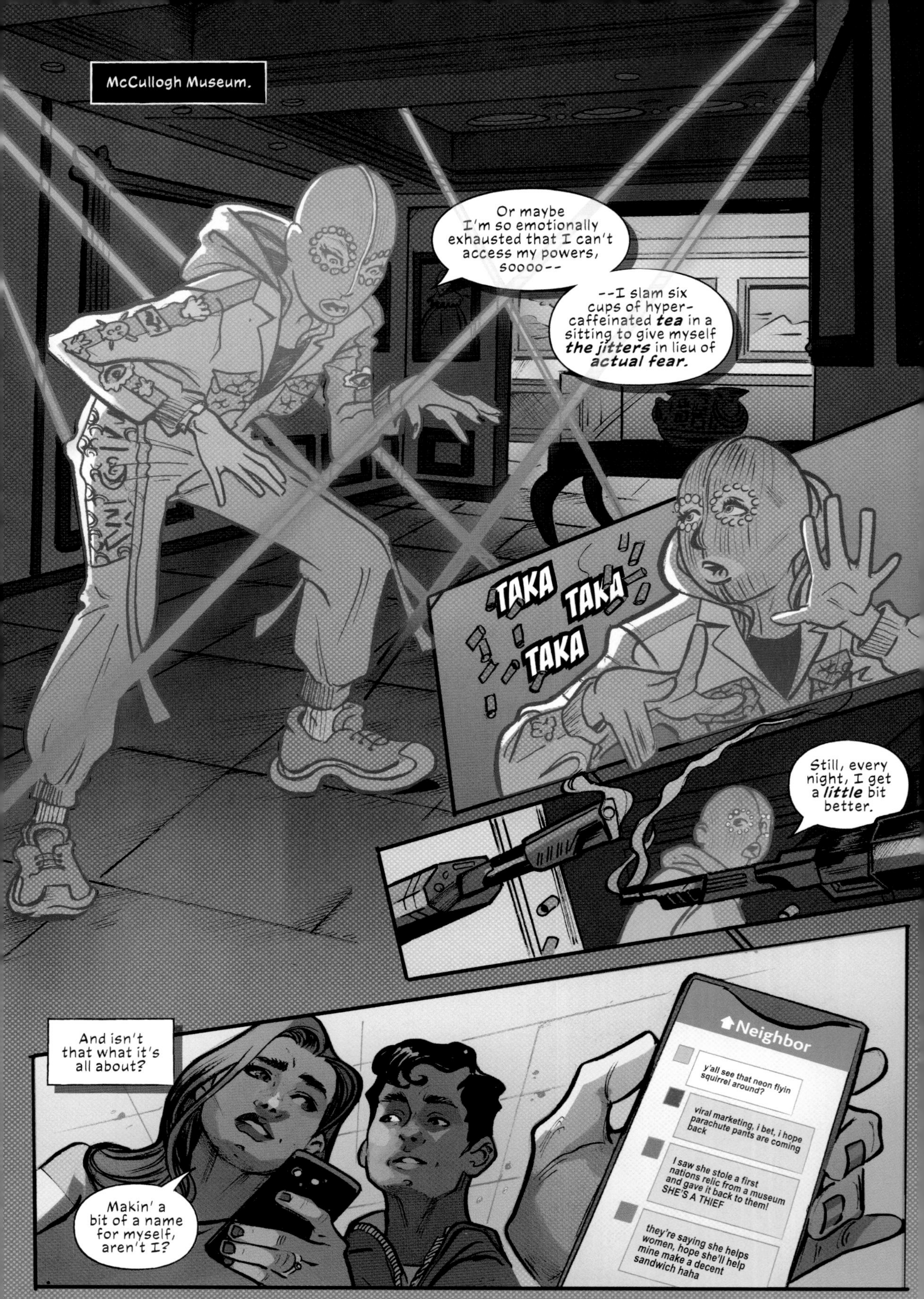

McCullogh Museum.
Or maybe I'm so emotionally exhausted that I can't access my powers, soooo--
--I slam six cups of hyper-caffeinated tea in a sitting to give myself the jitters in lieu of actual fear.
TAKA TAKA TAKA
Still, every night, I get a little bit better.
And isn't that what it's all about?
Neighbor
y'all see that neon flyin squirrel around?
viral marketing, i bet, i hope parachute pants are coming back
I saw she stole a first nations relic from a museum and gave it back to them! SHE'S A THIEF
they're saying she helps women, hope she'll help mine make a decent sandwich haha
Makin' a bit of a name for myself, aren't I?

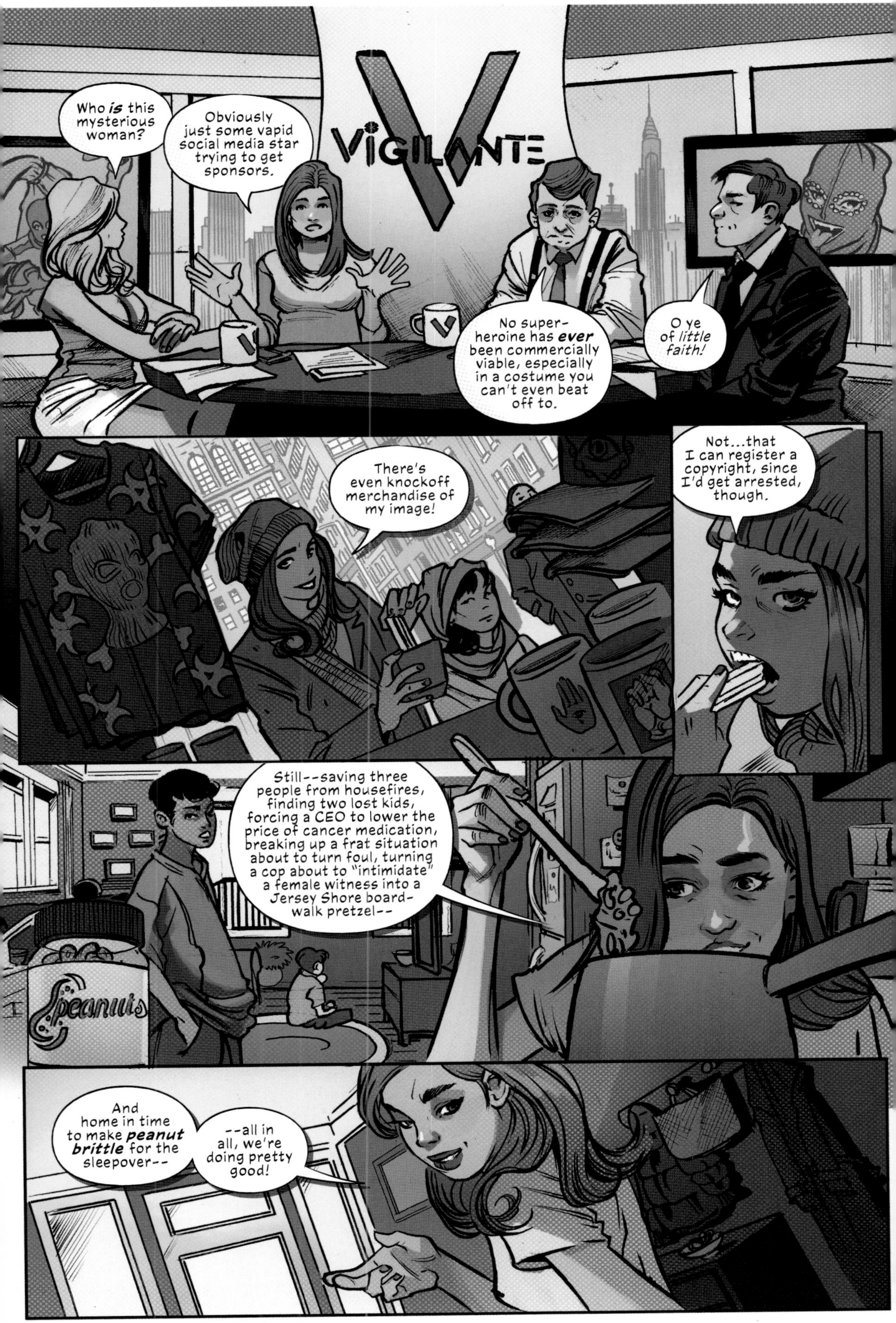
VIGILANTE
Who *is* this mysterious woman?
Obviously just some vapid social media star trying to get sponsors.
No super-heroine has ***ever*** been commercially viable, especially in a costume you can't even beat off to.
O ye of *little faith!*
There's even knockoff merchandise of my image!
Not...that I can register a copyright, since I'd get arrested, though.
Still--saving three people from housefires, finding two lost kids, forcing a CEO to lower the price of cancer medication, breaking up a frat situation about to turn foul, turning a cop about to "intimidate" a female witness into a Jersey Shore board-walk pretzel--
Peanuts
And home in time to make ***peanut brittle*** for the sleepover--
--all in all, we're doing pretty good!

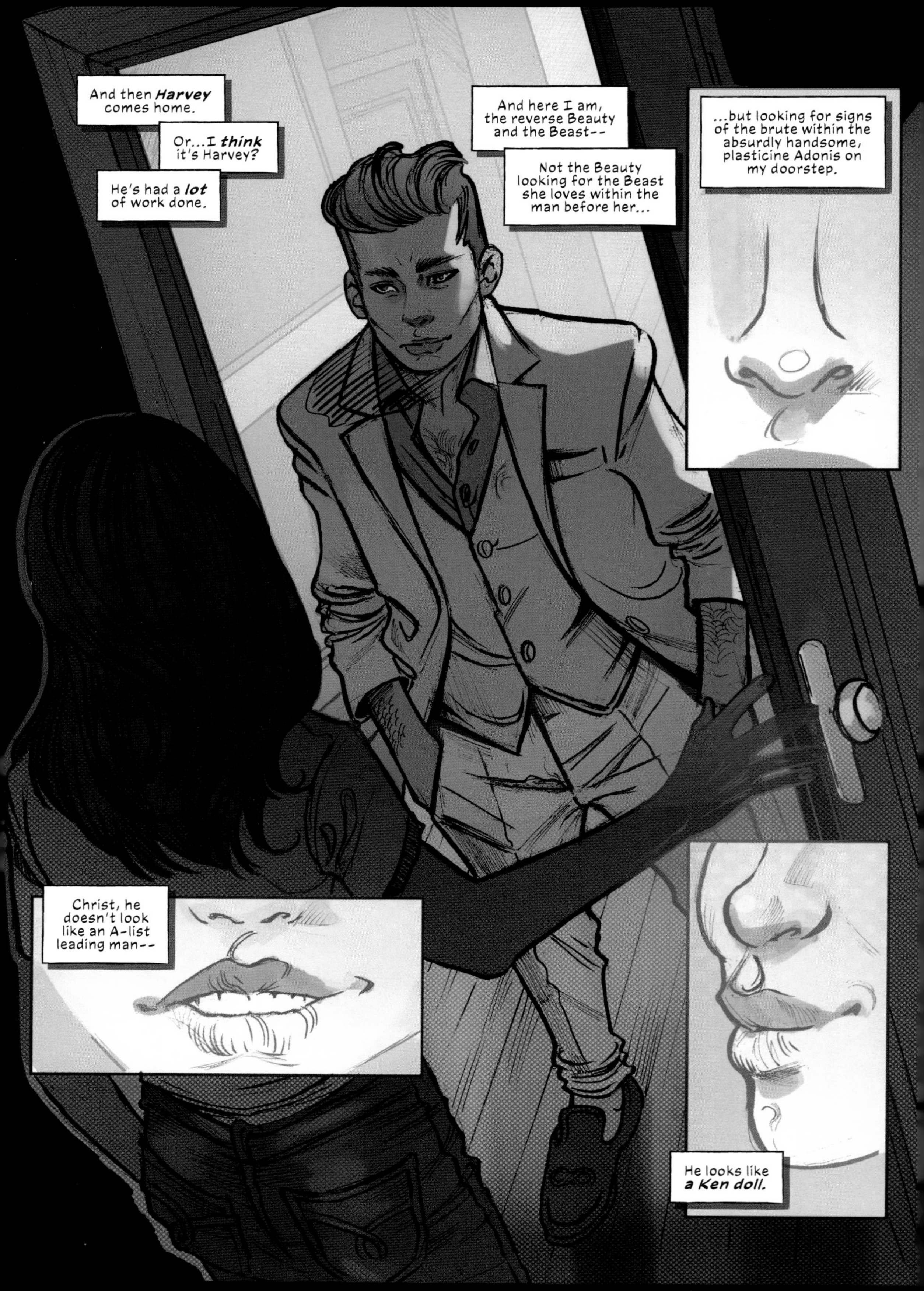
And then *Harvey* comes home.
Or...I *think* it's Harvey?
He's had a *lot* of work done.
And here I am, the reverse Beauty and the Beast--
Not the Beauty looking for the Beast she loves within the man before her...
...but looking for signs of the brute within the absurdly handsome, plasticine Adonis on my doorstep.
Christ, he doesn't look like an A-list leading man--
He looks like *a Ken doll.*

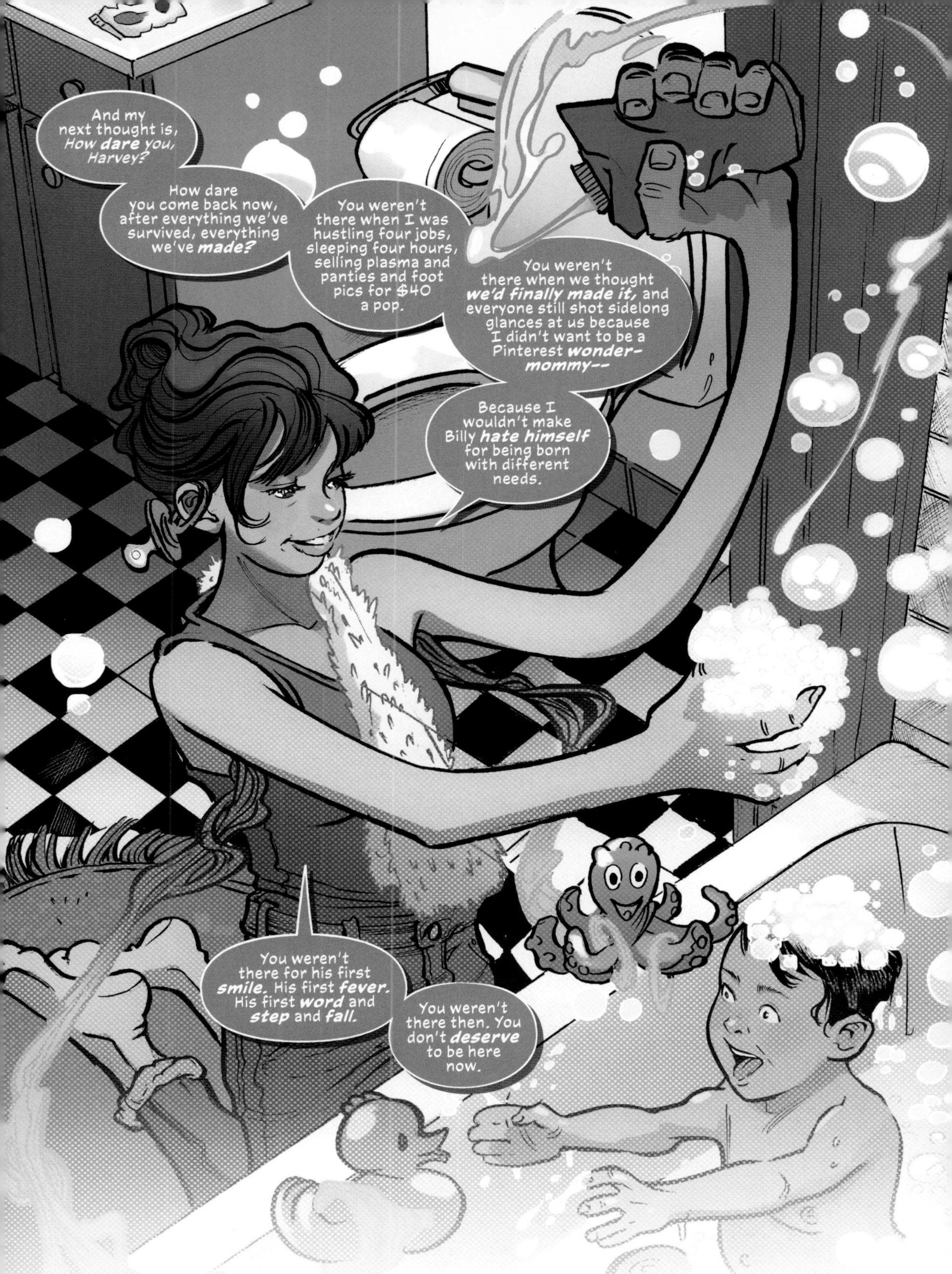
And my next thought is, *How **dare** you, Harvey?*
How dare you come back now, after everything we've survived, everything we've ***made?***
You weren't there when I was hustling four jobs, sleeping four hours, selling plasma and panties and foot pics for $40 a pop.
You weren't there when we thought ***we'd finally made it,*** and everyone still shot sidelong glances at us because I didn't want to be a Pinterest ***wonder-mommy--***
Because I wouldn't make Billy ***hate himself*** for being born with different needs.
You weren't there for his first ***smile.*** His first ***fever.*** His first ***word*** and ***step*** and ***fall.***
You weren't there then. You don't ***deserve*** to be here now.

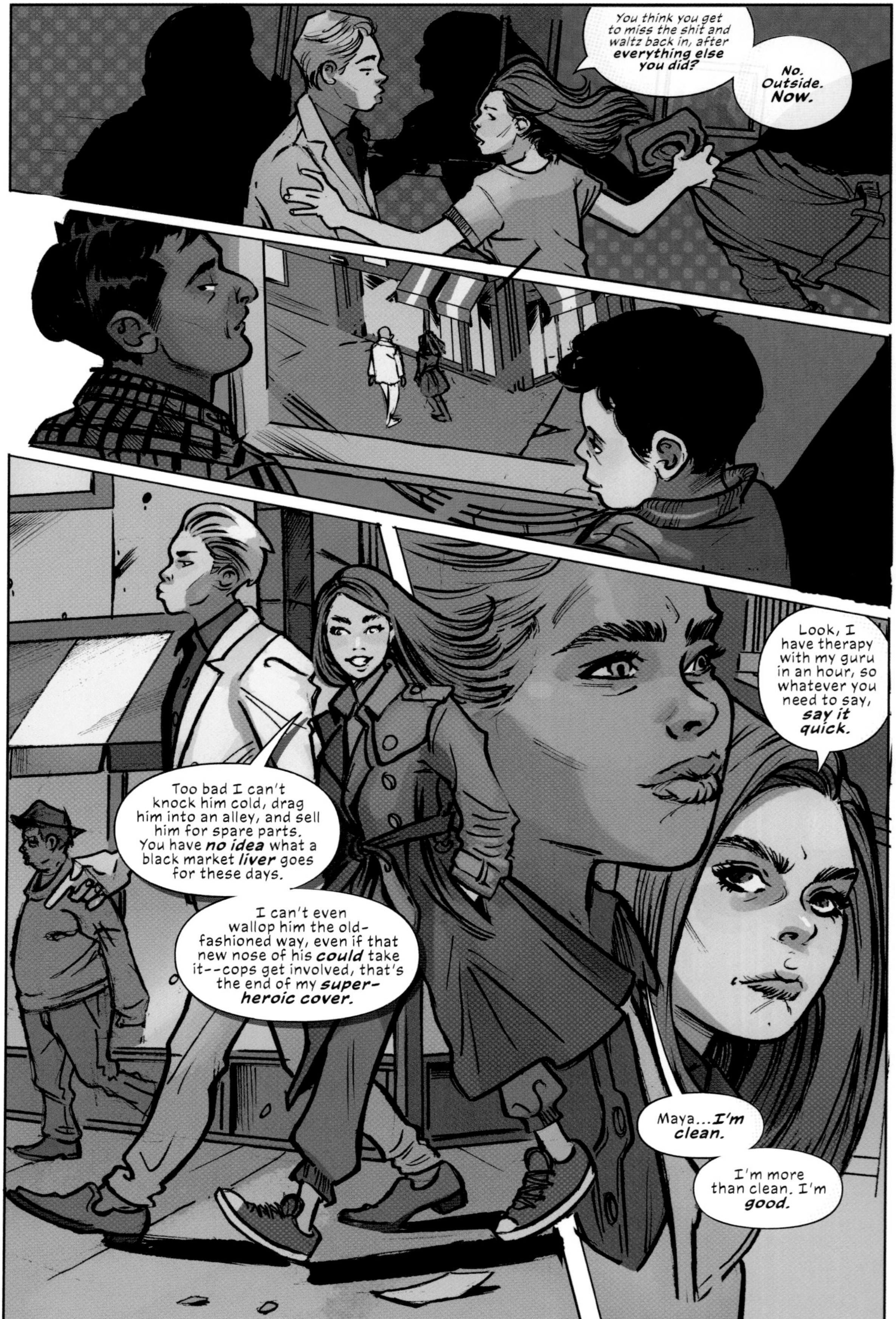
You think you get to miss the shit and waltz back in, after **everything else** you did?
No. Outside. Now.
Look, I have therapy with my guru in an hour, so whatever you need to say, ***say it quick.***
Too bad I can't knock him cold, drag him into an alley, and sell him for spare parts. You have ***no idea*** what a black market ***liver*** goes for these days.
I can't even wallop him the old-fashioned way, even if that new nose of his ***could*** take it--cops get involved, that's the end of my ***super-heroic cover.***
Maya... ***I'm clean.***
I'm more than clean. I'm ***good.***

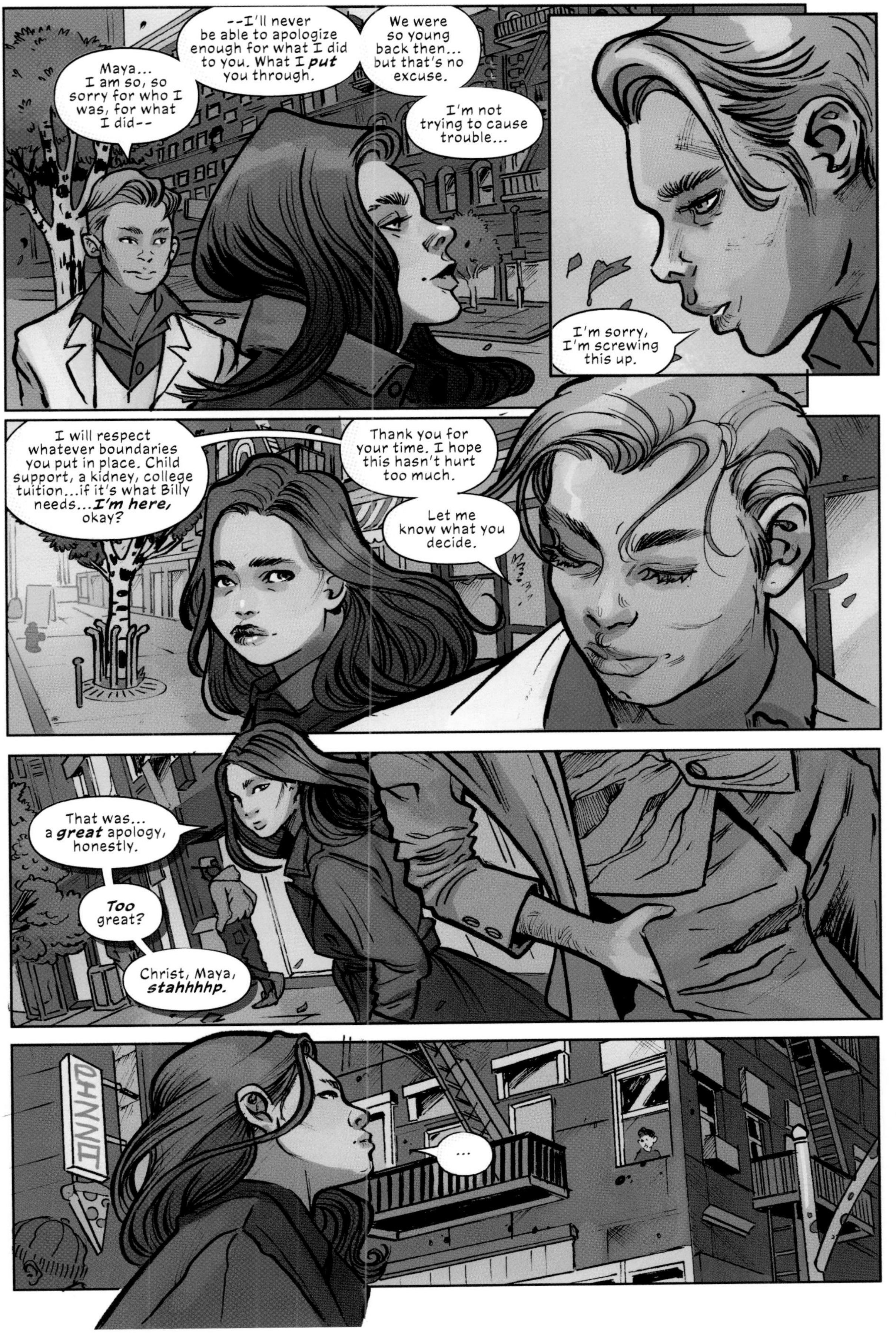
Maya... I am so, sorry for who I was, for what I did--
--I'll never be able to apologize enough for what I did to you. What I *put* you through.
We were so young back then... but that's no excuse.
I'm not trying to cause trouble...
I'm sorry, I'm screwing this up.
I will respect whatever boundaries you put in place. Child support, a kidney, college tuition...if it's what Billy needs...*I'm here,* okay?
Thank you for your time. I hope this hasn't hurt too much.
Let me know what you decide.
That was... a *great* apology, honestly.
Too great?
Christ, Maya, *stahhhhp.*
...

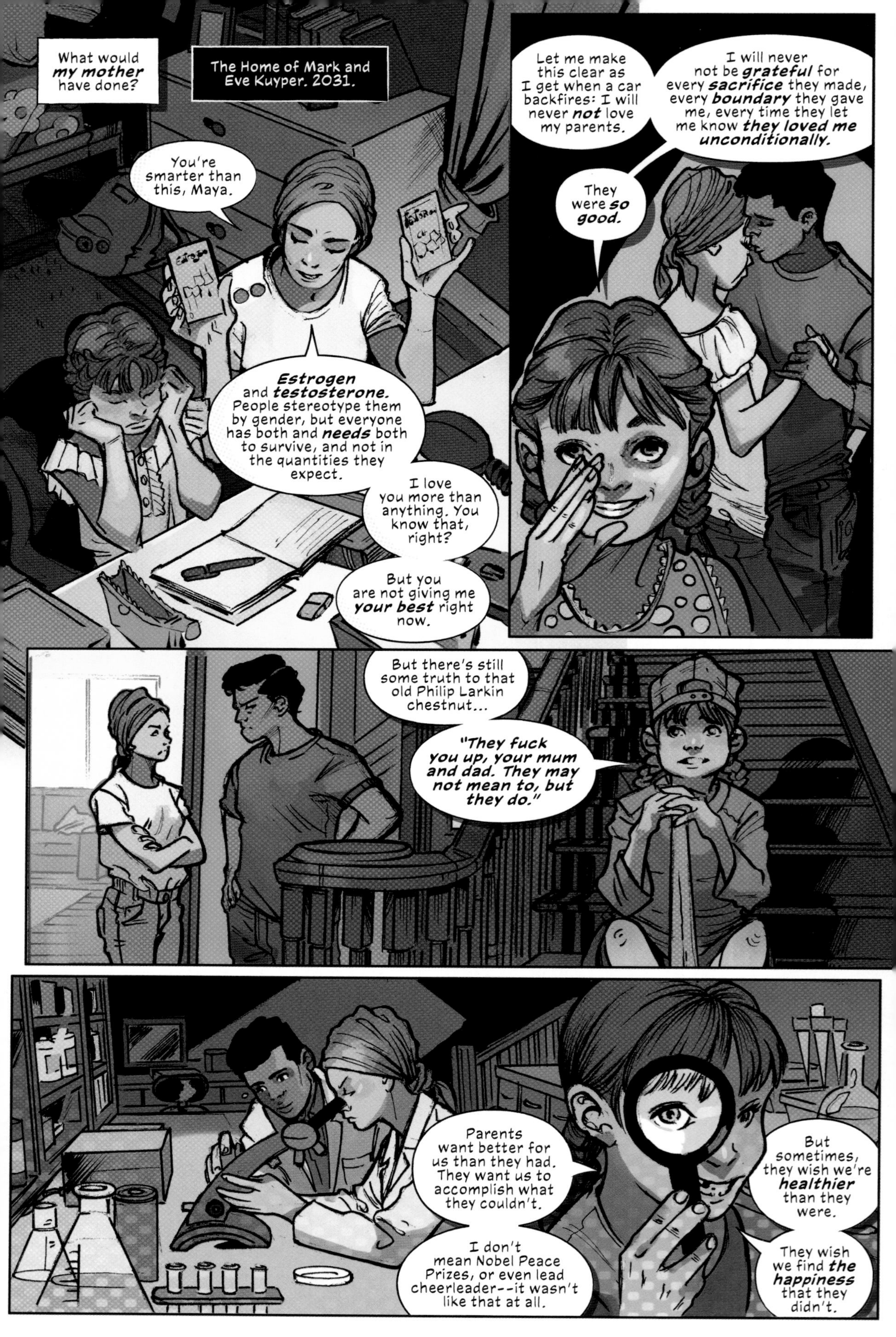

What would my mother have done?
The Home of Mark and Eve Kuyper. 2031.
You're smarter than this, Maya.
Estrogen and testosterone. People stereotype them by gender, but everyone has both and needs both to survive, and not in the quantities they expect.
I love you more than anything. You know that, right?
But you are not giving me your best right now.
Let me make this clear as I get when a car backfires: I will never not love my parents.
I will never not be grateful for every sacrifice they made, every boundary they gave me, every time they let me know they loved me unconditionally.
They were so good.
But there's still some truth to that old Philip Larkin chestnut...
"They fuck you up, your mum and dad. They may not mean to, but they do."
Parents want better for us than they had. They want us to accomplish what they couldn't.
I don't mean Nobel Peace Prizes, or even lead cheerleader--it wasn't like that at all.
But sometimes, they wish we're healthier than they were.
They wish we find the happiness that they didn't.

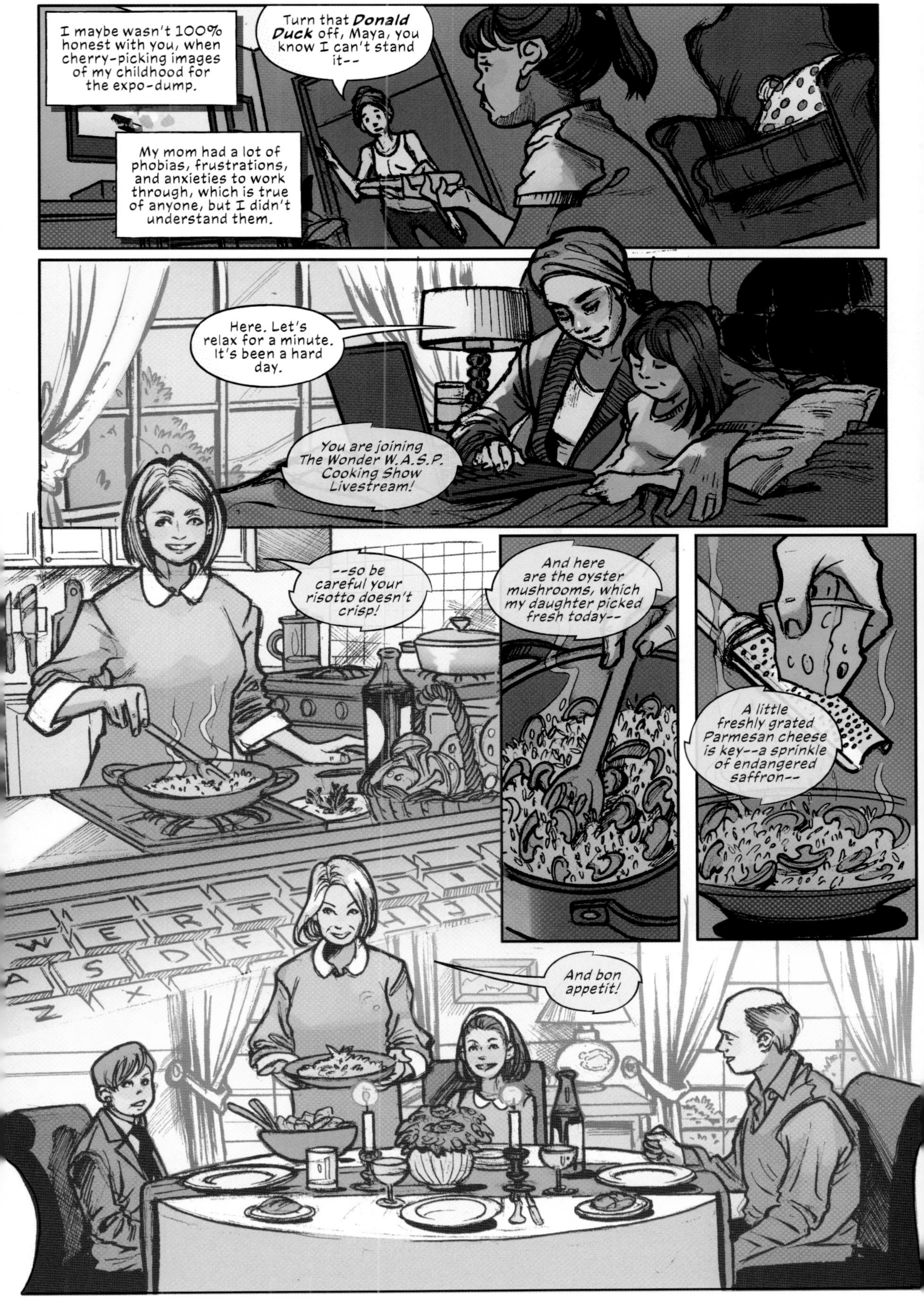
I maybe wasn't 100% honest with you, when cherry-picking images of my childhood for the expo-dump.
Turn that **Donald Duck** off, Maya, you know I can't stand it--
My mom had a lot of phobias, frustrations, and anxieties to work through, which is true of anyone, but I didn't understand them.
Here. Let's relax for a minute. It's been a hard day.
You are joining The Wonder W.A.S.P. Cooking Show Livestream!
--so be careful your risotto doesn't crisp!
And here are the oyster mushrooms, which my daughter picked fresh today--
A little freshly grated Parmesan cheese is key--a sprinkle of endangered saffron--
And bon appetit!

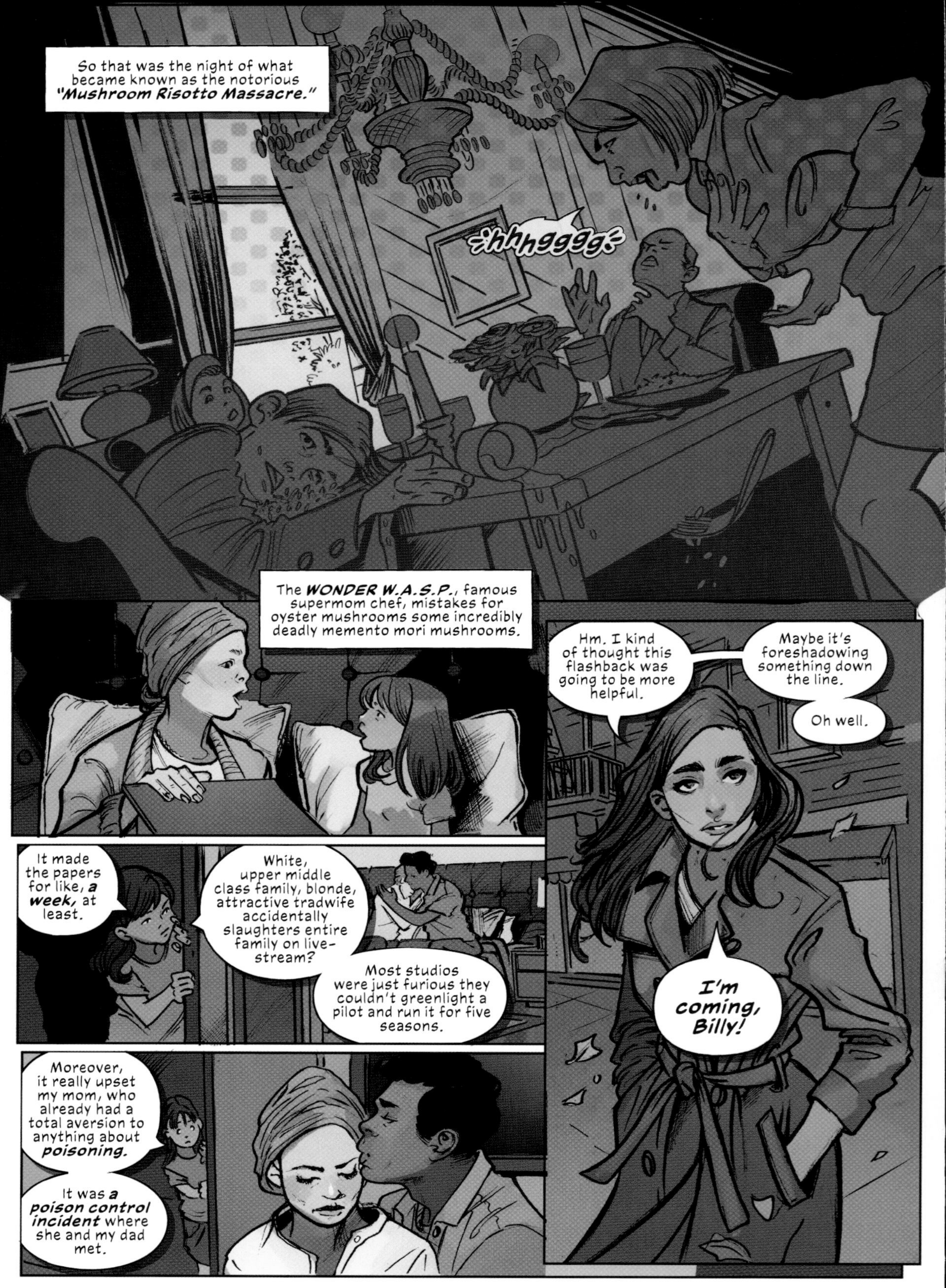
So that was the night of what became known as the notorious ***"Mushroom Risotto Massacre."***
-hhhggggg-
The ***WONDER W.A.S.P.***, famous supermom chef, mistakes for oyster mushrooms some incredibly deadly memento mori mushrooms.
Hm. I kind of thought this flashback was going to be more helpful.
Maybe it's foreshadowing something down the line.
Oh well.
It made the papers for like, ***a week,*** at least.
White, upper middle class family, blonde, attractive tradwife accidentally slaughters entire family on live-stream?
Most studios were just furious they couldn't greenlight a pilot and run it for five seasons.
I'm coming, Billy!
Moreover, it really upset my mom, who already had a total aversion to anything about ***poisoning.***
It was ***a poison control incident*** where she and my dad met.

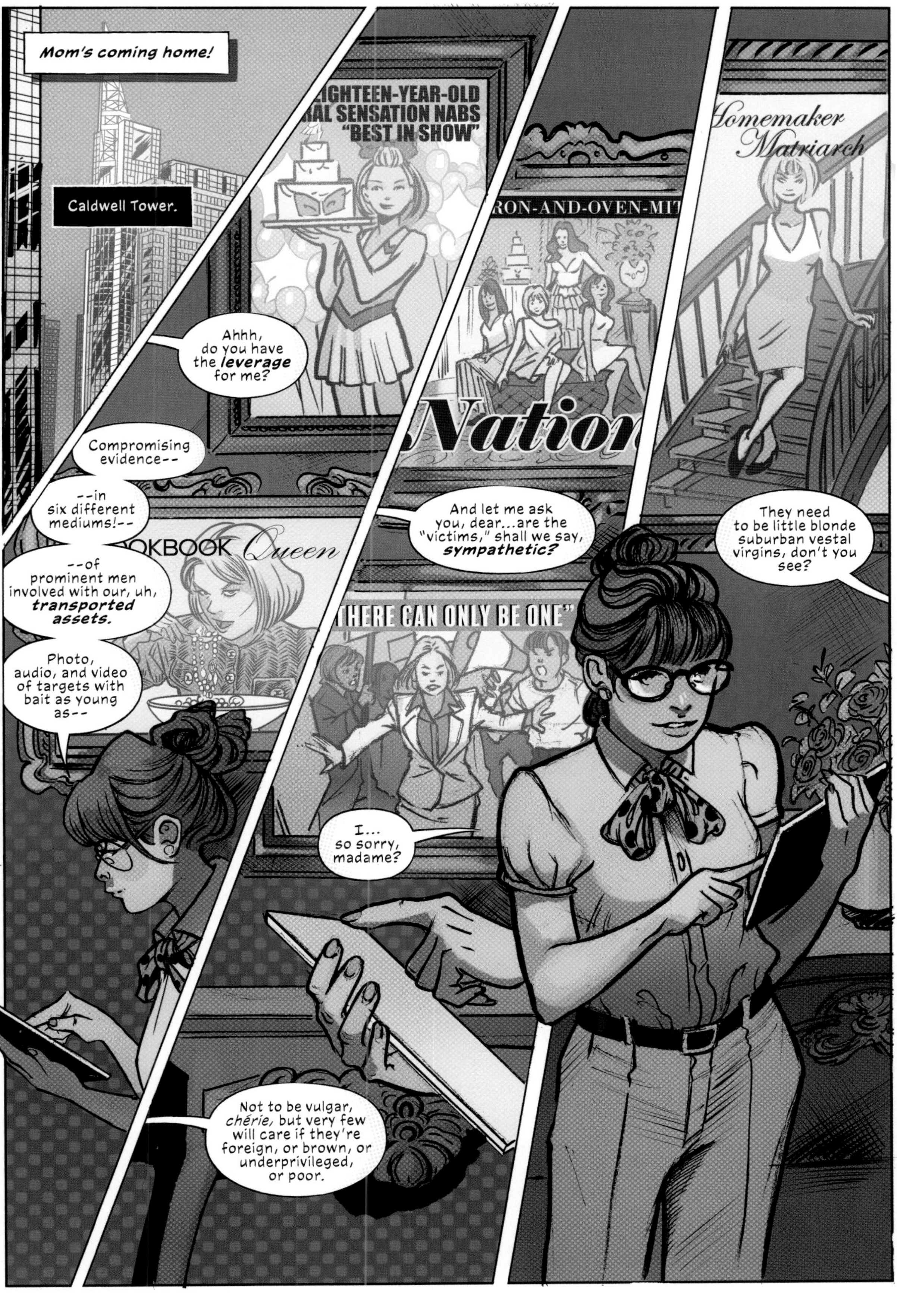

Mom's coming home!
Caldwell Tower.
EIGHTEEN-YEAR-OLD
RAL SENSATION NABS
"BEST IN SHOW"
RON-AND-OVEN-MIT
Nation
Homemaker Matriarch
Ahhh, do you have the leverage for me?
Compromising evidence--
--in six different mediums!--
--of prominent men involved with our, uh, transported assets.
Photo, audio, and video of targets with bait as young as--
OKBOOK Queen
And let me ask you, dear...are the "victims," shall we say, sympathetic?
They need to be little blonde suburban vestal virgins, don't you see?
"THERE CAN ONLY BE ONE"
I... so sorry, madame?
Not to be vulgar, chérie, but very few will care if they're foreign, or brown, or underprivileged, or poor.

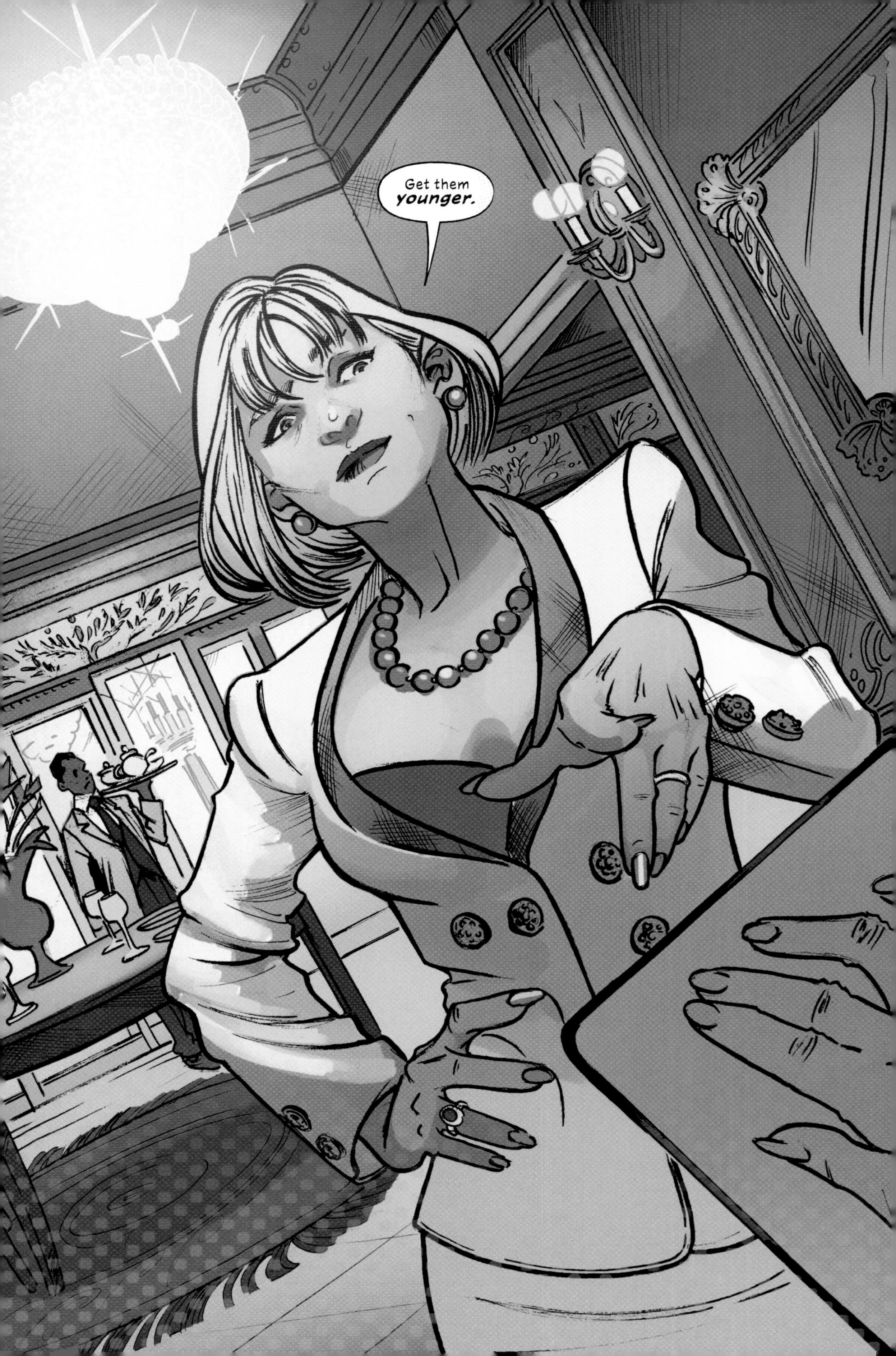
Get them *younger.*

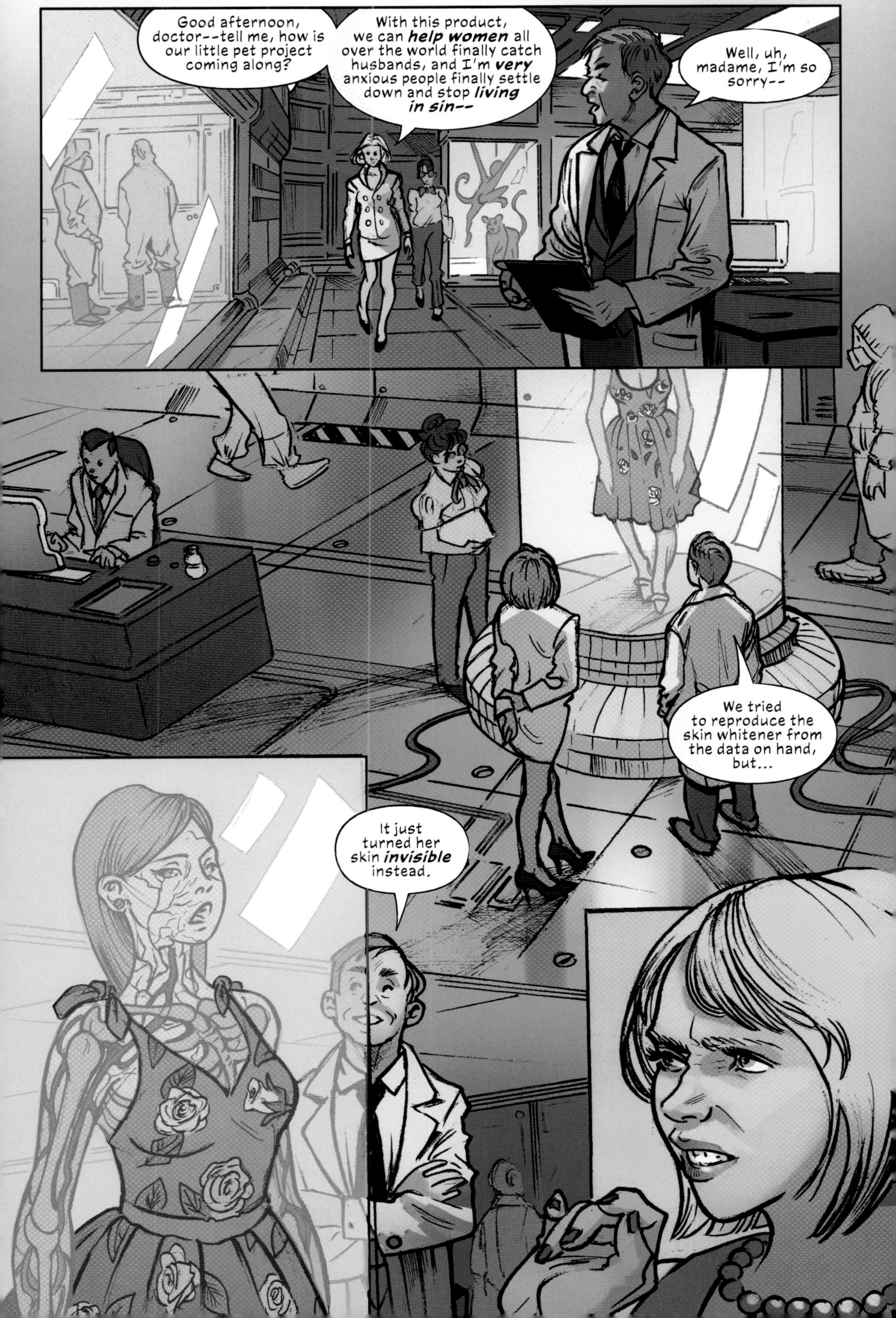
Good afternoon, doctor--tell me, how is our little pet project coming along?
With this product, we can help women all over the world finally catch husbands, and I'm very anxious people finally settle down and stop living in sin--
Well, uh, madame, I'm so sorry--
We tried to reproduce the skin whitener from the data on hand, but...
It just turned her skin invisible instead.

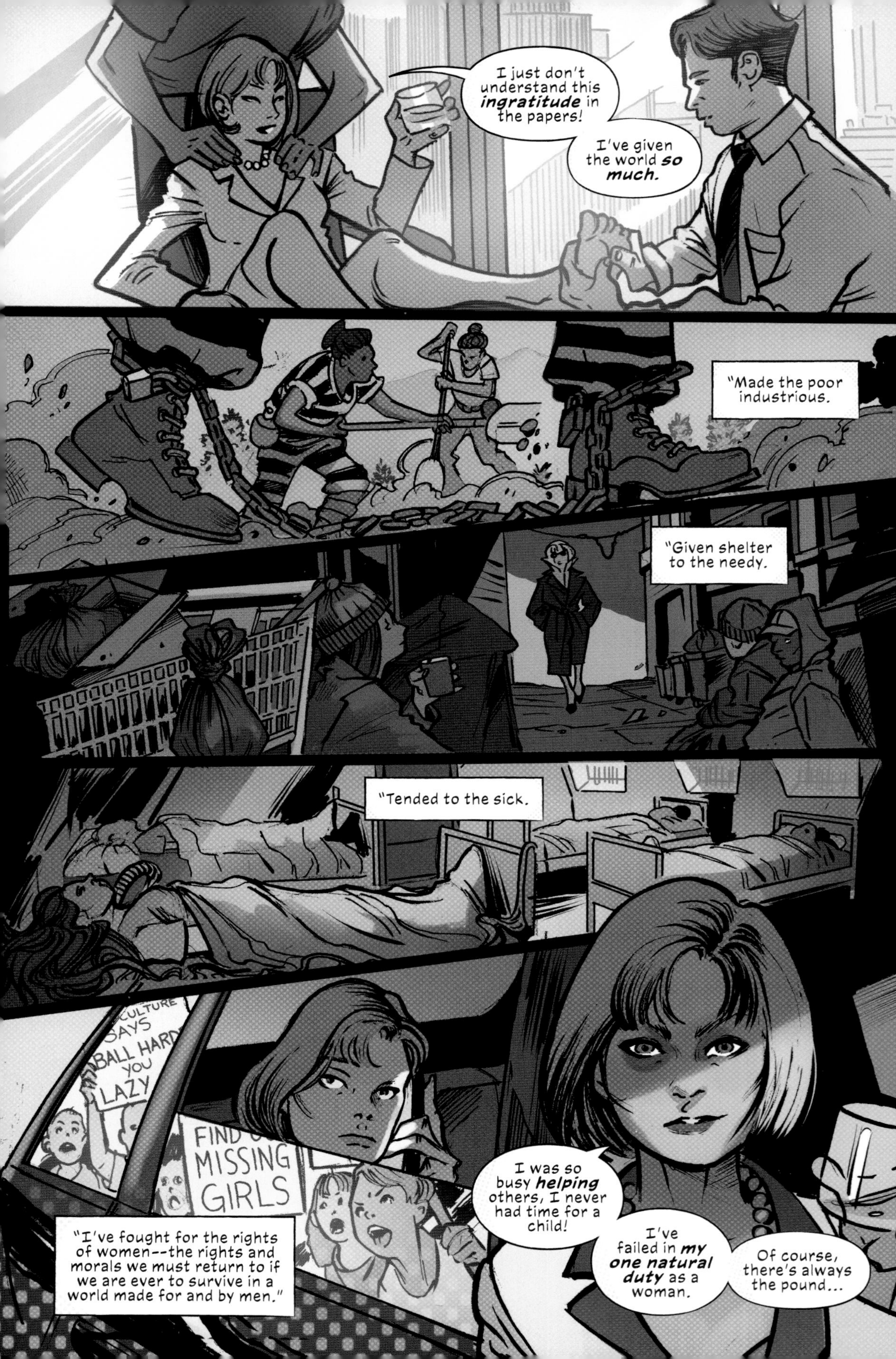

I just don't understand this *ingratitude* in the papers!
I've given the world ***so much.***
"Made the poor industrious.
"Given shelter to the needy.
"Tended to the sick.
CULTURE SAYS BALL HARD YOU LAZY
FIND MISSING GIRLS
"I've fought for the rights of women--the rights and morals we must return to if we are ever to survive in a world made for and by men."
I was so busy ***helping*** others, I never had time for a child!
I've failed in ***my one natural duty*** as a woman.
Of course, there's always the pound...

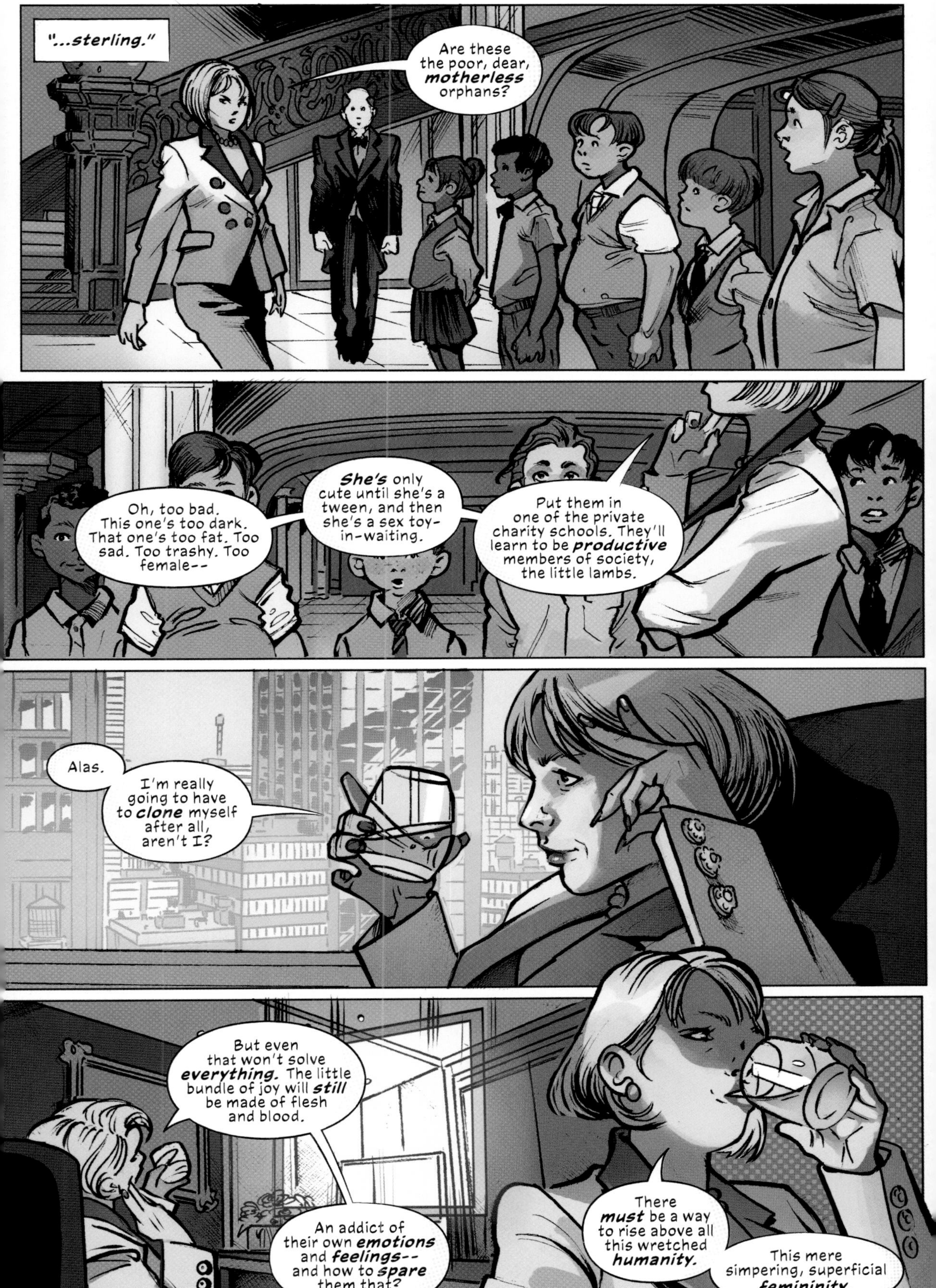
"...sterling."
Are these the poor, dear, motherless orphans?
Oh, too bad. This one's too dark. That one's too fat. Too sad. Too trashy. Too female--
She's only cute until she's a tween, and then she's a sex toy-in-waiting.
Put them in one of the private charity schools. They'll learn to be productive members of society, the little lambs.
Alas.
I'm really going to have to clone myself after all, aren't I?
But even that won't solve everything. The little bundle of joy will still be made of flesh and blood.
An addict of their own emotions and feelings--and how to spare them that?
There must be a way to rise above all this wretched humanity.
This mere simpering, superficial femininity.

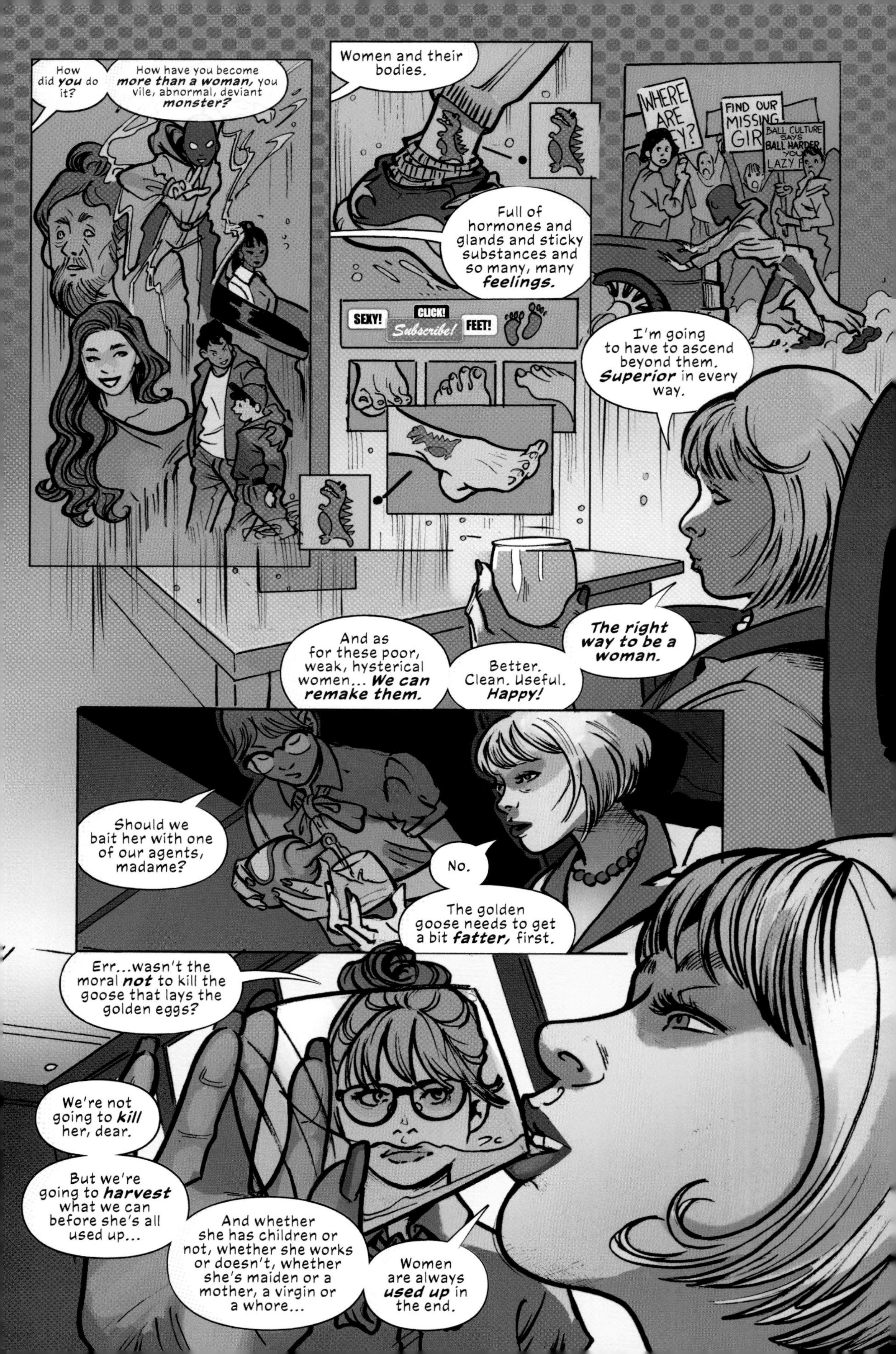
How did **you** do it?
How have you become **more than a woman,** you vile, abnormal, deviant **monster?**
Women and their bodies.
Full of hormones and glands and sticky substances and so many, many **feelings.**
SEXY!
CLICK!
Subscribe!
FEET!
WHERE ARE
FIND OUR MISSING
BALL CULTURE SAYS BALL HARDER YOU LAZY
I'm going to have to ascend beyond them. **Superior** in every way.
And as for these poor, weak, hysterical women... **We can remake them.**
Better. Clean. Useful. **Happy!**
The right way to be a woman.
Should we bait her with one of our agents, madame?
No.
The golden goose needs to get a bit **fatter,** first.
Err...wasn't the moral **not** to kill the goose that lays the golden eggs?
We're not going to **kill** her, dear.
But we're going to **harvest** what we can before she's all used up...
And whether she has children or not, whether she works or doesn't, whether she's maiden or a mother, a virgin or a whore...
Women are always **used up** in the end.

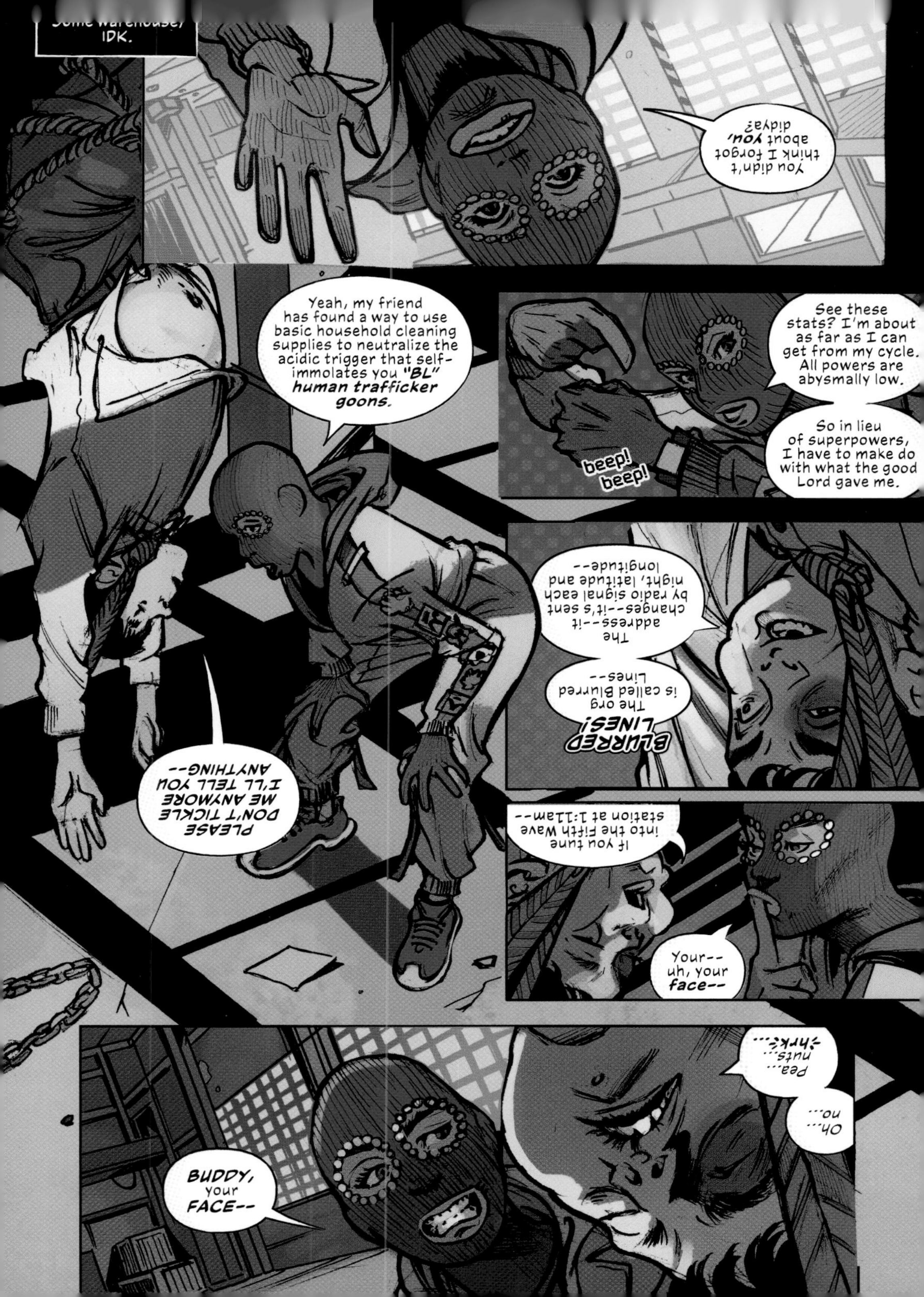
IDK.
You didn't think I forgot about *you*, didya?
Yeah, my friend has found a way to use basic household cleaning supplies to neutralize the acidic trigger that self-immolates you ***"BL" human trafficker goons.***
PLEASE DON'T TICKLE ME ANYMORE I'LL TELL YOU ANYTHING--
See these stats? I'm about as far as I can get from my cycle. All powers are abysmally low.
beep! beep!
So in lieu of superpowers, I have to make do with what the good Lord gave me.
BLURRED LINES!
The org is called Blurred Lines--
The address--it changes--it's sent by radio signal each night, latitude and longitude--
If you tune into the Fifth Wave station at 1:11am--
Your--uh, your *face--*
Oh... no...
Pea... nuts... *hrk...*
BUDDY, your ***FACE--***

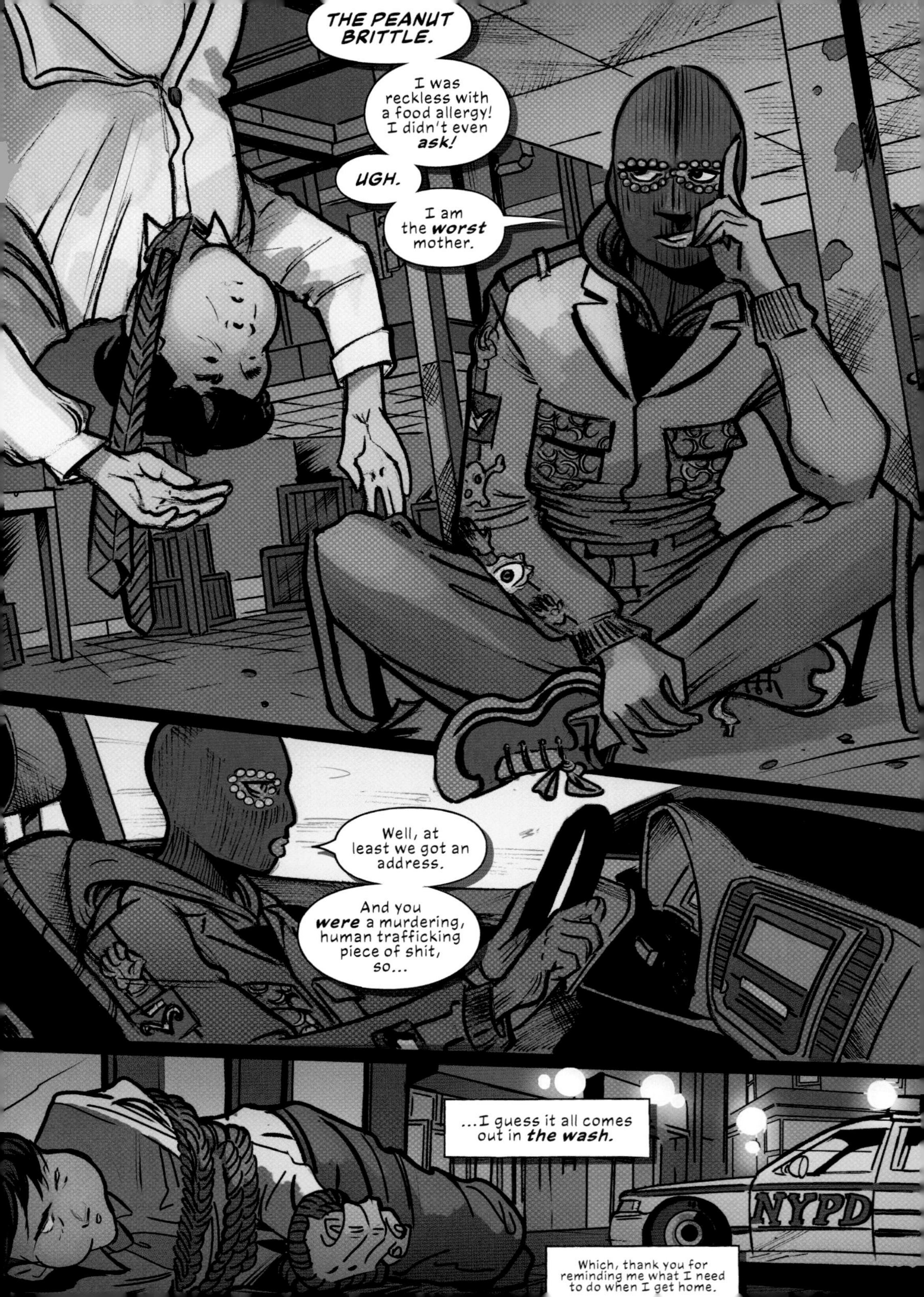

THE PEANUT BRITTLE.
I was reckless with a food allergy! I didn't even ask!
UGH.
I am the worst mother.
Well, at least we got an address.
And you were a murdering, human trafficking piece of shit, so...
...I guess it all comes out in the wash.
NYPD
Which, thank you for reminding me what I need to do when I get home.

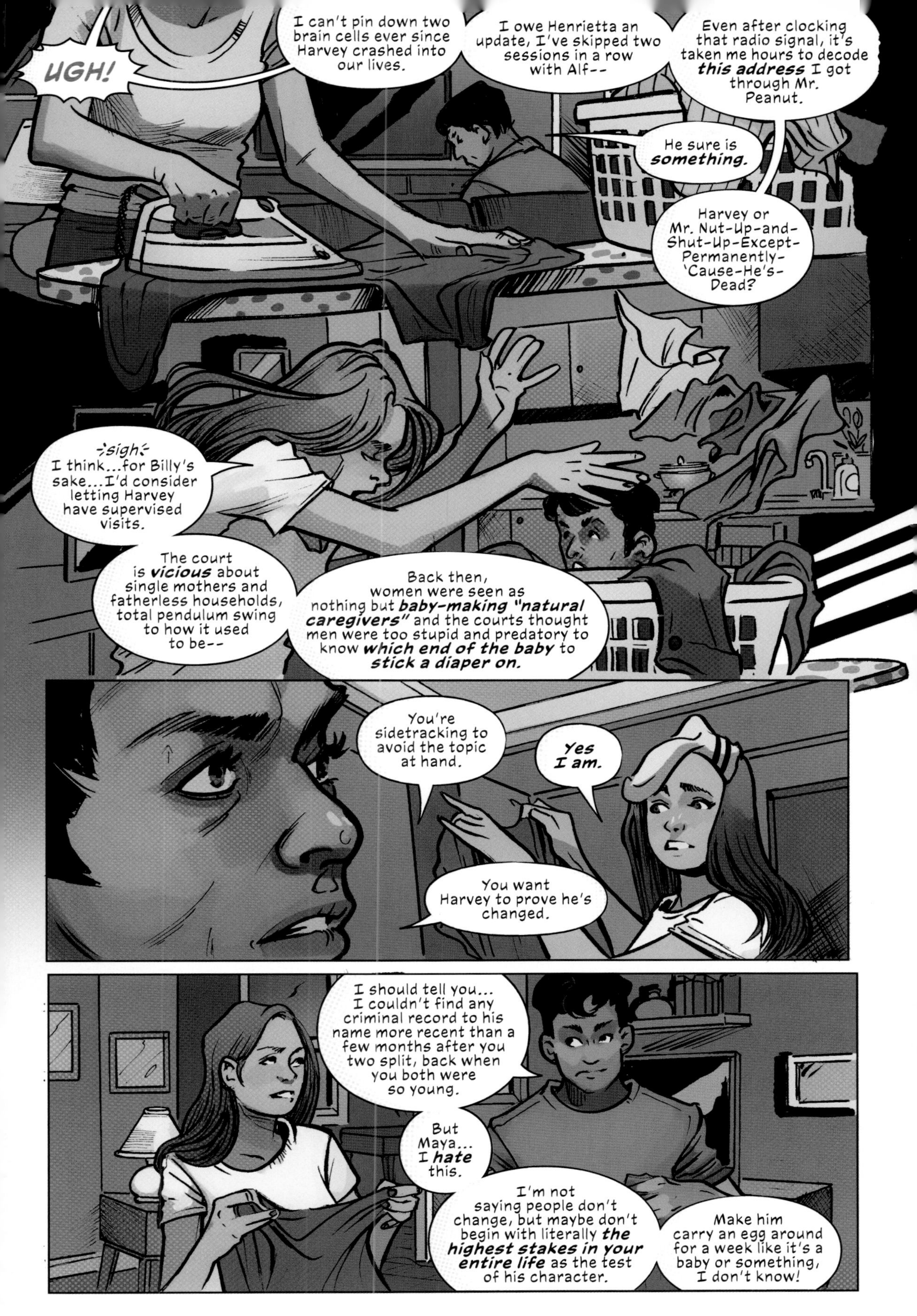
UGH!
I can't pin down two brain cells ever since Harvey crashed into our lives.
I owe Henrietta an update, I've skipped two sessions in a row with Alf--
Even after clocking that radio signal, it's taken me hours to decode **this address** I got through Mr. Peanut.
He sure is **something.**
Harvey or Mr. Nut-Up-and-Shut-Up-Except-Permanently-'Cause-He's-Dead?
-sigh- I think...for Billy's sake...I'd consider letting Harvey have supervised visits.
The court is **vicious** about single mothers and fatherless households, total pendulum swing to how it used to be--
Back then, women were seen as nothing but **baby-making "natural caregivers"** and the courts thought men were too stupid and predatory to know **which end of the baby** to **stick a diaper on.**
You're sidetracking to avoid the topic at hand.
Yes I am.
You want Harvey to prove he's changed.
I should tell you... I couldn't find any criminal record to his name more recent than a few months after you two split, back when you both were so young.
But Maya... I **hate** this.
I'm not saying people don't change, but maybe don't begin with literally **the highest stakes in your entire life** as the test of his character.
Make him carry an egg around for a week like it's a baby or something, I don't know!

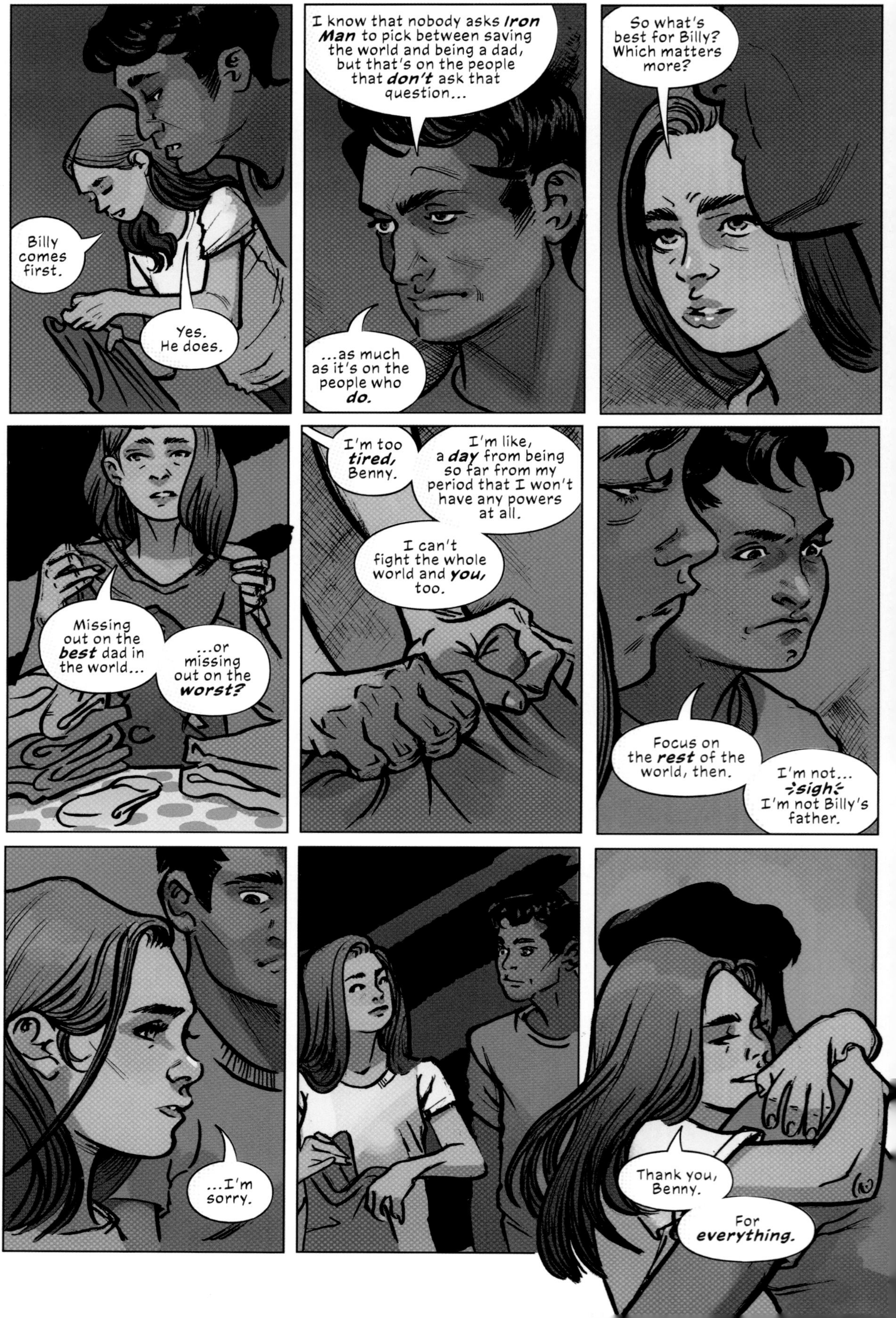
Billy comes first.
Yes. He does.
I know that nobody asks *Iron Man* to pick between saving the world and being a dad, but that's on the people that *don't* ask that question...
...as much as it's on the people who *do.*
So what's best for Billy? Which matters more?
Missing out on the *best* dad in the world...
...or missing out on the *worst?*
I'm too *tired,* Benny.
I'm like, a *day* from being so far from my period that I won't have any powers at all.
I can't fight the whole world and *you,* too.
Focus on the *rest* of the world, then.
I'm not... *sigh* I'm not Billy's father.
...I'm sorry.
Thank you, Benny.
For *everything.*

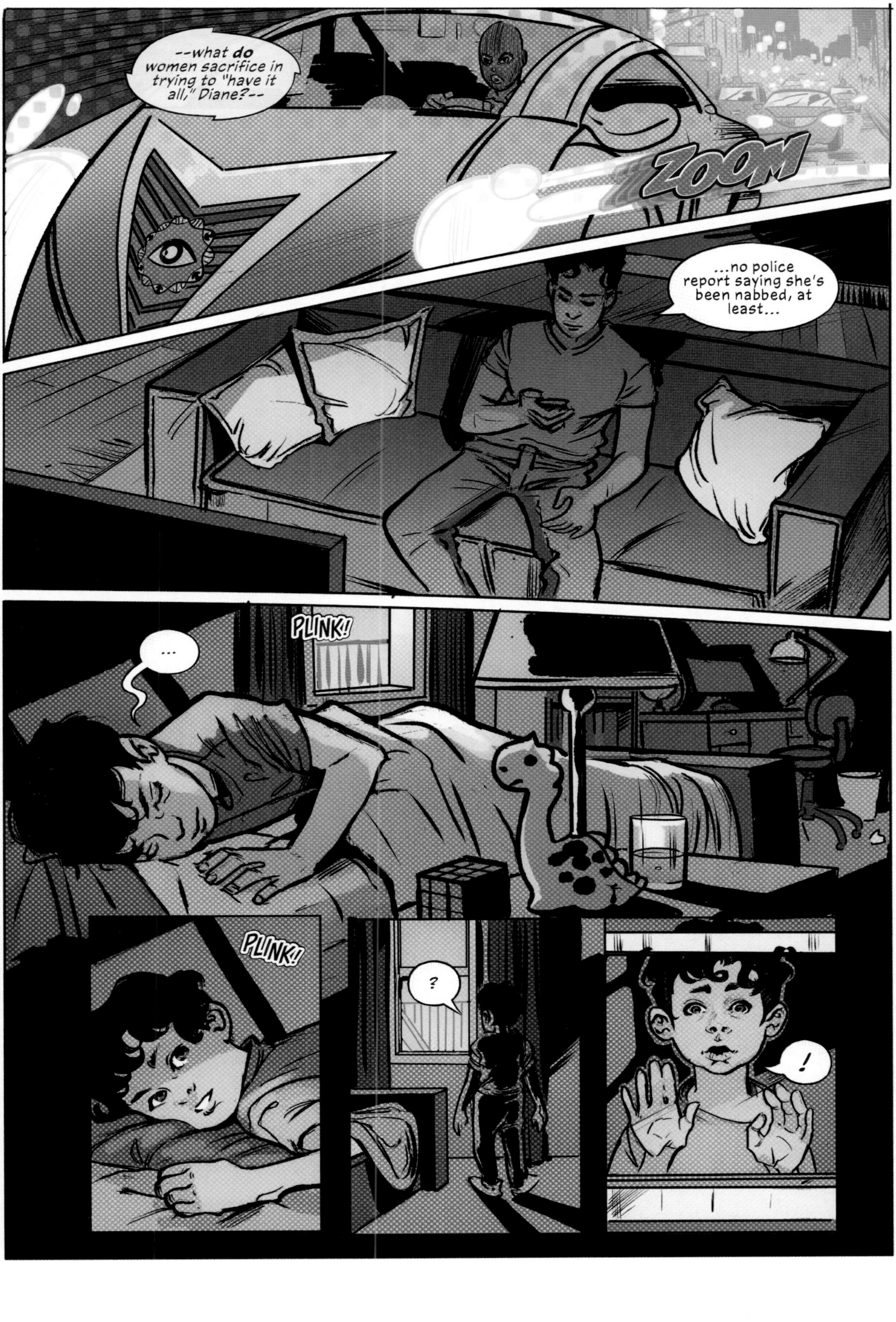
--what do women sacrifice in trying to "have it all," Diane?--
ZOOM
...no police report saying she's been nabbed, at least...
PLINK!
...
PLINK!
?
!

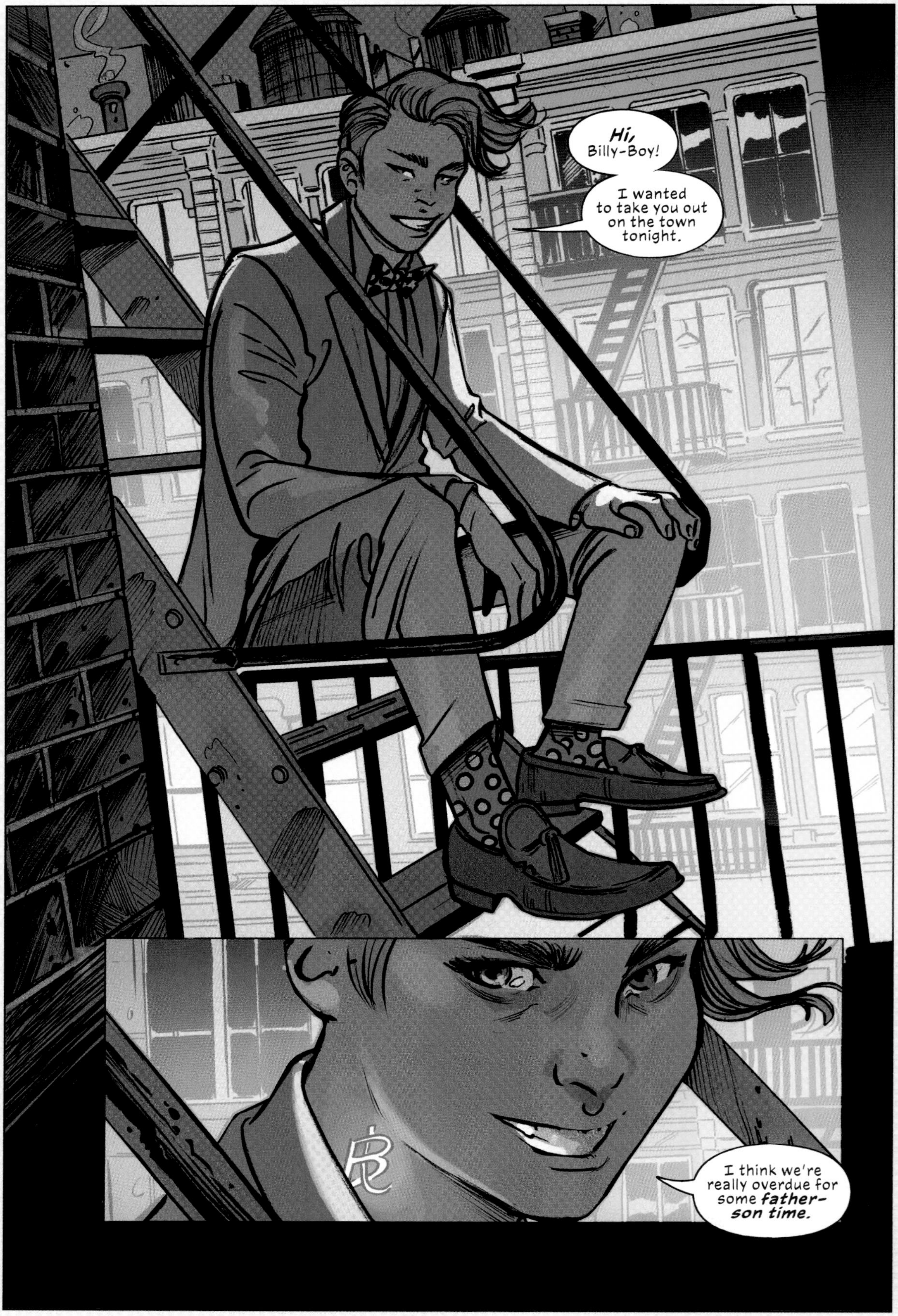
Hi, Billy-Boy!
I wanted to take you out on the town tonight.
I think we're really overdue for some father-son time.

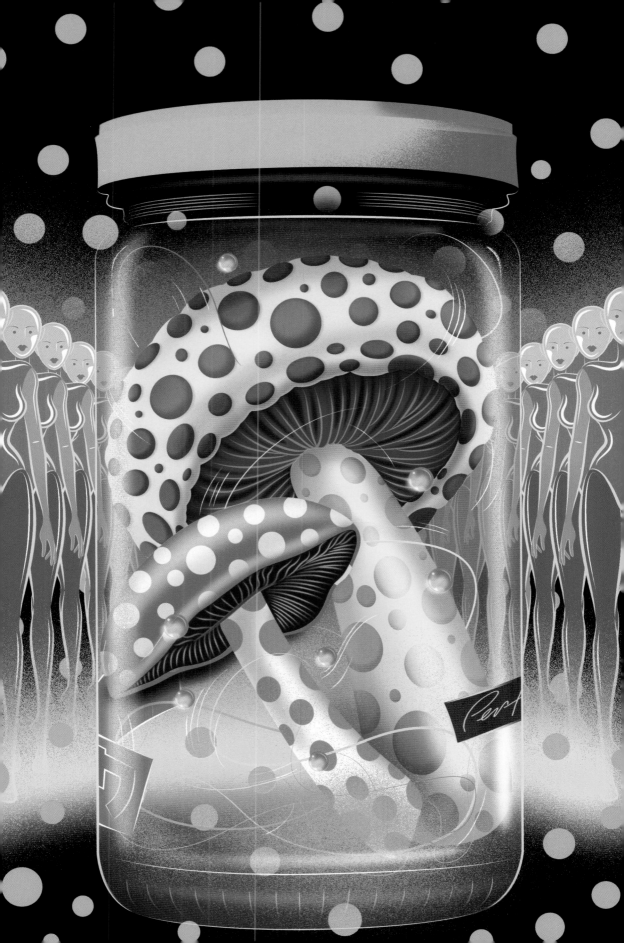

MOM

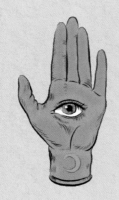

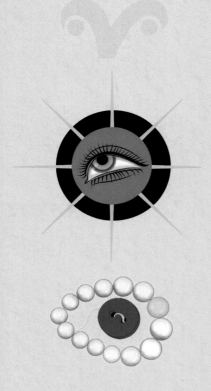

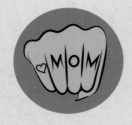

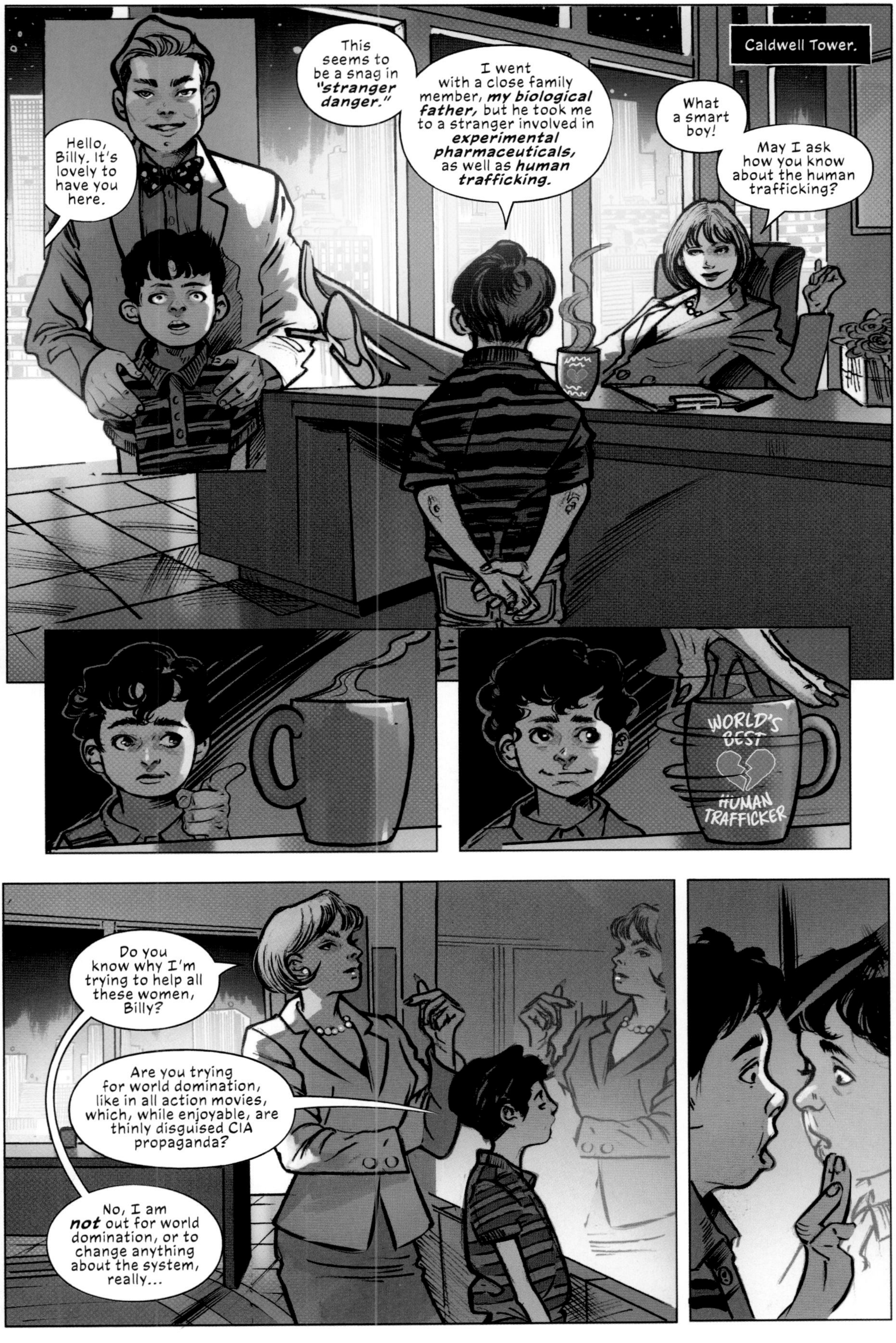
Caldwell Tower.
Hello, Billy. It's lovely to have you here.
This seems to be a snag in *"stranger danger."*
I went with a close family member, ***my biological father,*** but he took me to a stranger involved in ***experimental pharmaceuticals,*** as well as ***human trafficking.***
What a smart boy!
May I ask how you know about the human trafficking?
WORLD'S BEST HUMAN TRAFFICKER
Do you know why I'm trying to help all these women, Billy?
Are you trying for world domination, like in all action movies, which, while enjoyable, are thinly disguised CIA propaganda?
No, I am ***not*** out for world domination, or to change anything about the system, really...

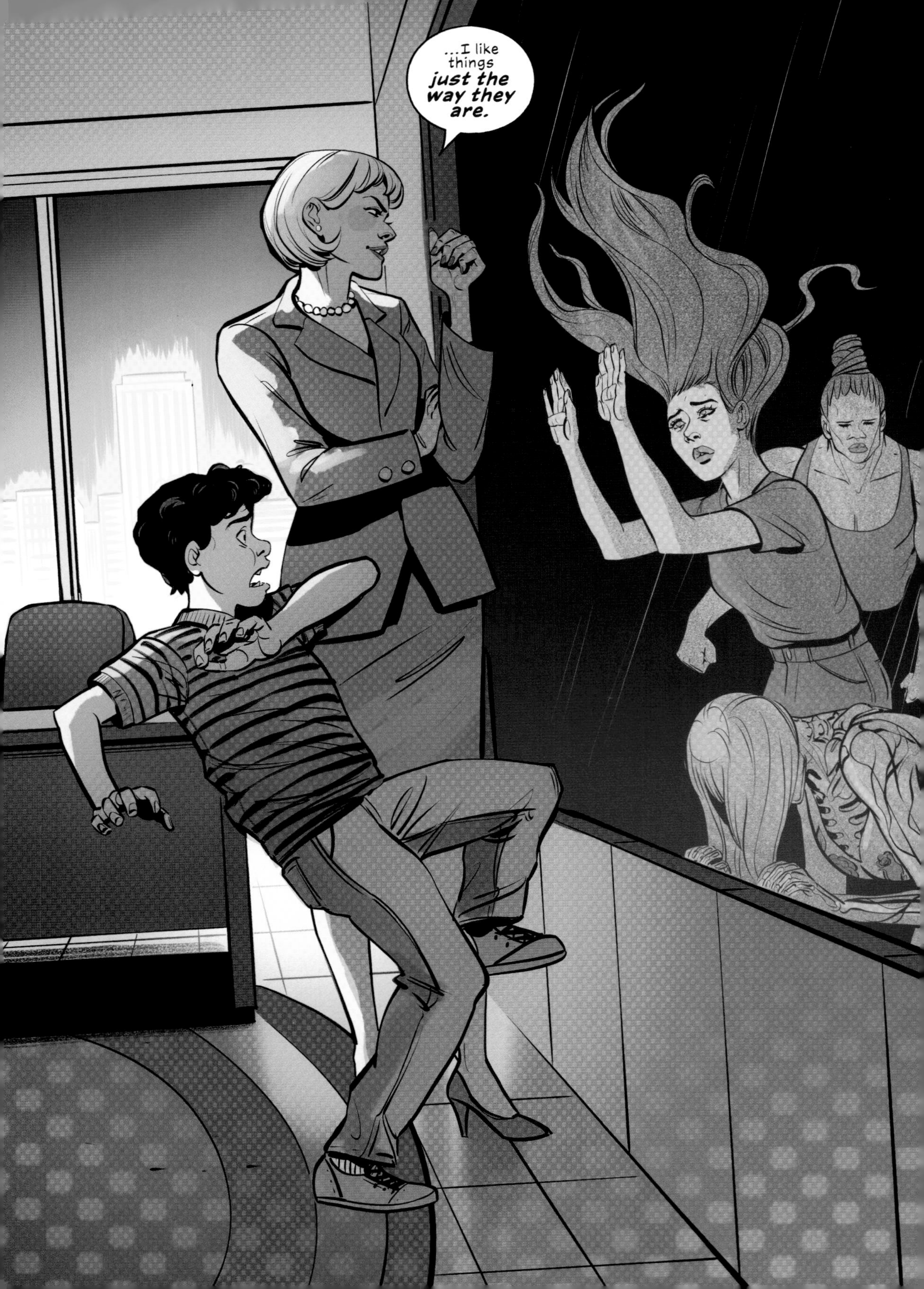
...I like things *just the way they are.*

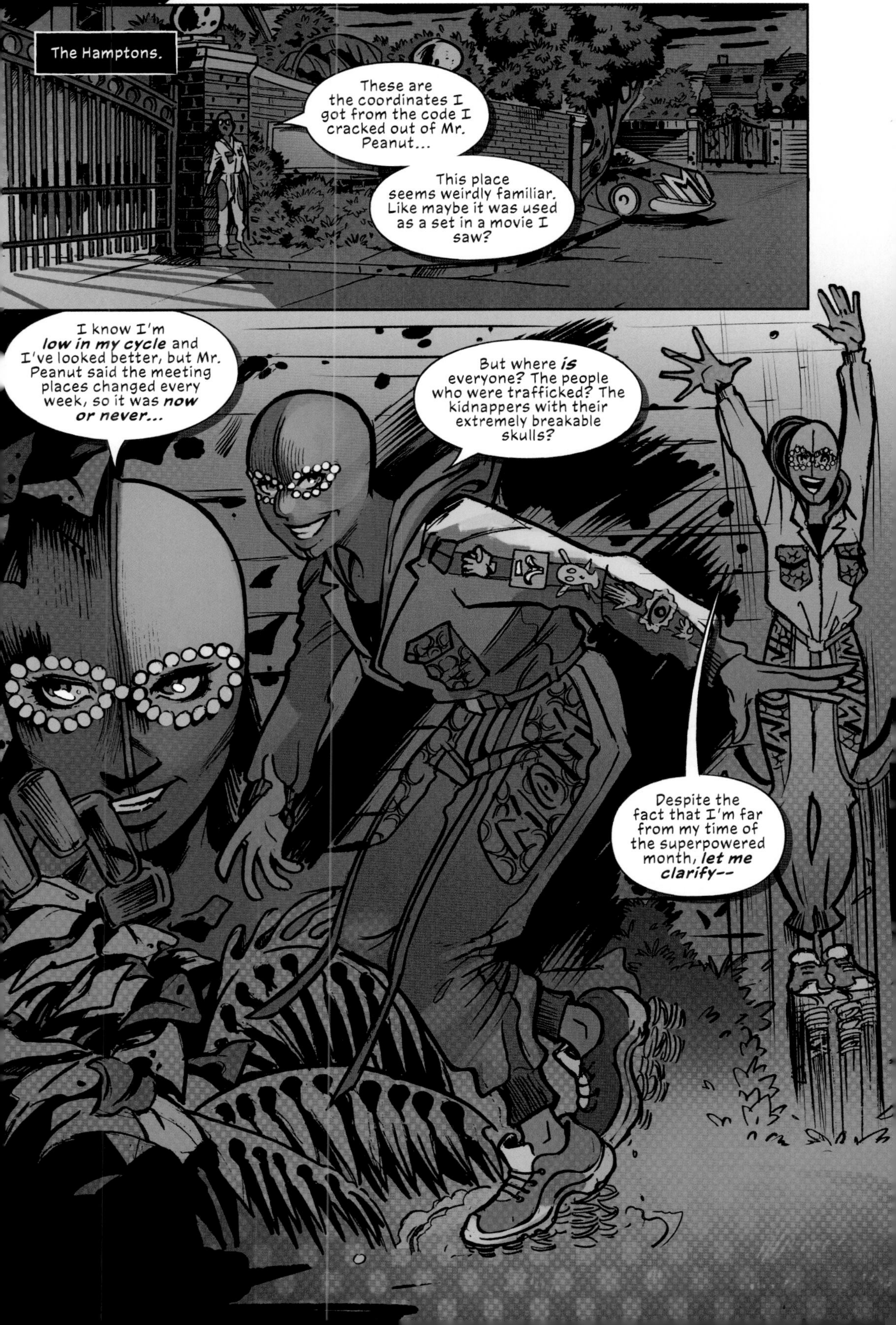
The Hamptons.
These are the coordinates I got from the code I cracked out of Mr. Peanut...
This place seems weirdly familiar. Like maybe it was used as a set in a movie I saw?
I know I'm **low in my cycle** and I've looked better, but Mr. Peanut said the meeting places changed every week, so it was **now or never...**
But where **is** everyone? The people who were trafficked? The kidnappers with their extremely breakable skulls?
Despite the fact that I'm far from my time of the superpowered month, **let me clarify--**

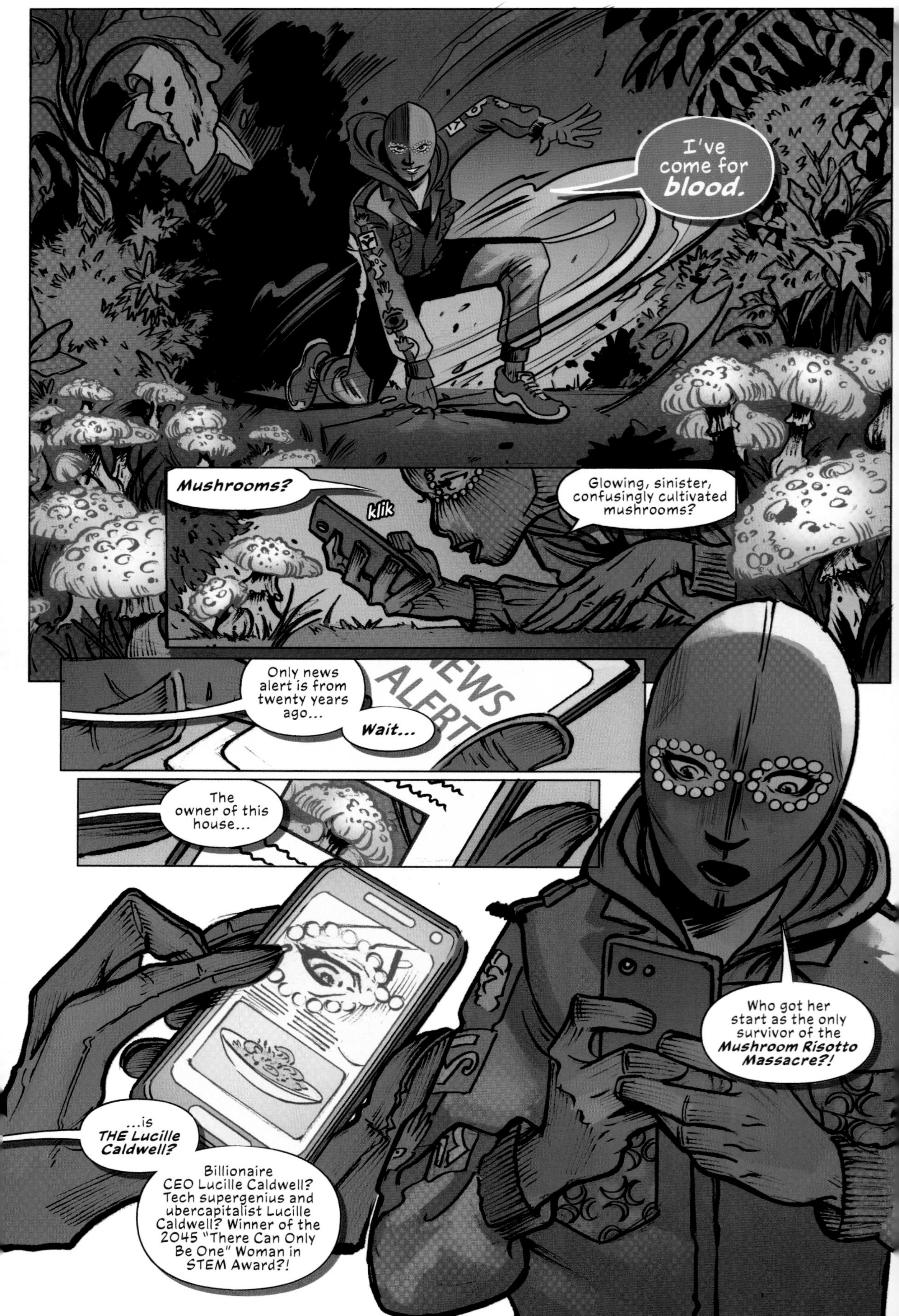

I've come for *blood.*
Mushrooms?
klik
Glowing, sinister, confusingly cultivated mushrooms?
Only news alert is from twenty years ago...
Wait...
NEWS ALERT
The owner of this house...
...is *THE Lucille Caldwell?*
Billionaire CEO Lucille Caldwell? Tech supergenius and ubercapitalist Lucille Caldwell? Winner of the 2045 "There Can Only Be One" Woman in STEM Award?!
Who got her start as the only survivor of the *Mushroom Risotto Massacre?!*

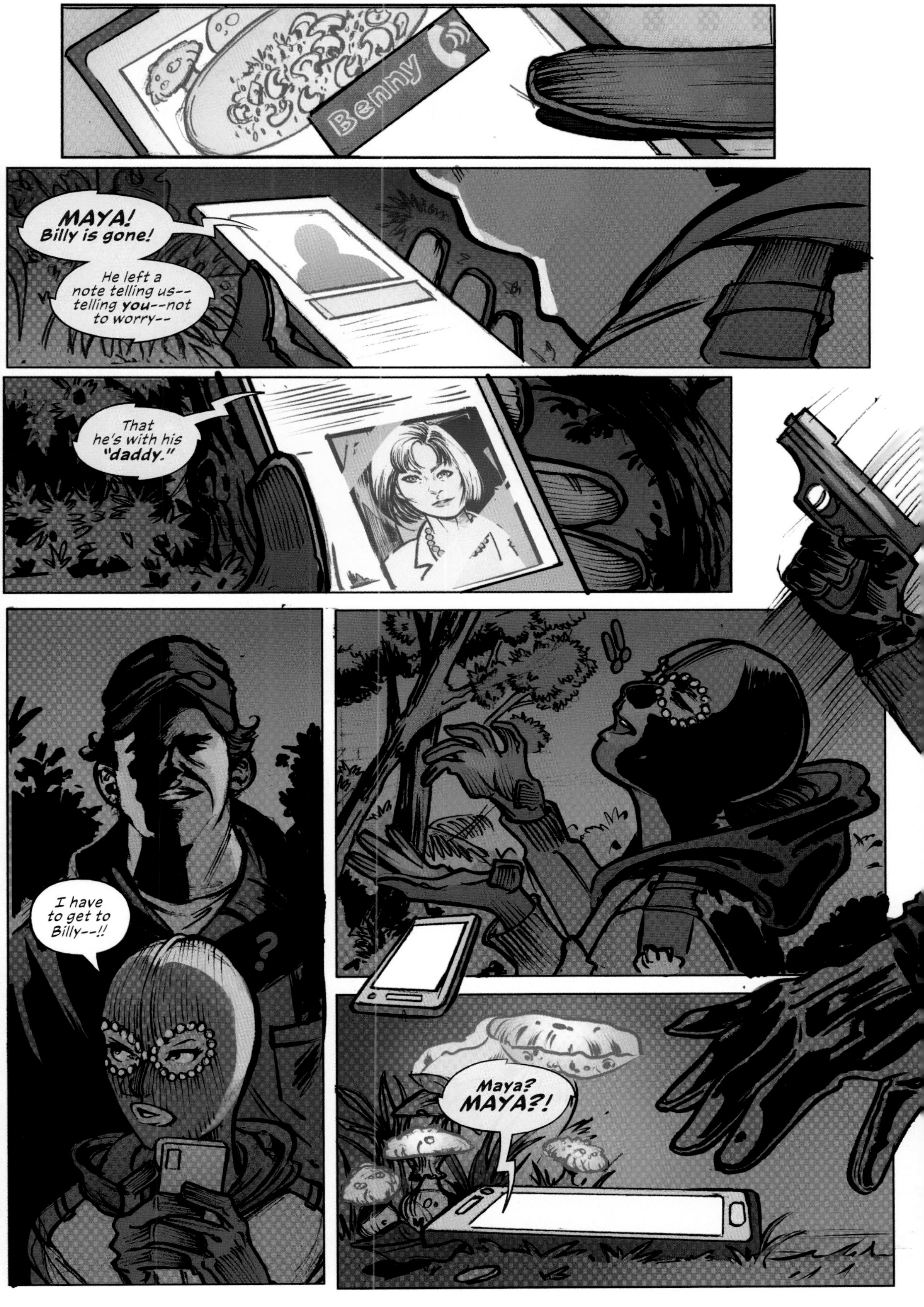
Benny
MAYA! Billy is gone!
He left a note telling us-- telling you--not to worry--
That he's with his "daddy."
I have to get to Billy--!!
?
!!
Maya? MAYA?!

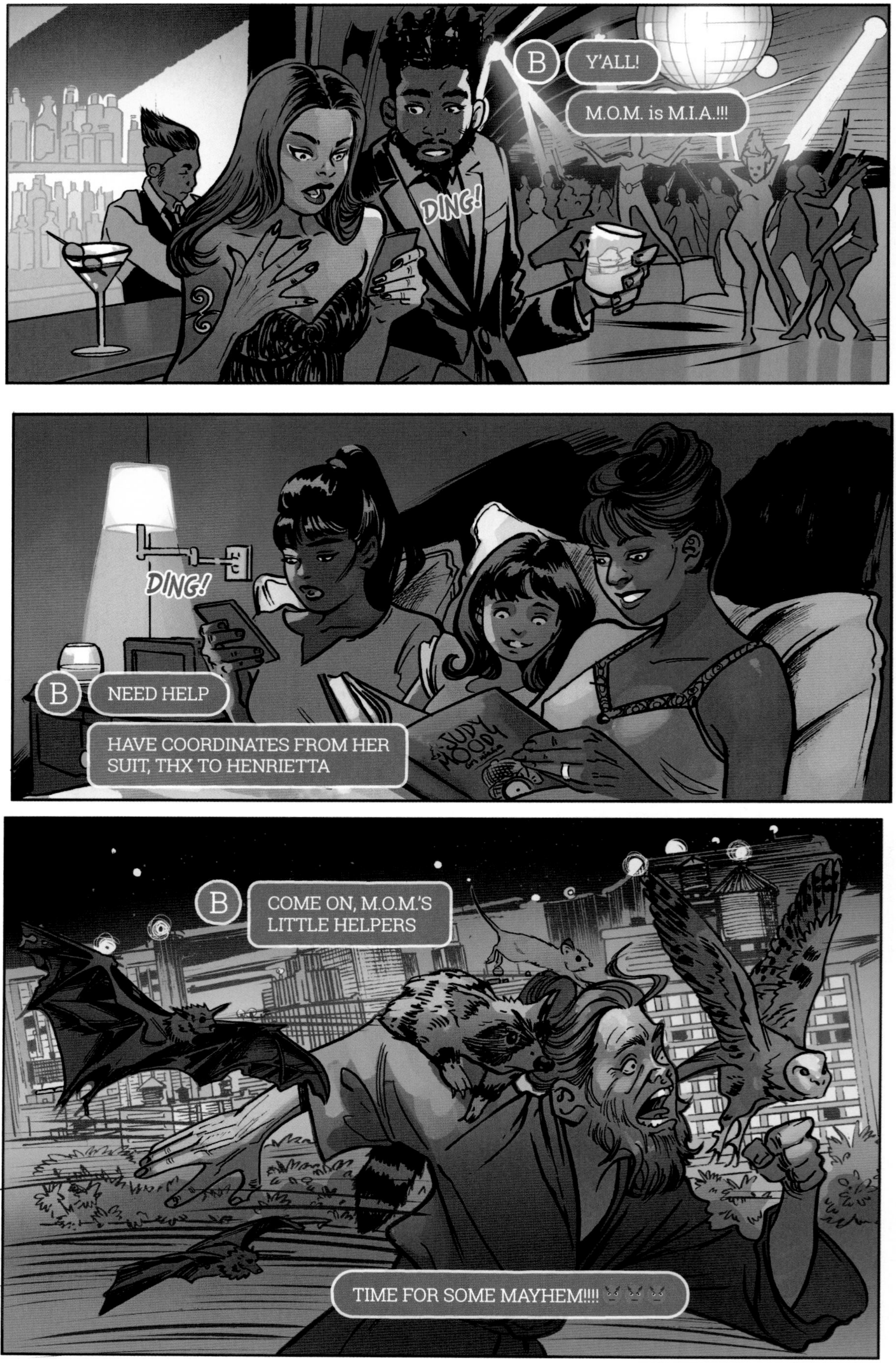
B
Y'ALL!
M.O.M. is M.I.A.!!!
DING!
DING!
B
NEED HELP
HAVE COORDINATES FROM HER SUIT, THX TO HENRIETTA
JUDY MOODY
B
COME ON, M.O.M.'S LITTLE HELPERS
TIME FOR SOME MAYHEM!!!!

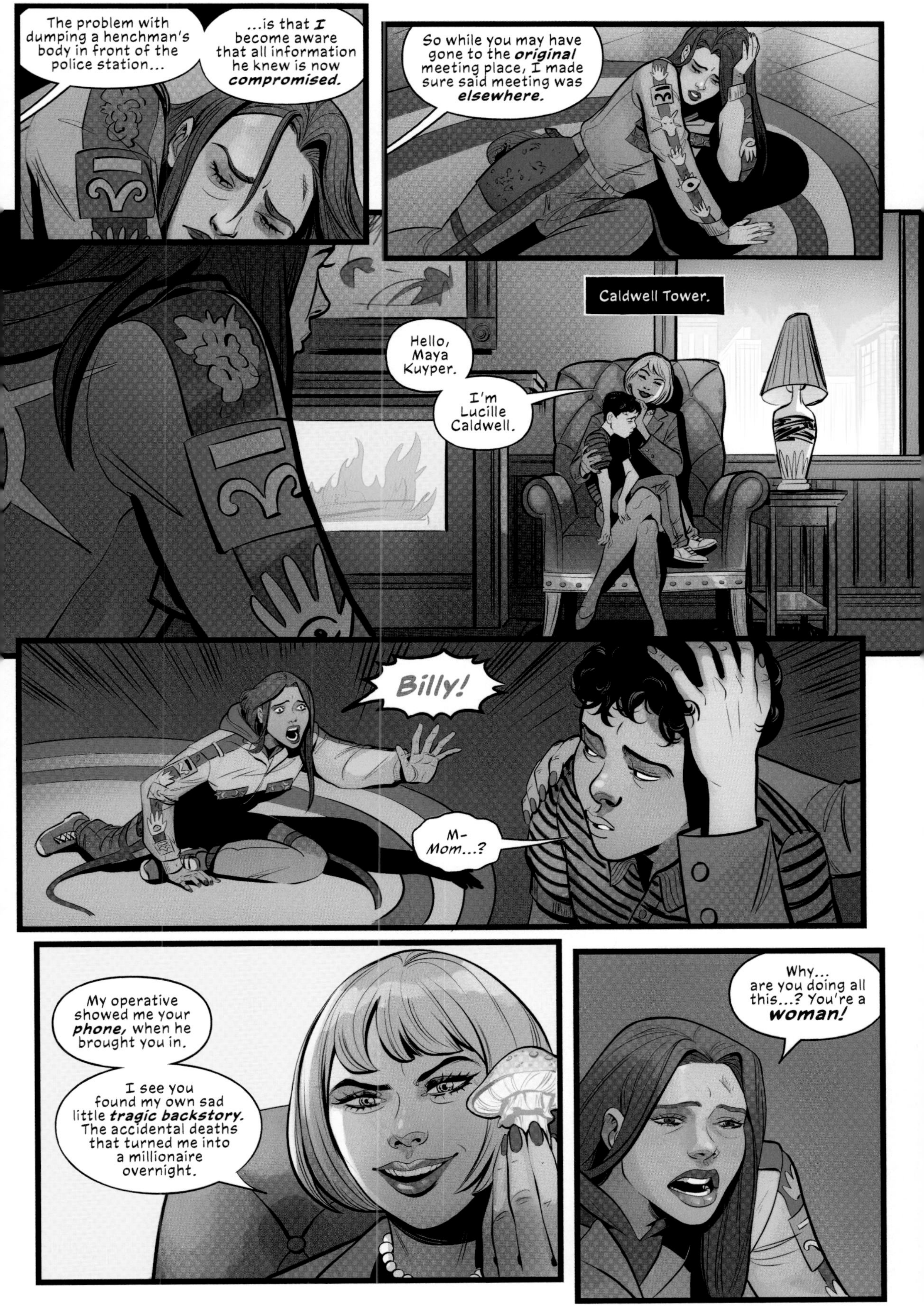
The problem with dumping a henchman's body in front of the police station...
...is that I become aware that all information he knew is now compromised.
So while you may have gone to the original meeting place, I made sure said meeting was elsewhere.
Caldwell Tower.
Hello, Maya Kuyper.
I'm Lucille Caldwell.
Billy!
M- Mom...?
My operative showed me your phone, when he brought you in.
I see you found my own sad little tragic backstory. The accidental deaths that turned me into a millionaire overnight.
Why... are you doing all this...? You're a woman!

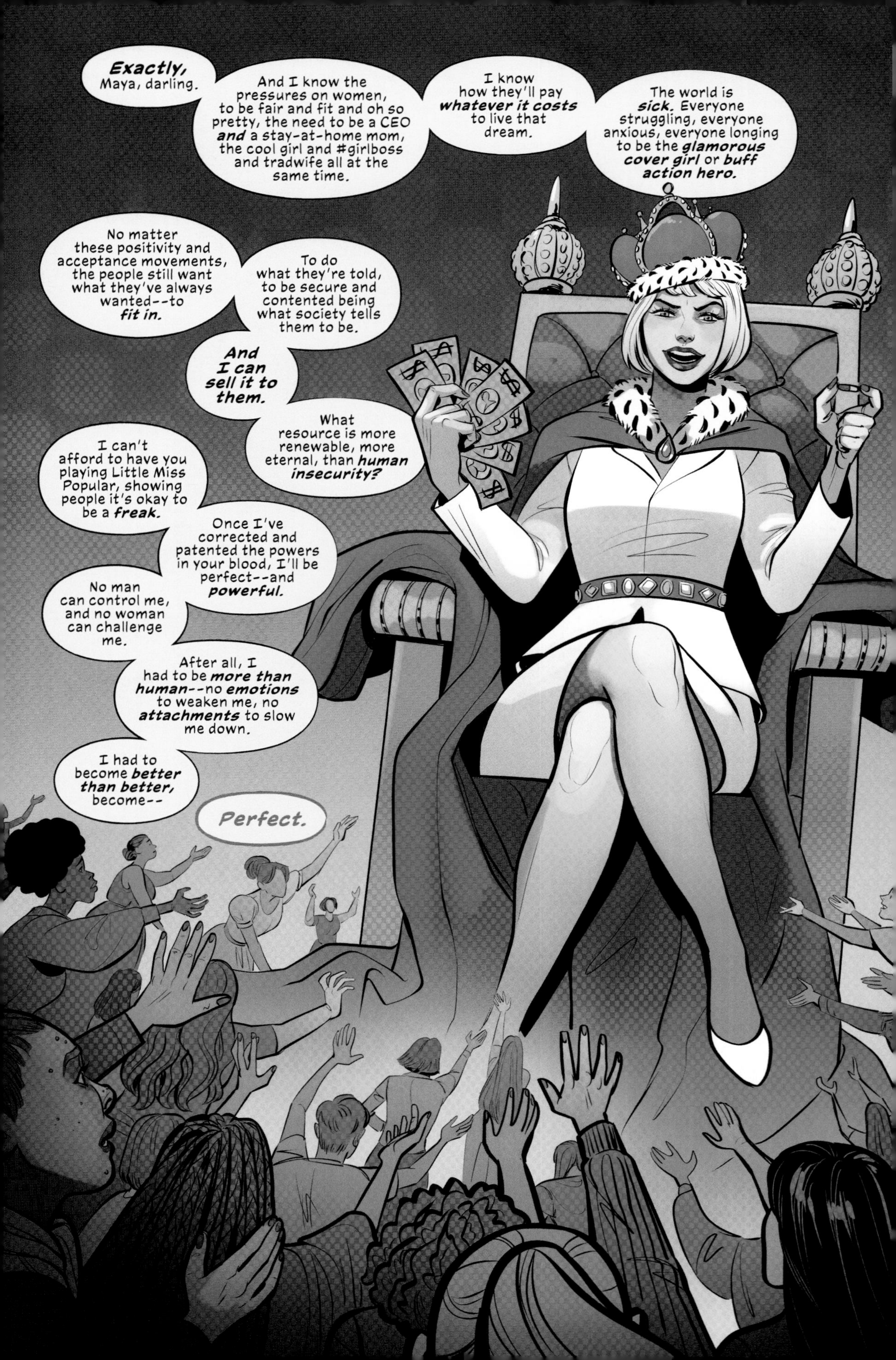
Exactly, Maya, darling.
And I know the pressures on women, to be fair and fit and oh so pretty, the need to be a CEO and a stay-at-home mom, the cool girl and #girlboss and tradwife all at the same time.
I know how they'll pay whatever it costs to live that dream.
The world is sick. Everyone struggling, everyone anxious, everyone longing to be the glamorous cover girl or buff action hero.
No matter these positivity and acceptance movements, the people still want what they've always wanted--to fit in.
To do what they're told, to be secure and contented being what society tells them to be.
And I can sell it to them.
What resource is more renewable, more eternal, than human insecurity?
I can't afford to have you playing Little Miss Popular, showing people it's okay to be a freak.
Once I've corrected and patented the powers in your blood, I'll be perfect--and powerful.
No man can control me, and no woman can challenge me.
After all, I had to be more than human--no emotions to weaken me, no attachments to slow me down.
I had to become better than better, become--
Perfect.

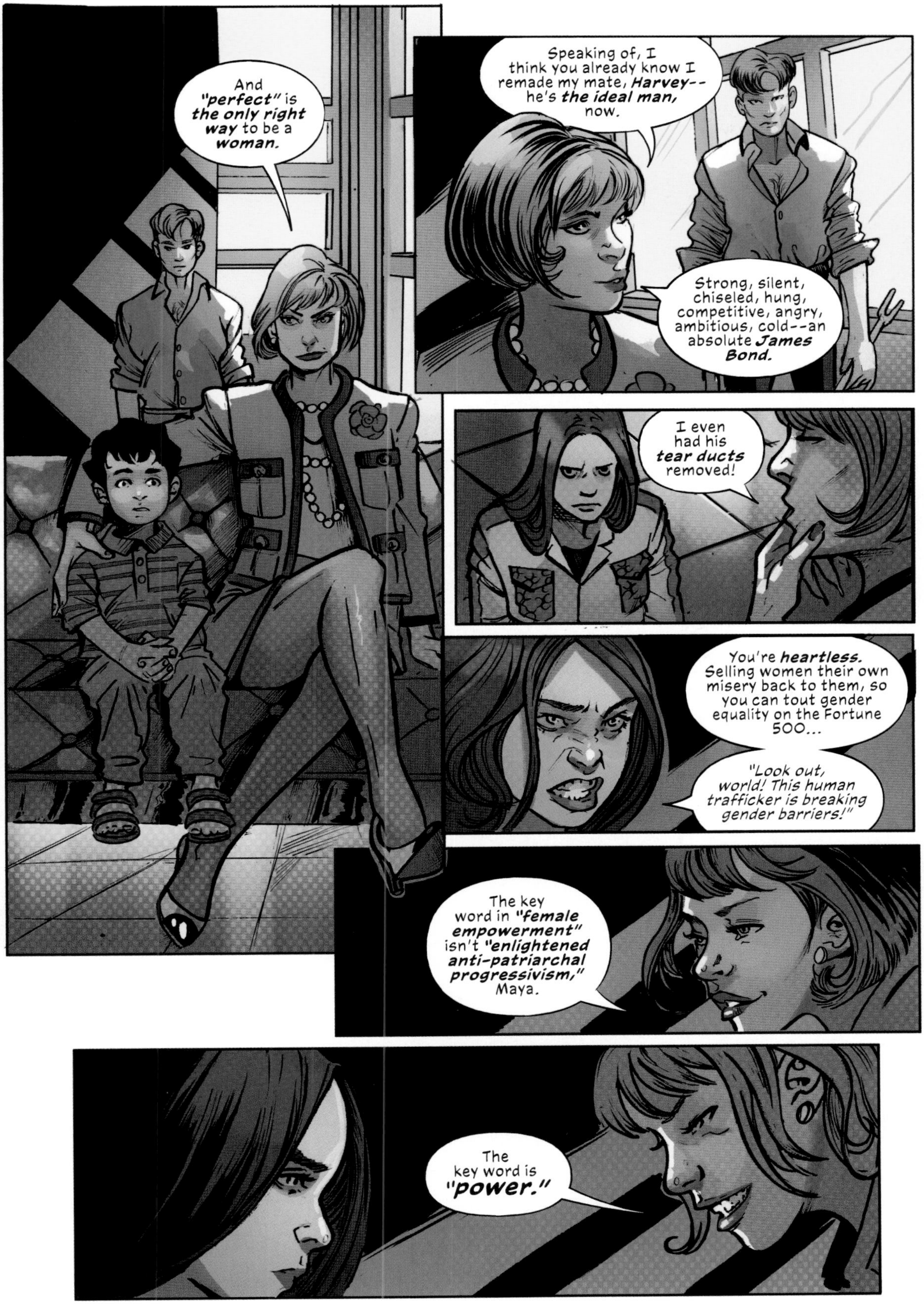
And "perfect" is the only right way to be a woman.
Speaking of, I think you already know I remade my mate, Harvey-- he's the ideal man, now.
Strong, silent, chiseled, hung, competitive, angry, ambitious, cold--an absolute James Bond.
I even had his tear ducts removed!
You're heartless. Selling women their own misery back to them, so you can tout gender equality on the Fortune 500...
"Look out, world! This human trafficker is breaking gender barriers!"
The key word in "female empowerment" isn't "enlightened anti-patriarchal progressivism," Maya.
The key word is "power."

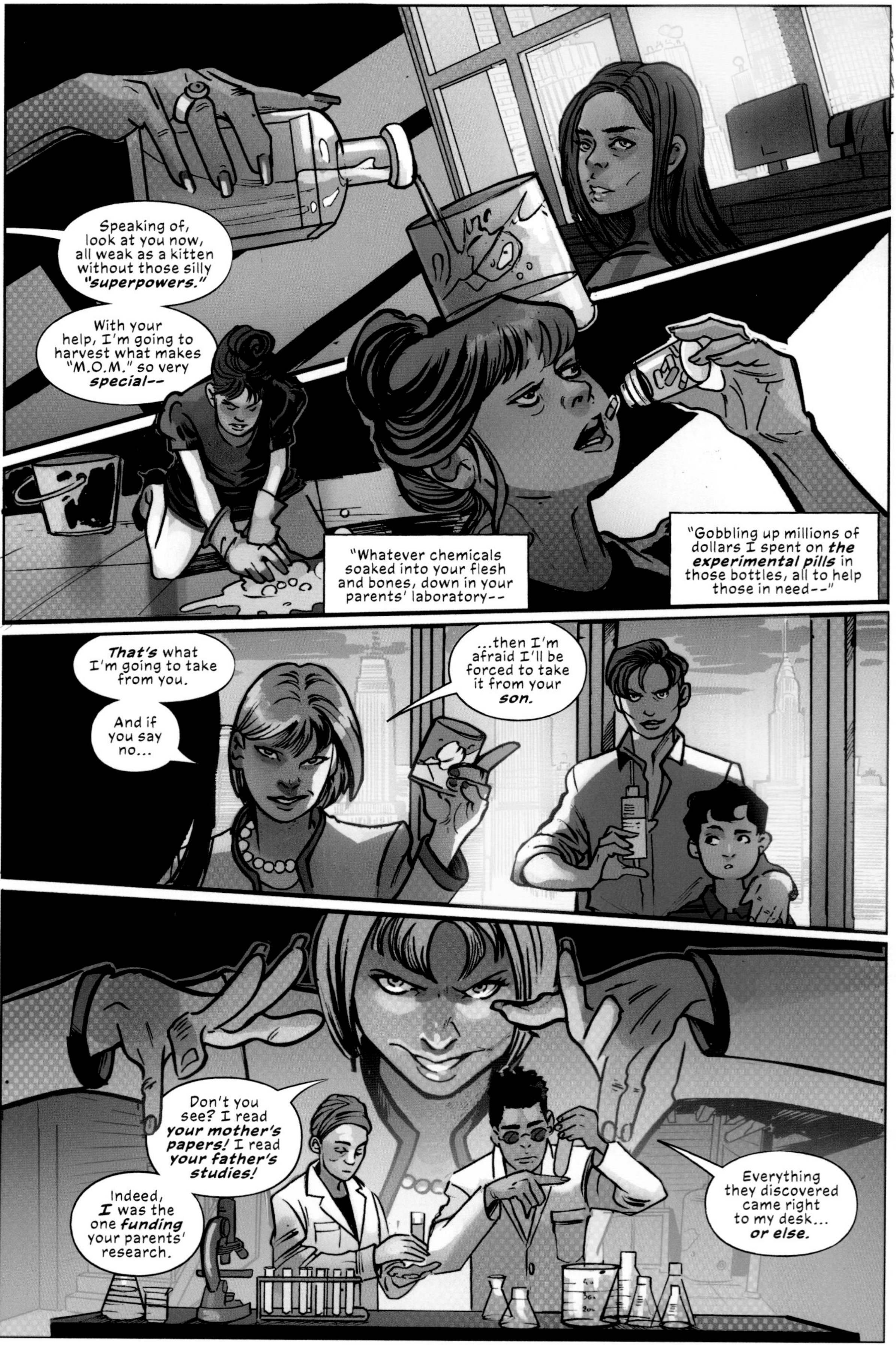
Speaking of, look at you now, all weak as a kitten without those silly "superpowers."
With your help, I'm going to harvest what makes "M.O.M." so very special--
"Whatever chemicals soaked into your flesh and bones, down in your parents' laboratory--
"Gobbling up millions of dollars I spent on the experimental pills in those bottles, all to help those in need--"
That's what I'm going to take from you.
And if you say no...
...then I'm afraid I'll be forced to take it from your son.
Don't you see? I read your mother's papers! I read your father's studies!
Indeed, I was the one funding your parents' research.
Everything they discovered came right to my desk... or else.

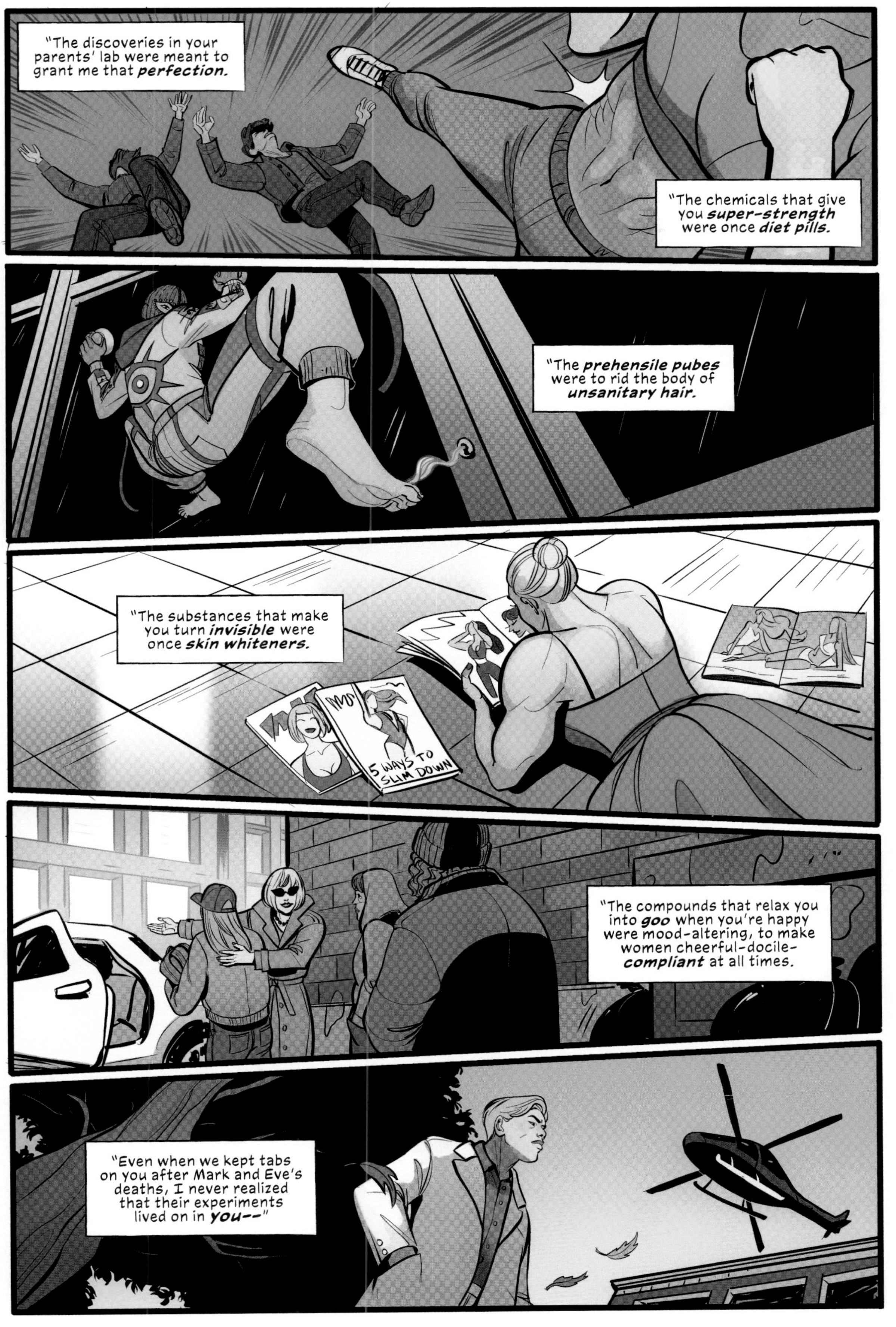
"The discoveries in your parents' lab were meant to grant me that *perfection.*
"The chemicals that give you ***super-strength*** were once ***diet pills.***
"The ***prehensile pubes*** were to rid the body of ***unsanitary hair.***
"The substances that make you turn ***invisible*** were once ***skin whiteners.***
5 WAYS TO SLIM DOWN
"The compounds that relax you into ***goo*** when you're happy were mood-altering, to make women cheerful-docile-***compliant*** at all times.
"Even when we kept tabs on you after Mark and Eve's deaths, I never realized that their experiments lived on in ***you--***"

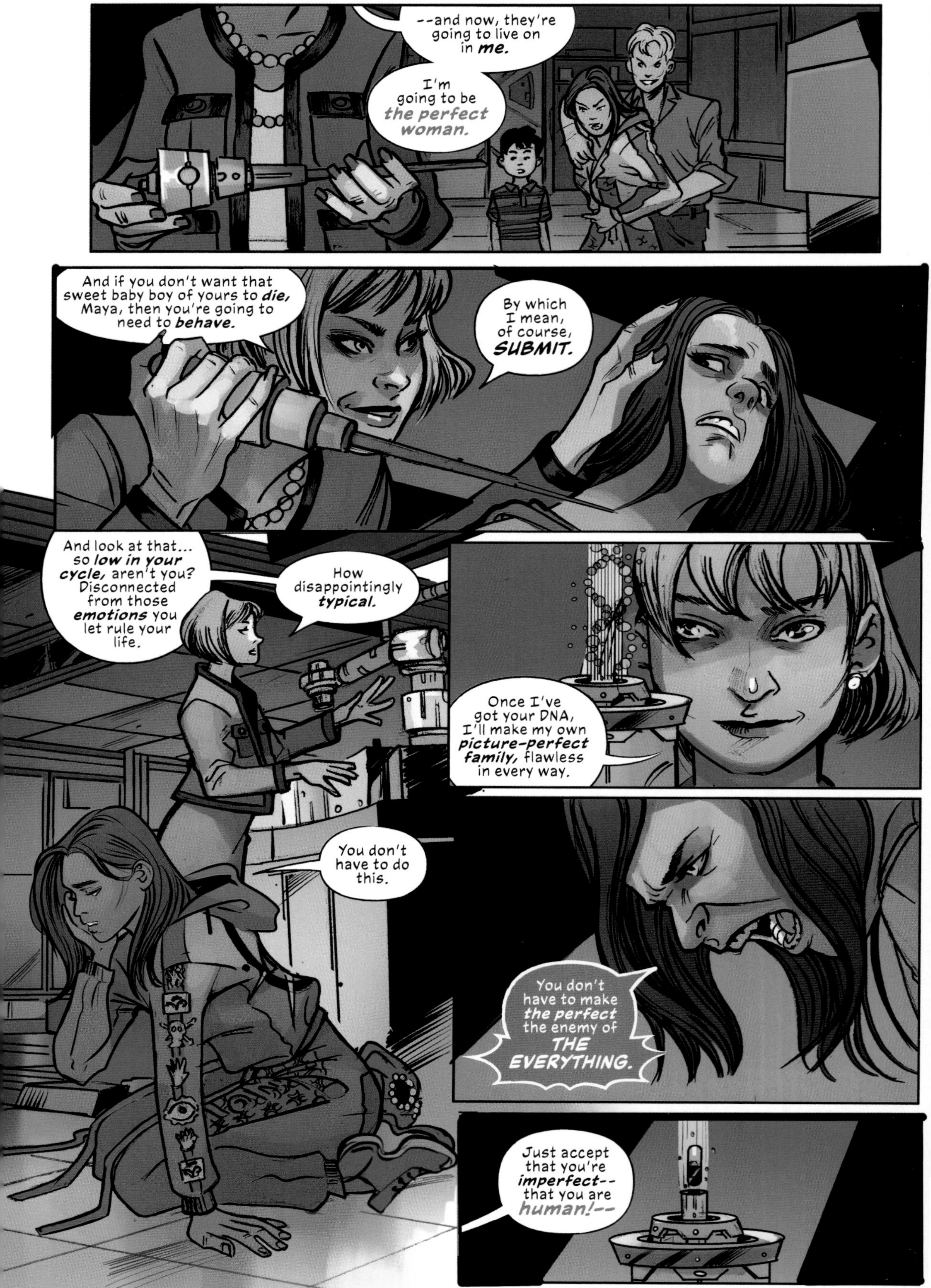
--and now, they're going to live on in *me.*
I'm going to be *the perfect woman.*
And if you don't want that sweet baby boy of yours to *die,* Maya, then you're going to need to *behave.*
By which I mean, of course, *SUBMIT.*
And look at that... so *low in your cycle,* aren't you? Disconnected from those *emotions* you let rule your life.
How disappointingly *typical.*
Once I've got your DNA, I'll make my own *picture-perfect family,* flawless in every way.
You don't have to do this.
You don't have to make *the perfect* the enemy of *THE EVERYTHING.*
Just accept that you're *imperfect--* that you are *human!--*

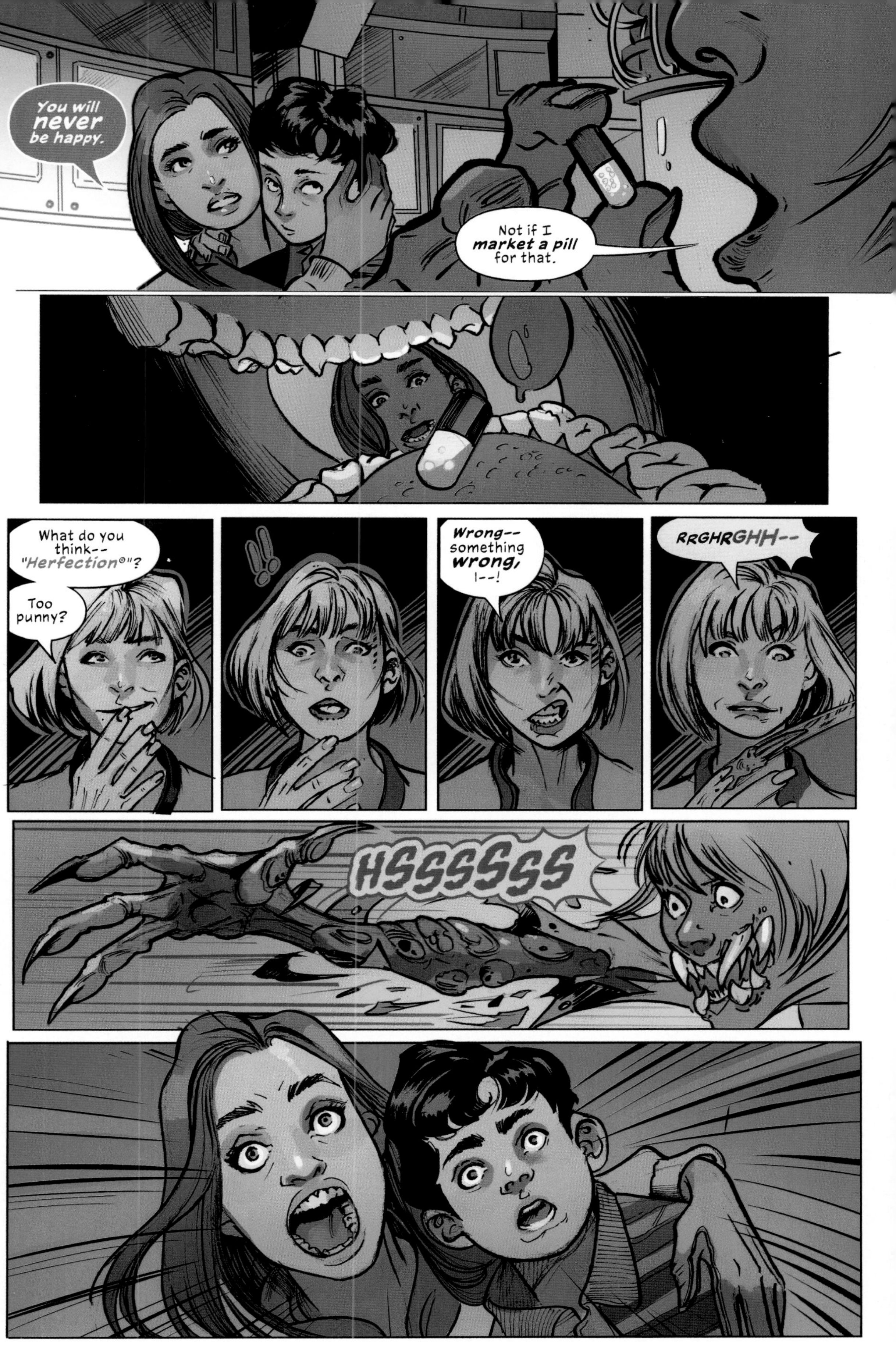
You will never be happy.
Not if I market a pill for that.
What do you think-- "Herfection®"?
Too punny?
!!
Wrong-- something wrong, I--!
RRGHRGHH--
HSSSSSS

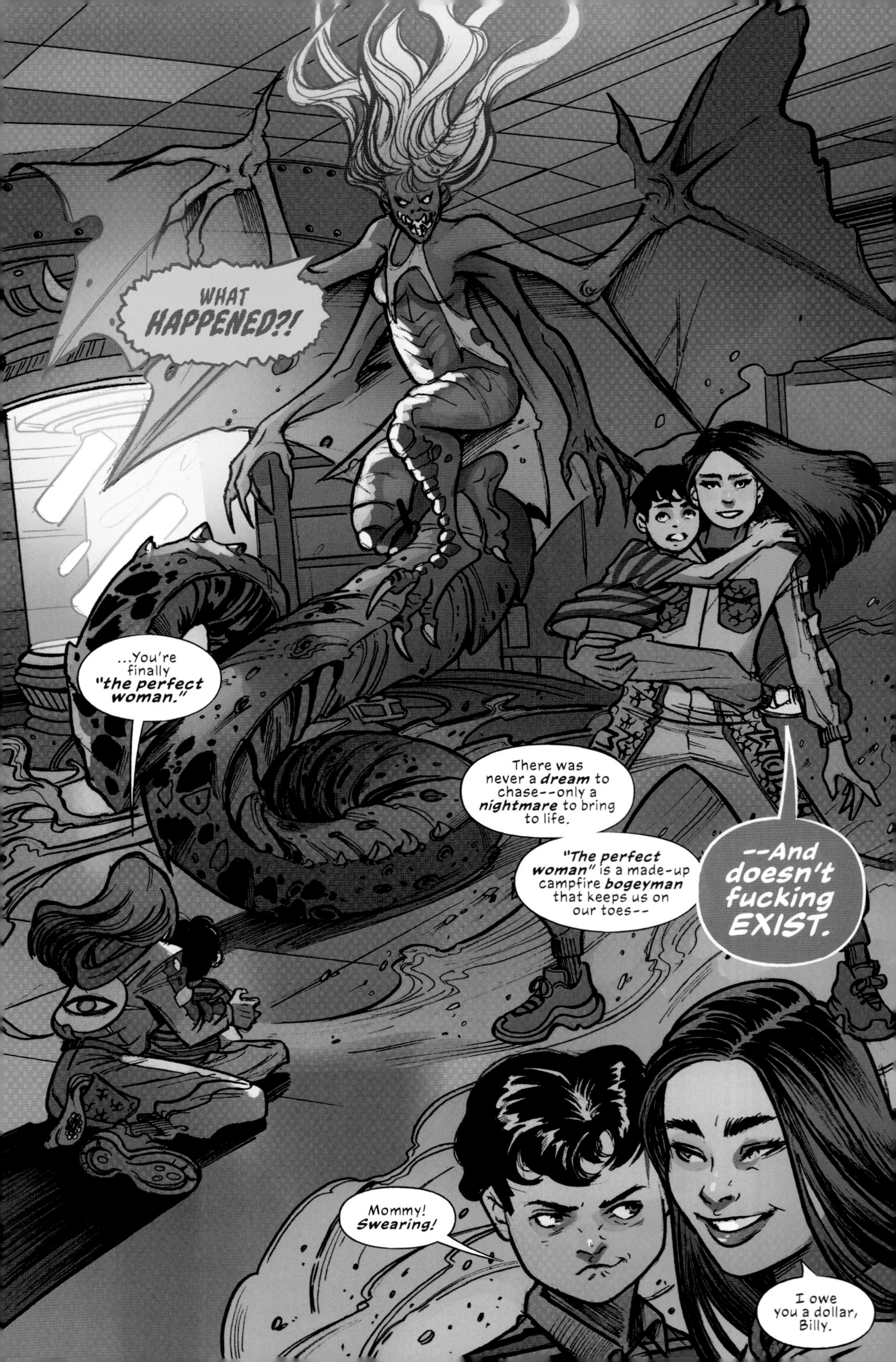
WHAT HAPPENED?!
...You're finally "the perfect woman."
There was never a dream to chase--only a nightmare to bring to life.
"The perfect woman" is a made-up campfire bogeyman that keeps us on our toes--
--And doesn't fucking EXIST.
Mommy! Swearing!
I owe you a dollar, Billy.

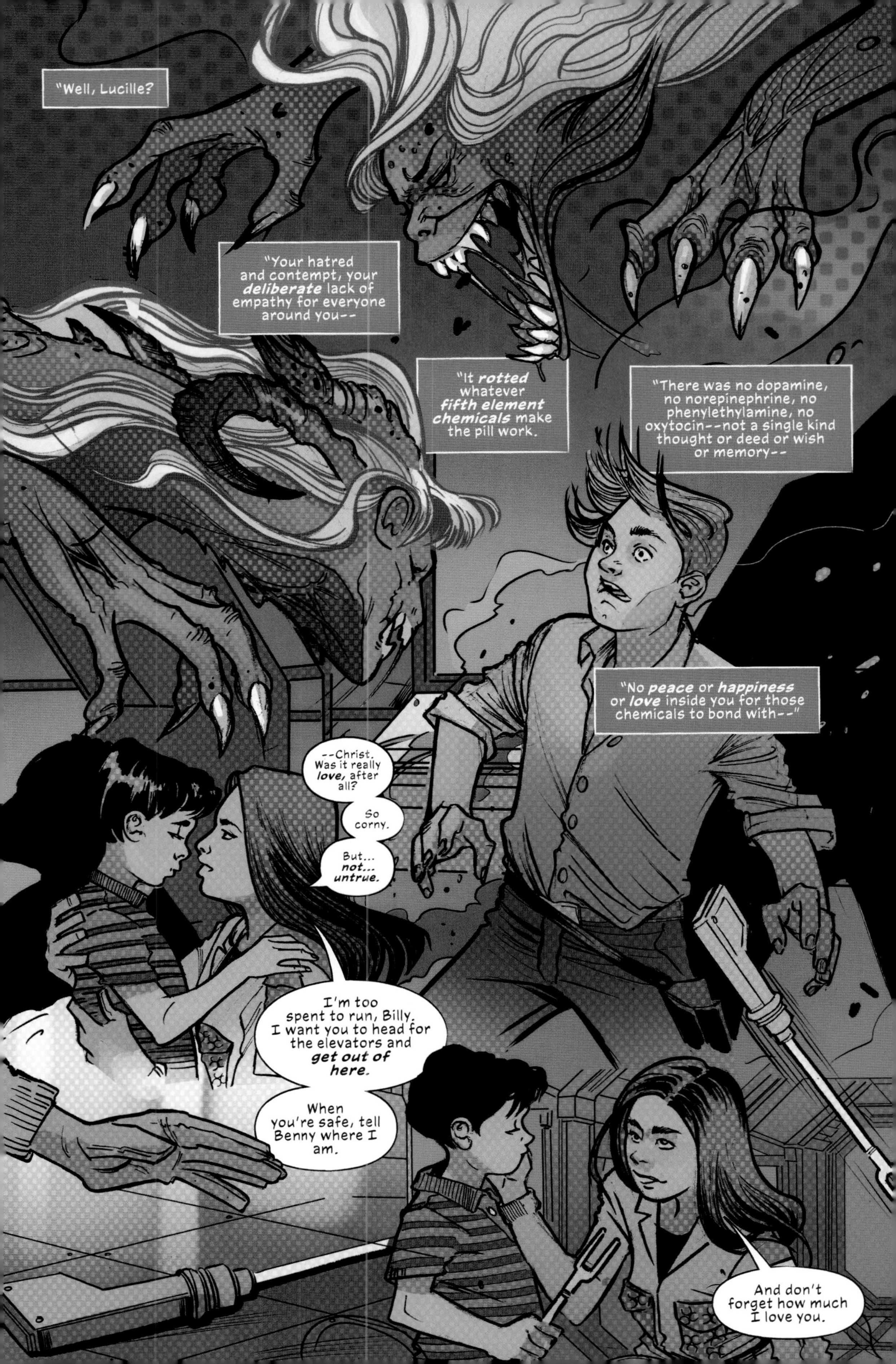
"Well, Lucille?
"Your hatred and contempt, your *deliberate* lack of empathy for everyone around you--
"It *rotted* whatever *fifth element chemicals* make the pill work.
"There was no dopamine, no norepinephrine, no phenylethylamine, no oxytocin--not a single kind thought or deed or wish or memory--
"No *peace* or *happiness* or *love* inside you for those chemicals to bond with--"
--Christ. Was it really *love*, after all?
So corny.
But... *not... untrue.*
I'm too spent to run, Billy. I want you to head for the elevators and *get out of here.*
When you're safe, tell Benny where I am.
And don't forget how much I love you.

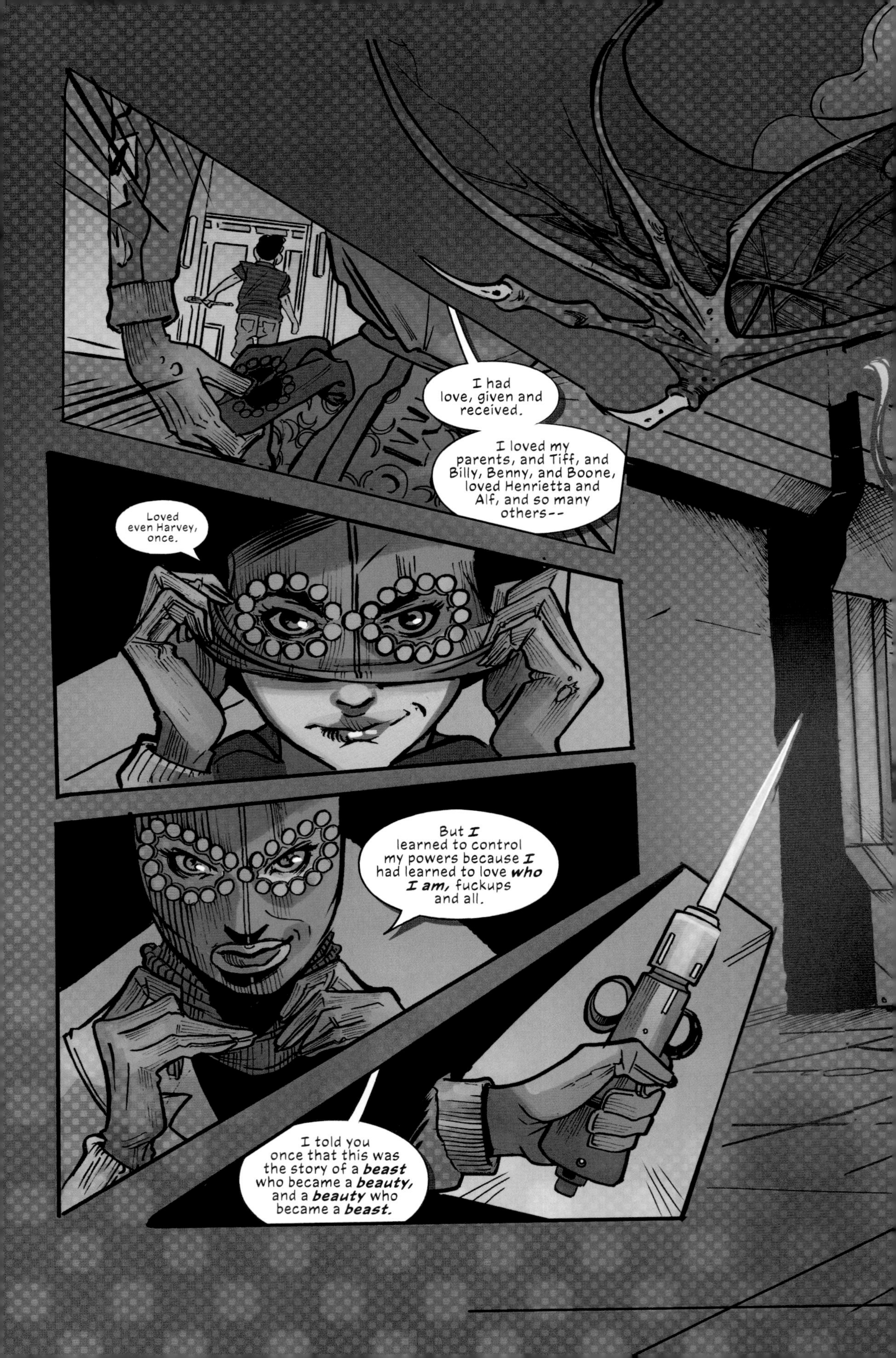

I had love, given and received.
I loved my parents, and Tiff, and Billy, Benny, and Boone, loved Henrietta and Alf, and so many others--
Loved even Harvey, once.
But I learned to control my powers because I had learned to love who I am, fuckups and all.
I told you once that this was the story of a beast who became a beauty, and a beauty who became a beast.

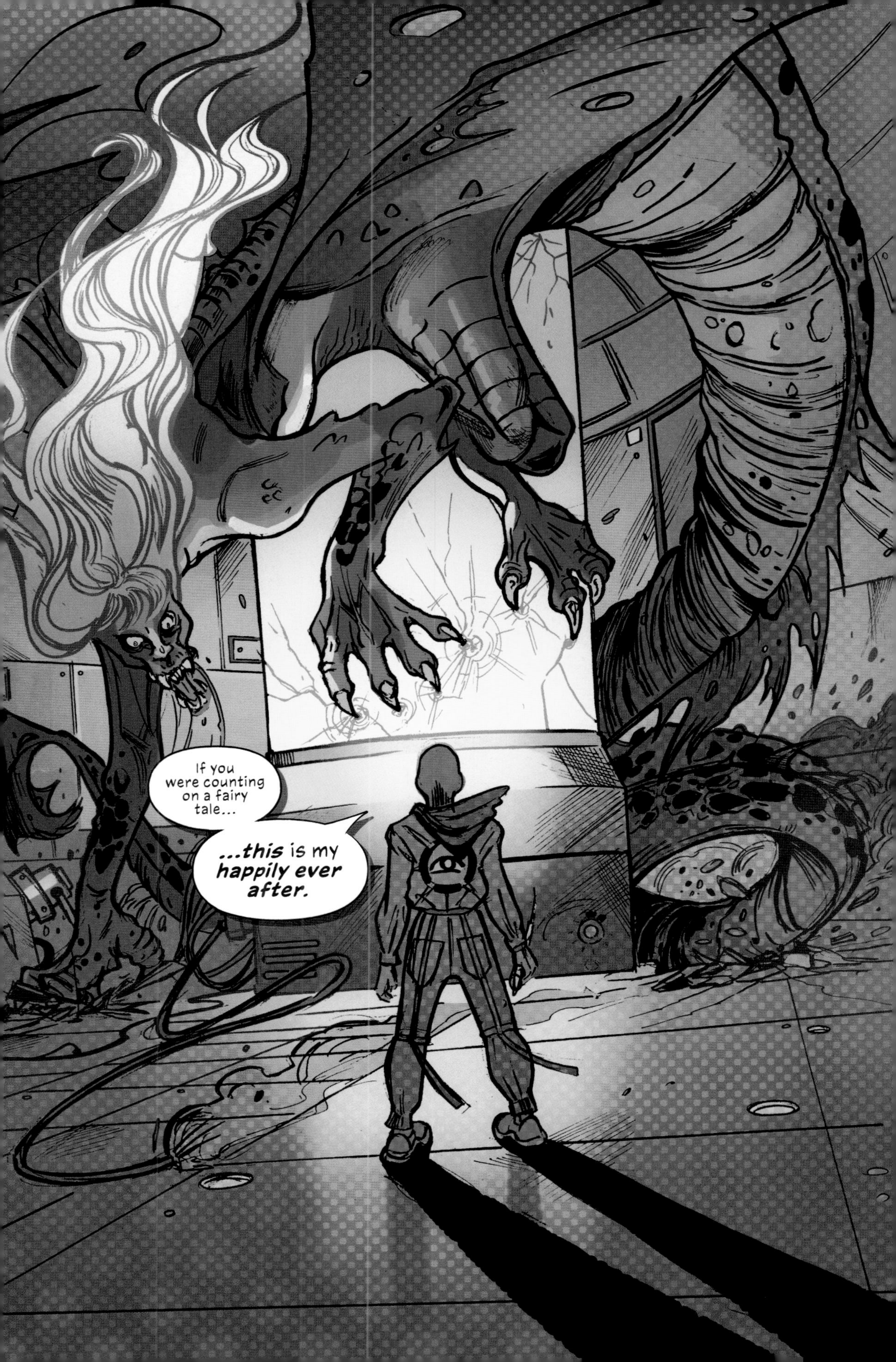
If you were counting on a fairy tale...
...*this* is my *happily ever after.*

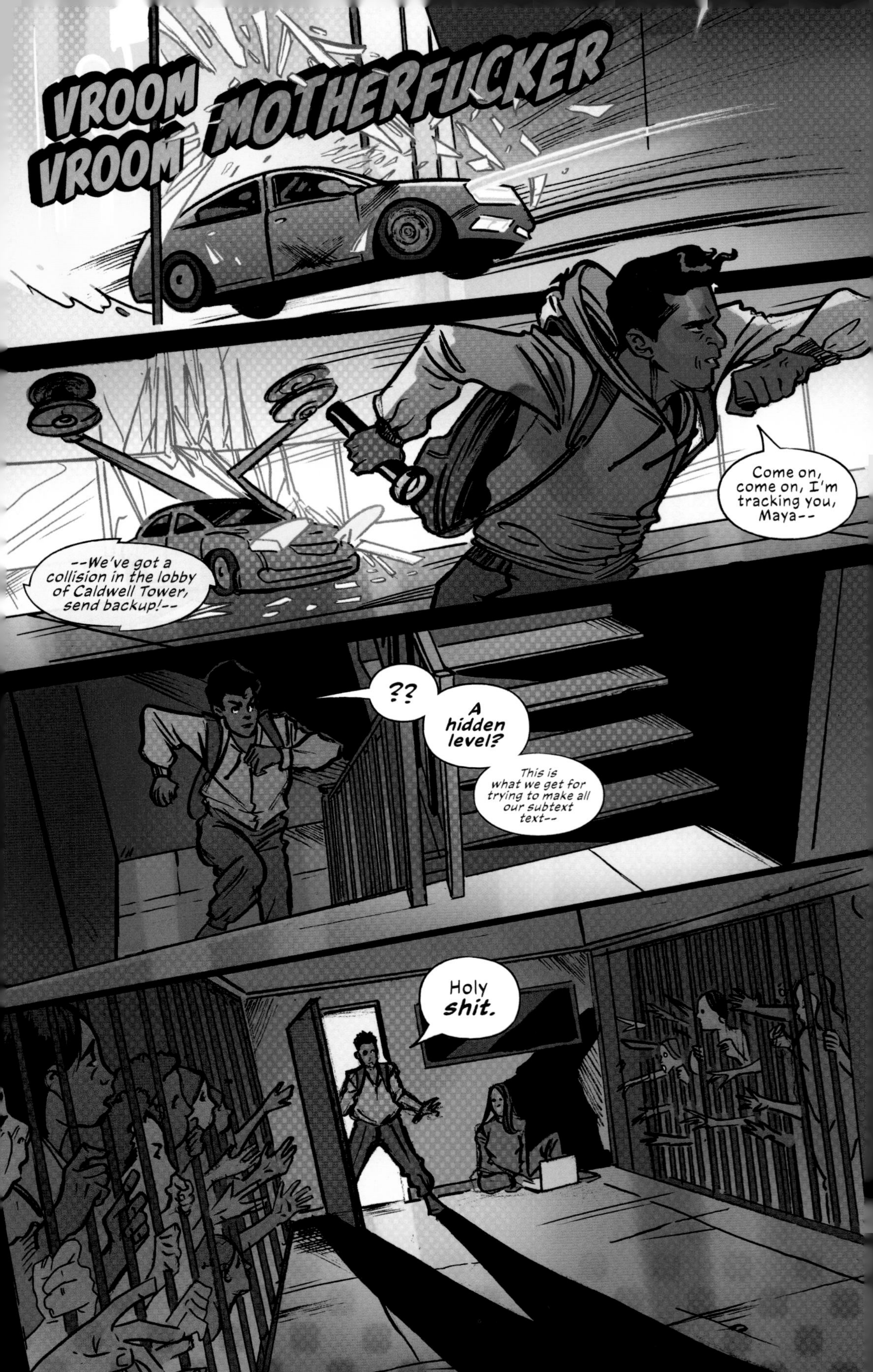

VROOM VROOM
MOTHERFUCKER
Come on, come on, I'm tracking you, Maya--
--We've got a collision in the lobby of Caldwell Tower, send backup!--
??
A hidden level?
This is what we get for trying to make all our subtext text--
Holy shit.

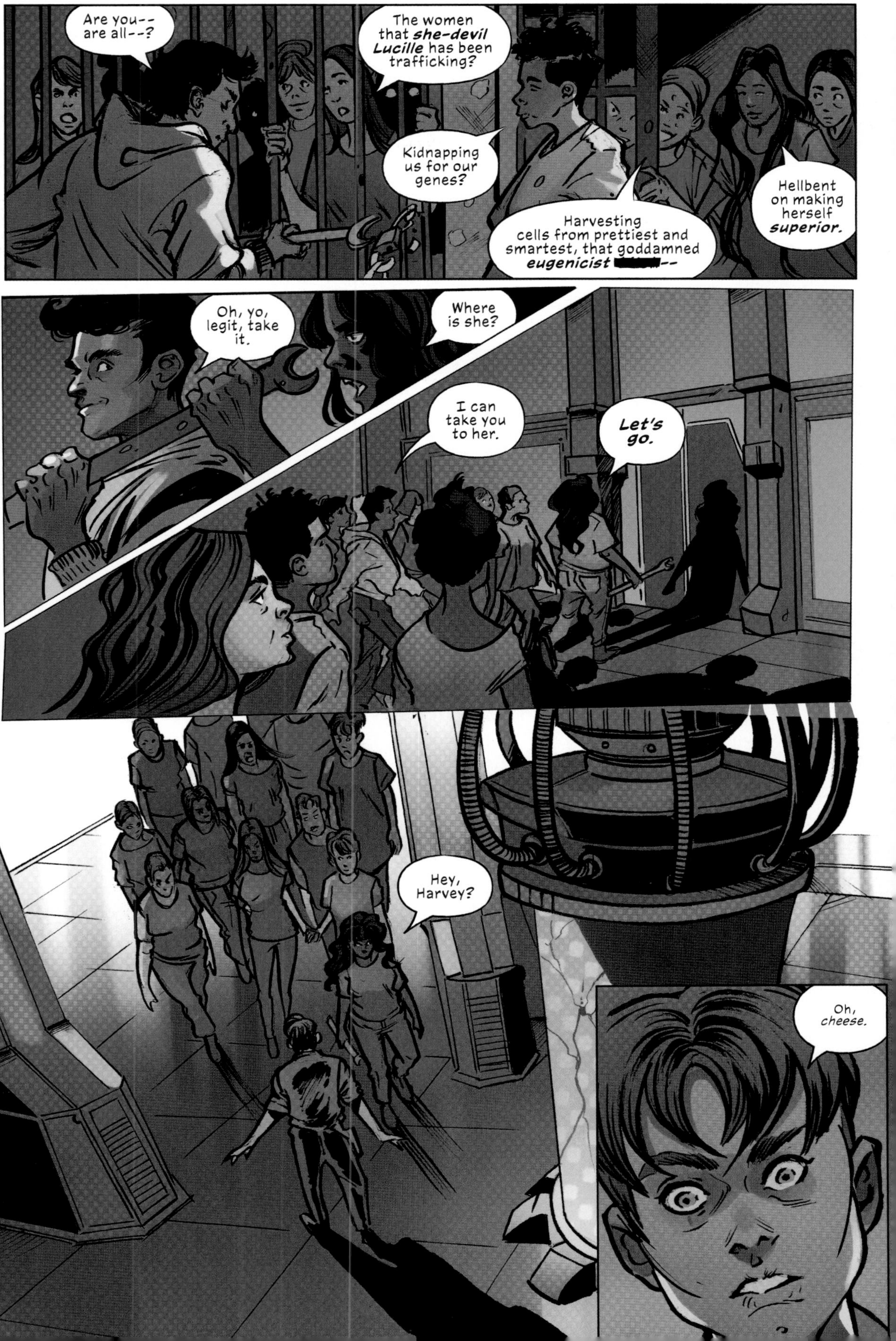

Are you-- are all--?
The women that *she-devil Lucille* has been trafficking?
Kidnapping us for our genes?
Harvesting cells from prettiest and smartest, that goddamned *eugenicist* [redacted]--
Hellbent on making herself *superior.*
Oh, yo, legit, take it.
Where is she?
I can take you to her.
Let's go.
Hey, Harvey?
Oh, *cheese.*

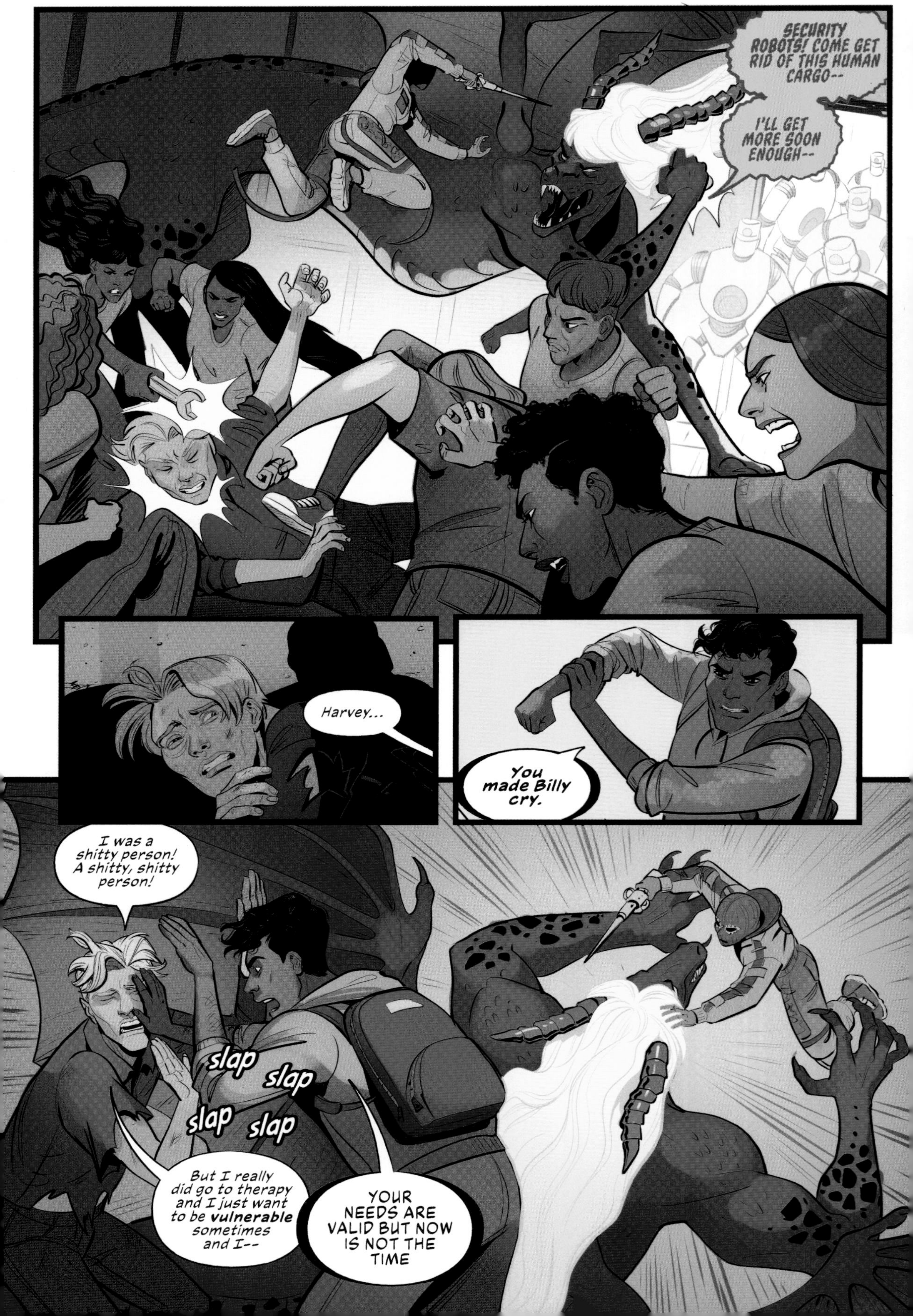
SECURITY ROBOTS! COME GET RID OF THIS HUMAN CARGO--
I'LL GET MORE SOON ENOUGH--
Harvey...
You made Billy cry.
I was a shitty person! A shitty, shitty person!
slap slap slap slap
But I really did go to therapy and I just want to be **vulnerable** sometimes and I--
YOUR NEEDS ARE VALID BUT NOW IS NOT THE TIME

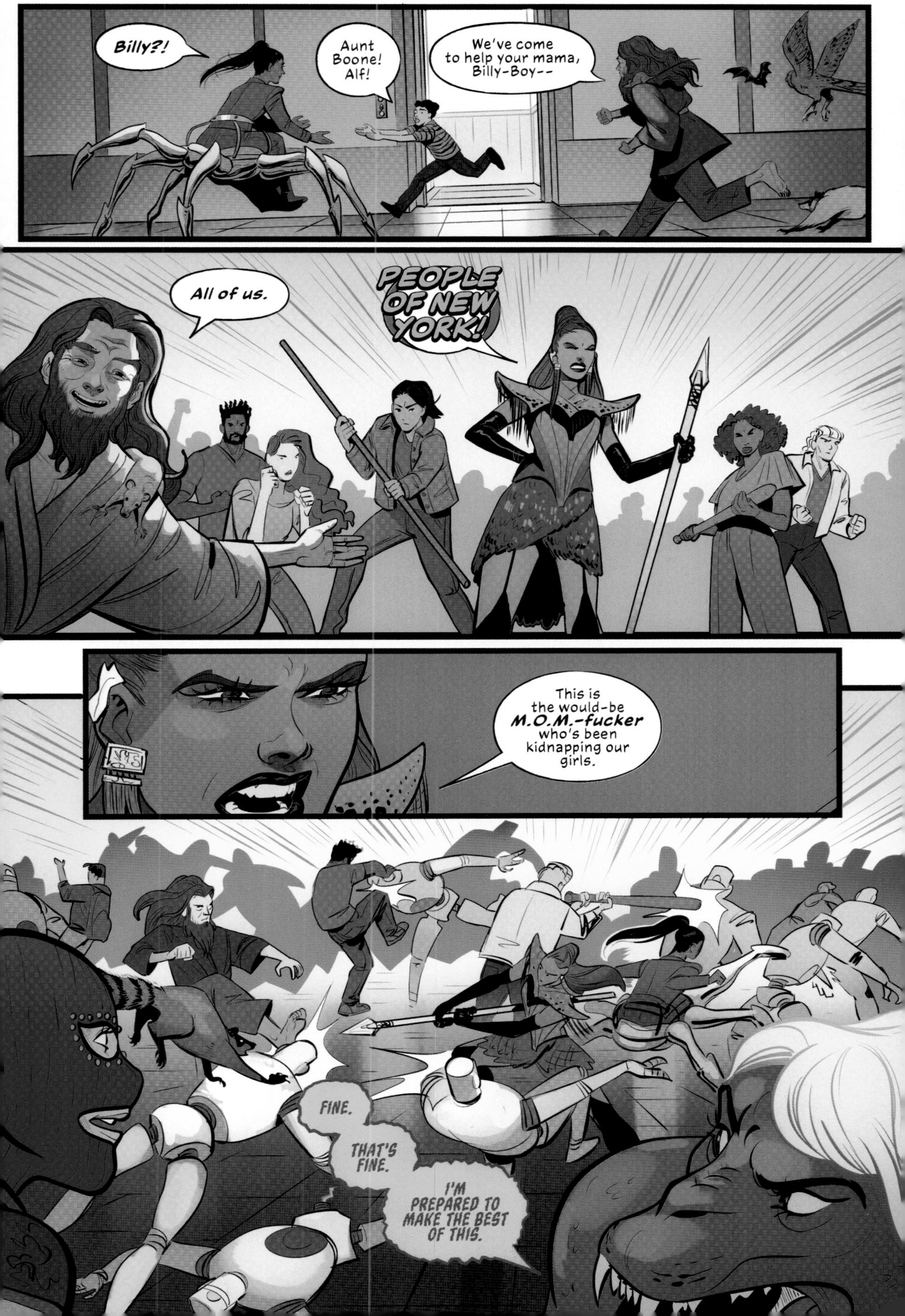
Billy?!
Aunt Boone! Alf!
We've come to help your mama, Billy-Boy--
All of us.
PEOPLE OF NEW YORK!
This is the would-be M.O.M.-fucker who's been kidnapping our girls.
FINE.
THAT'S FINE.
I'M PREPARED TO MAKE THE BEST OF THIS.

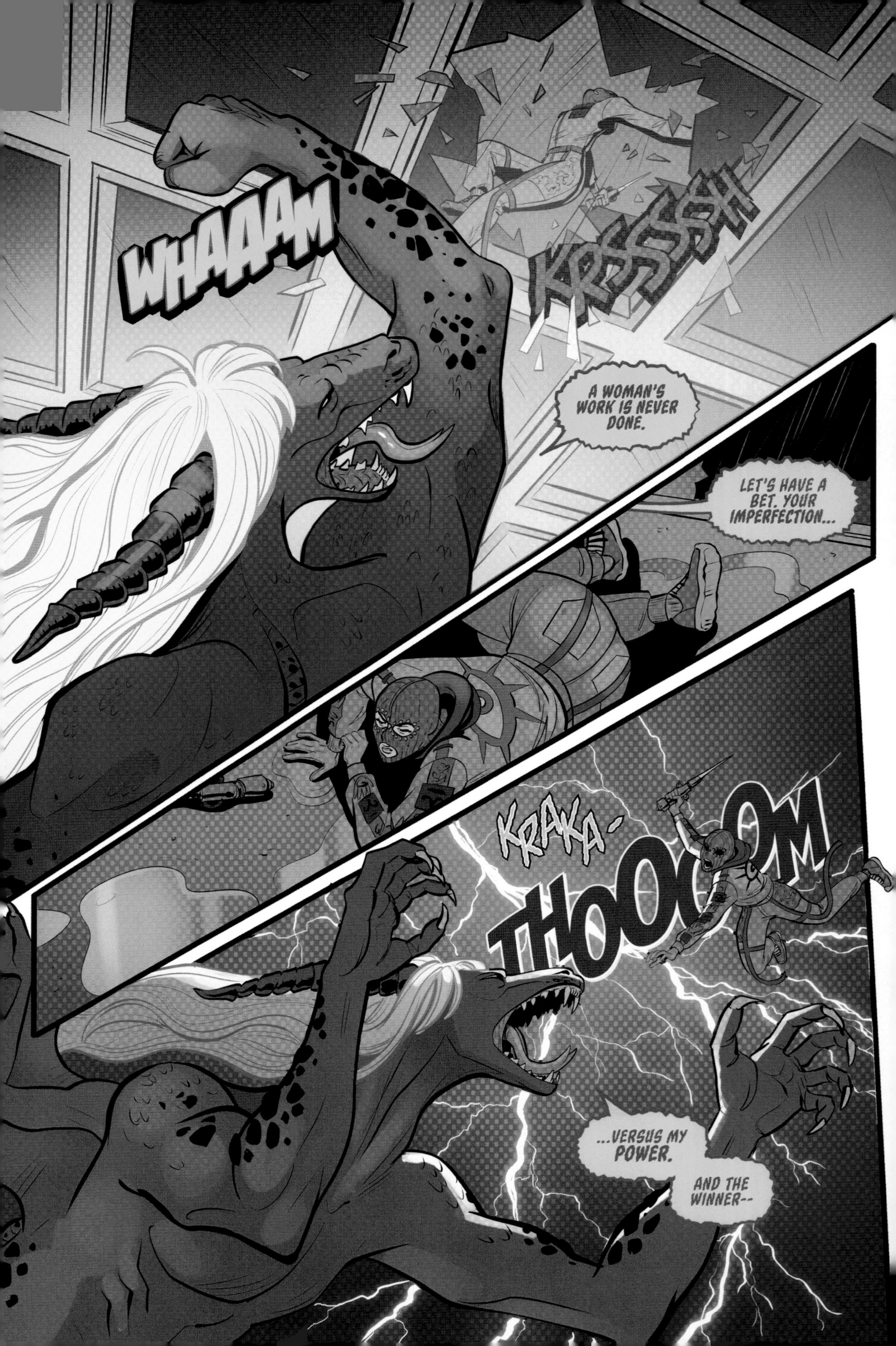
WHAAAM
KRSSSH
A WOMAN'S WORK IS NEVER DONE.
LET'S HAVE A BET. YOUR IMPERFECTION...
KRAKA-
THOOOOM
...VERSUS MY POWER.
AND THE WINNER--

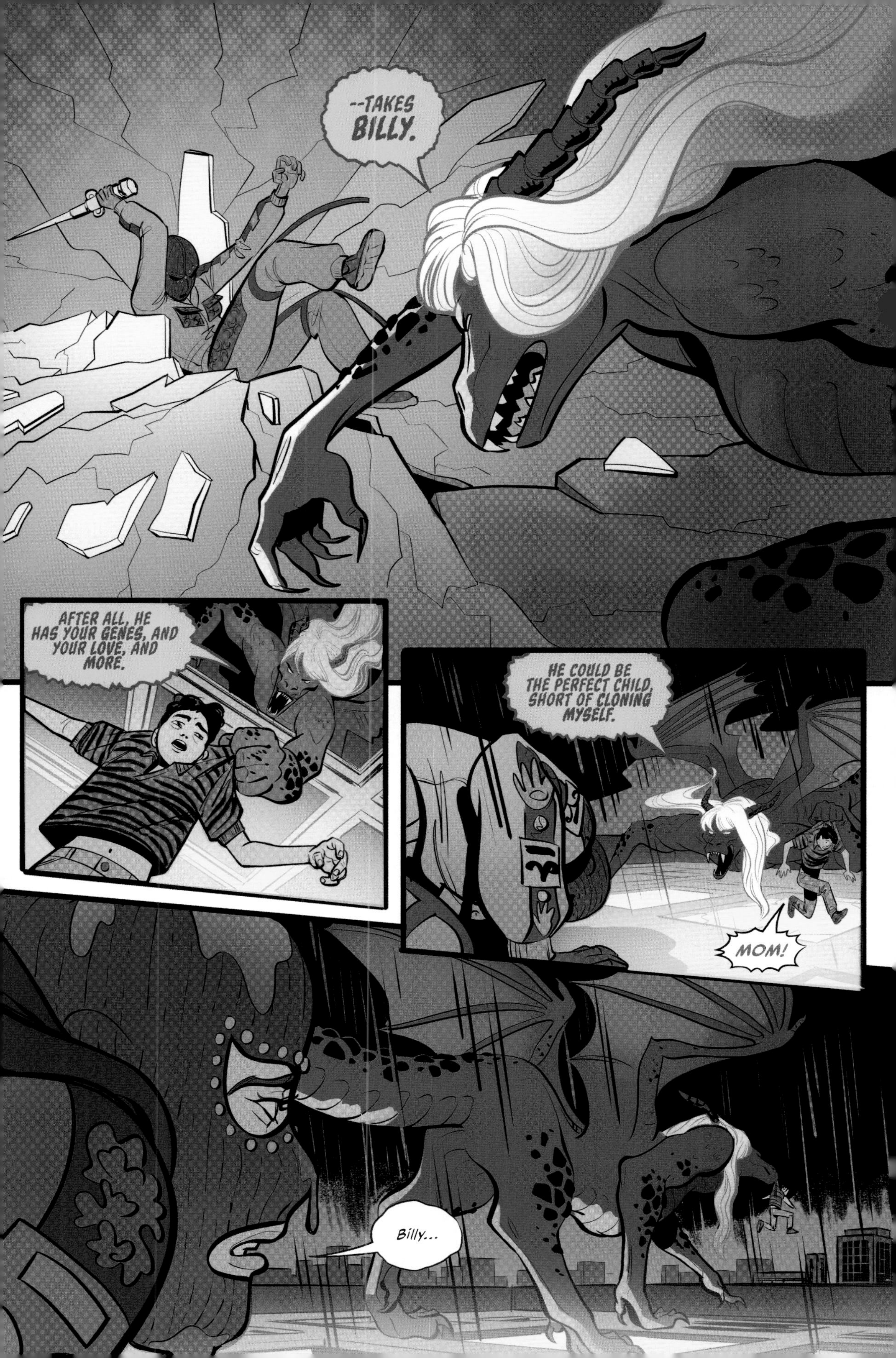
--TAKES BILLY.
AFTER ALL, HE HAS YOUR GENES, AND YOUR LOVE, AND MORE.
HE COULD BE THE PERFECT CHILD, SHORT OF CLONING MYSELF.
MOM!
Billy...

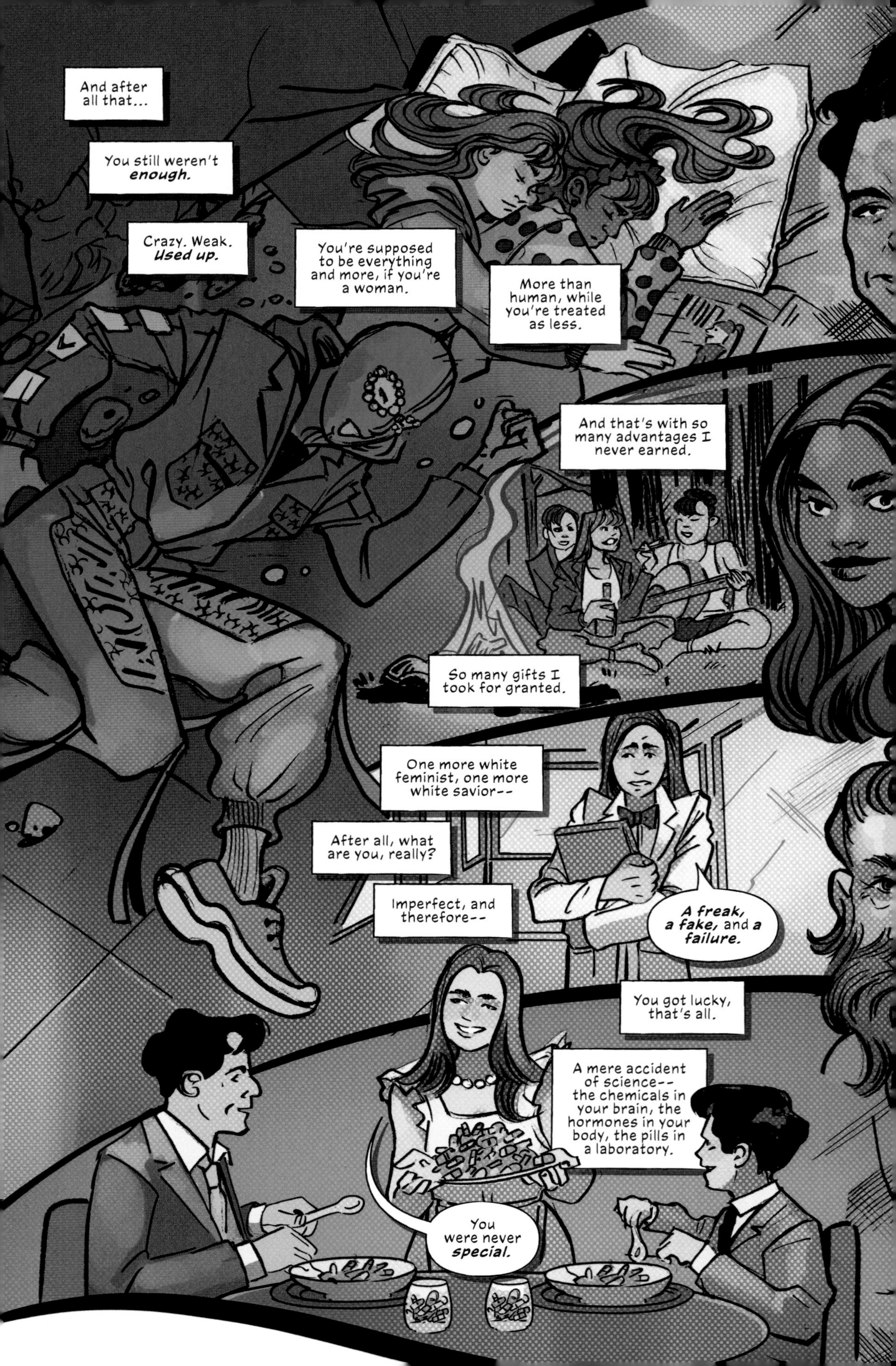

And after all that...
You still weren't ***enough.***
Crazy. Weak. ***Used up.***
You're supposed to be everything and more, if you're a woman.
More than human, while you're treated as less.
And that's with so many advantages I never earned.
So many gifts I took for granted.
One more white feminist, one more white savior--
After all, what are you, really?
Imperfect, and therefore--
A freak, a fake, and a ***failure.***
You got lucky, that's all.
A mere accident of science--the chemicals in your brain, the hormones in your body, the pills in a laboratory.
You were never ***special.***

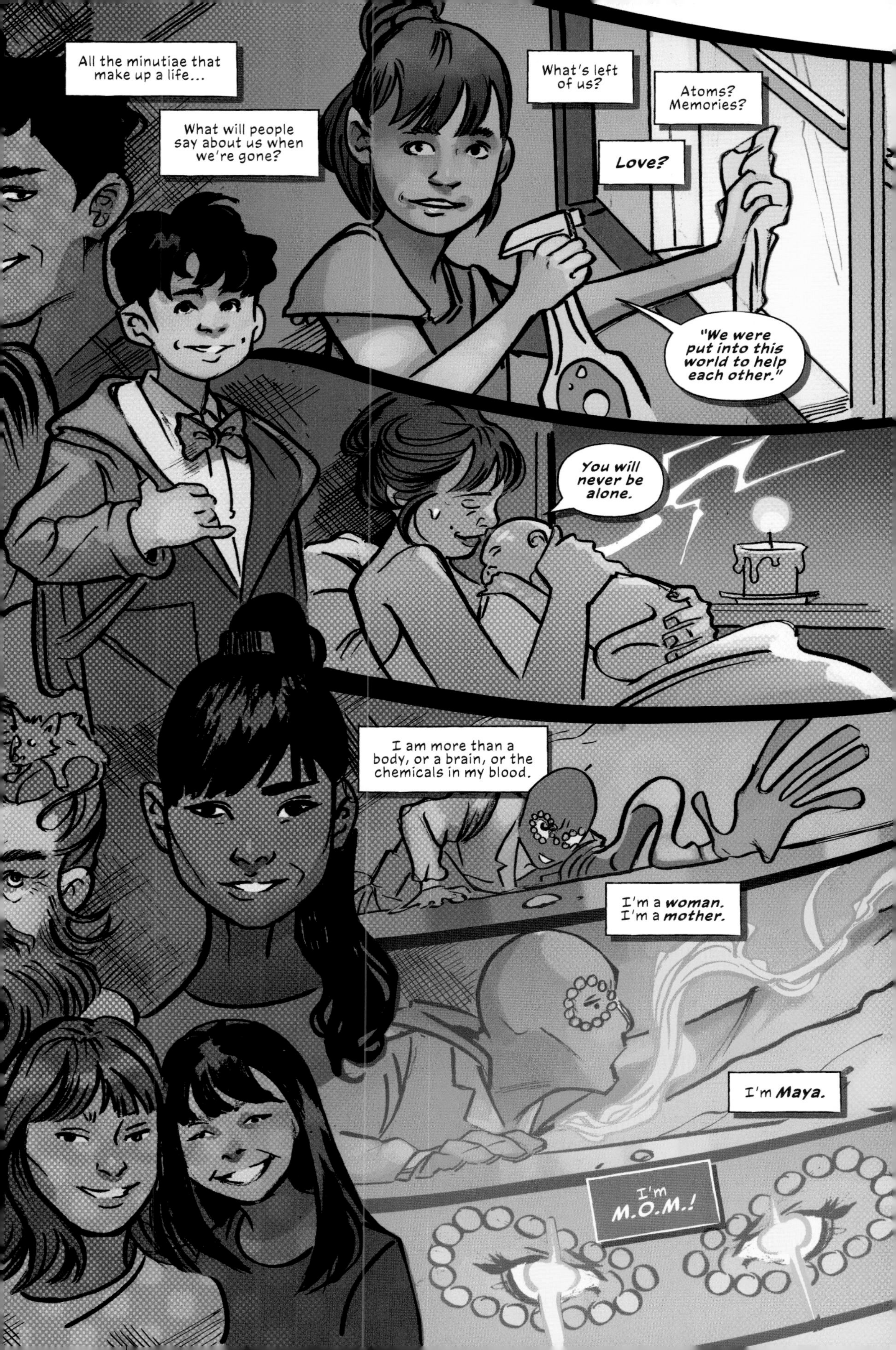

All the minutiae that make up a life...
What will people say about us when we're gone?
What's left of us?
Atoms? Memories?
Love?
"We were put into this world to help each other."
You will never be alone.
I am more than a body, or a brain, or the chemicals in my blood.
I'm a woman. I'm a mother.
I'm Maya.
I'm M.O.M.!

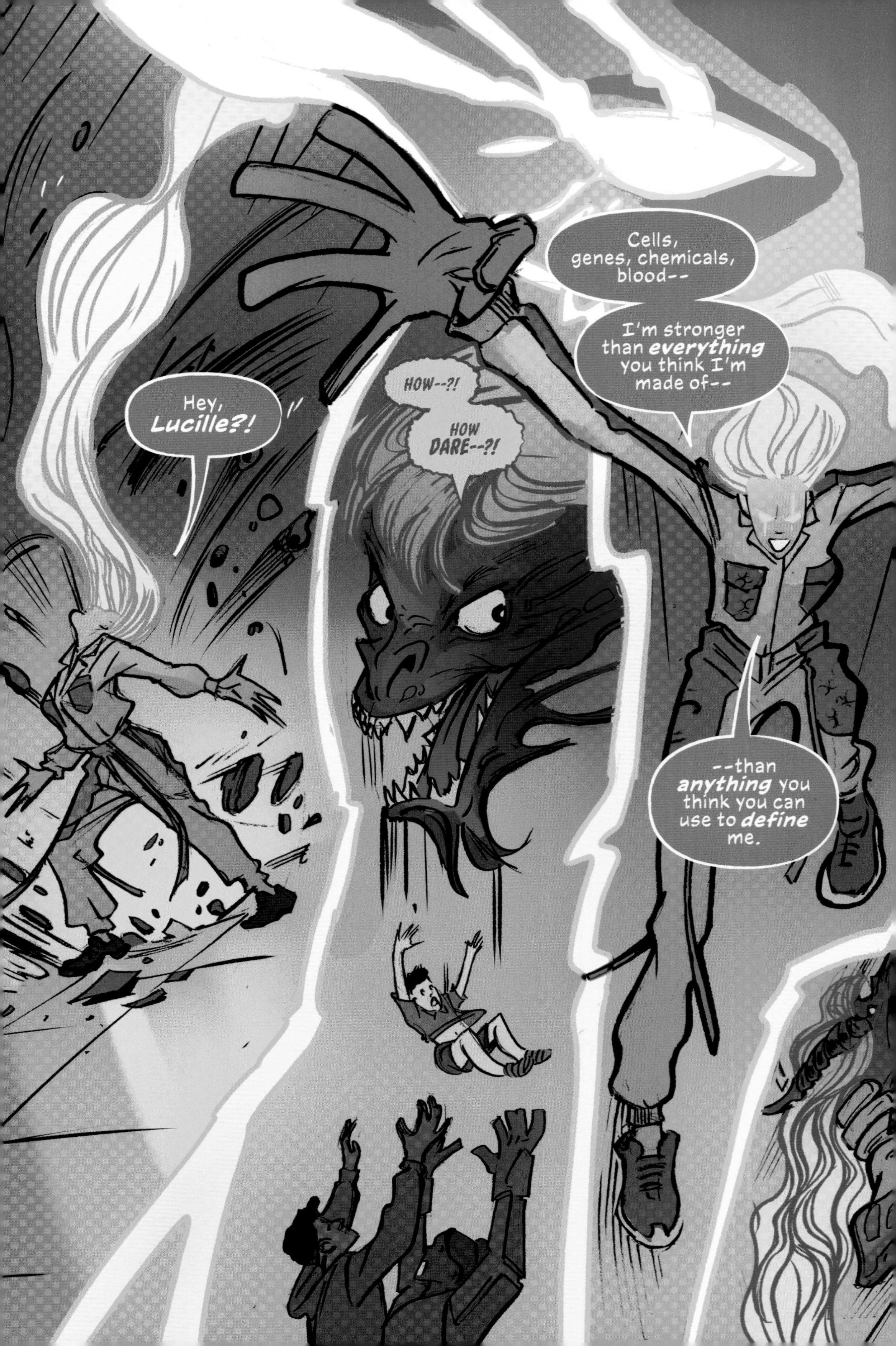
Hey, Lucille?!
HOW--?!
HOW DARE--?!
Cells, genes, chemicals, blood--
I'm stronger than *everything* you think I'm made of--
--than *anything* you think you can use to *define* me.

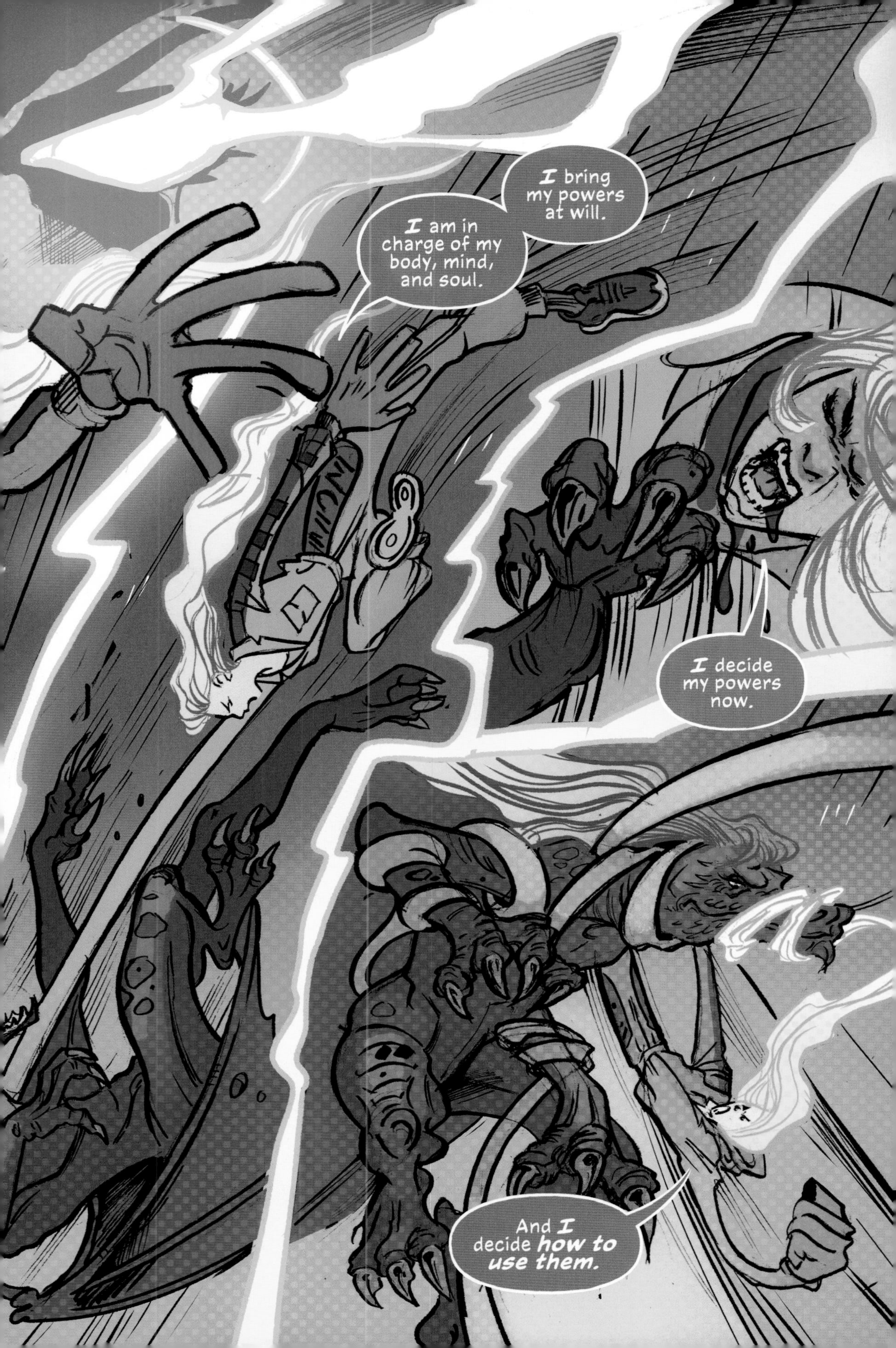

I am in charge of my body, mind, and soul.
I bring my powers at will.
I decide my powers now.
And *I* decide ***how to use them.***

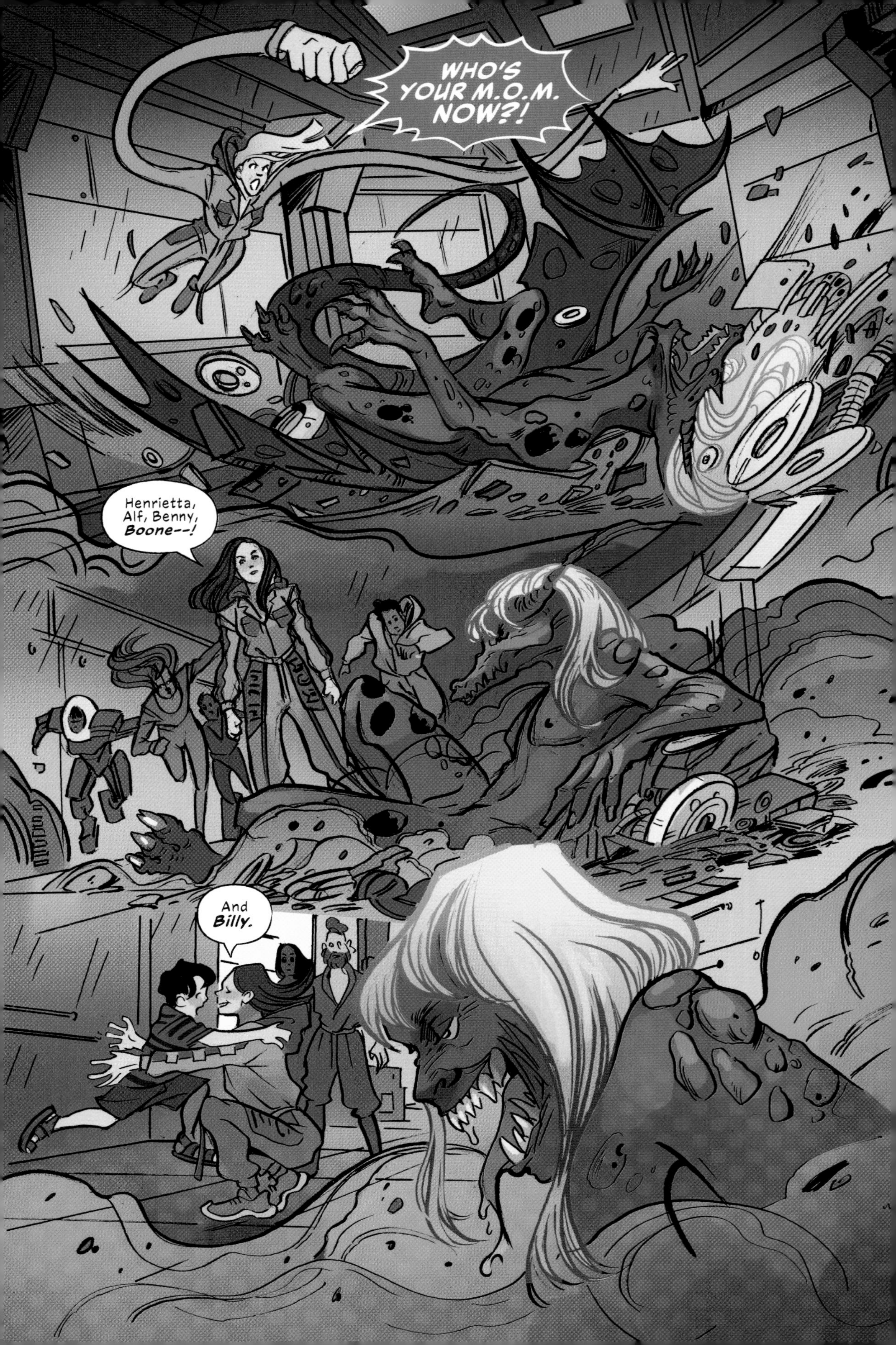
WHO'S YOUR M.O.M. NOW?!
Henrietta, Alf, Benny, Boone--!
And Billy.

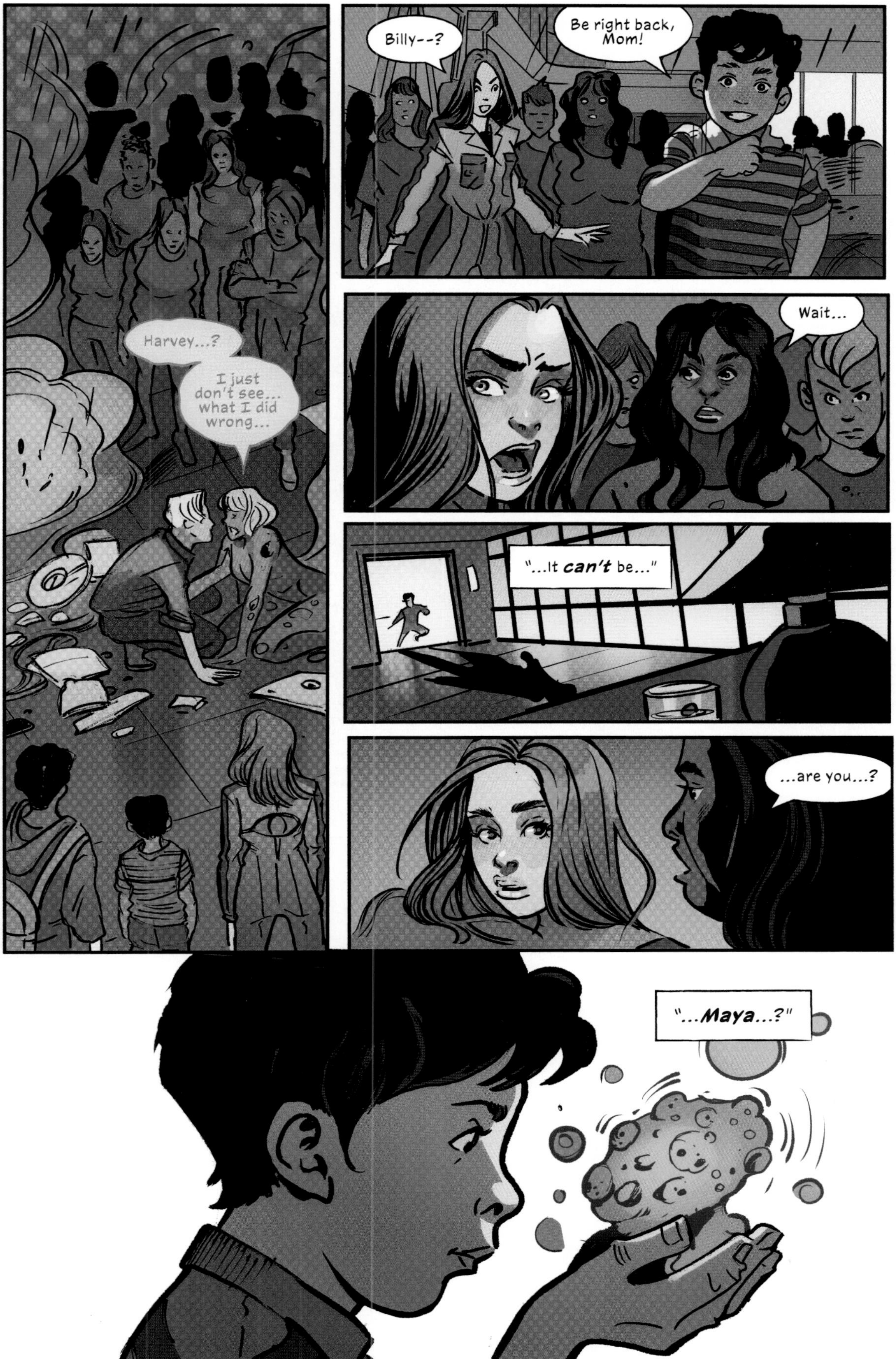

Harvey...?
I just don't see... what I did wrong...
Billy--?
Be right back, Mom!
Wait...
"...It can't be..."
...are you...?
"...Maya...?"

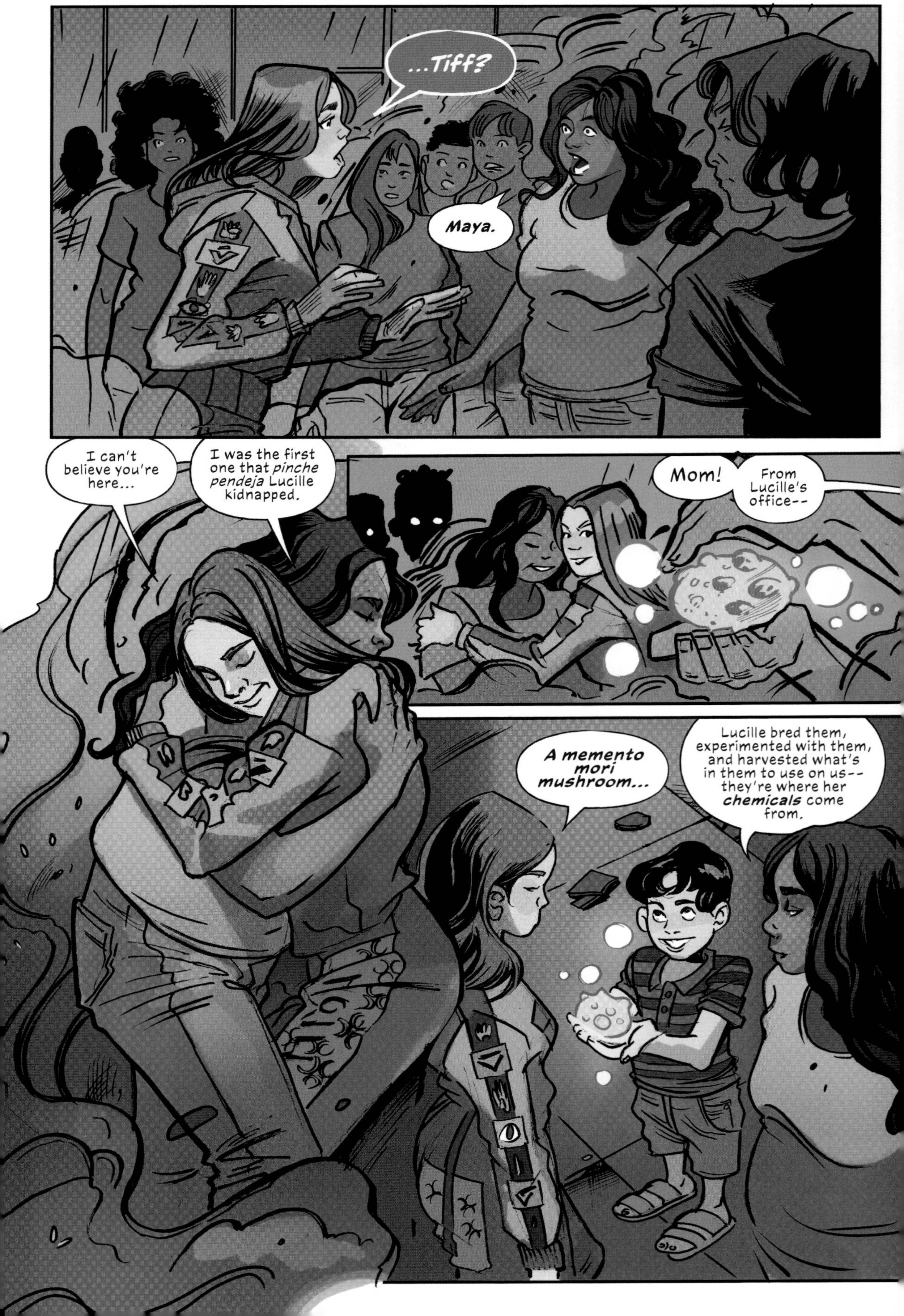
...Tiff?
Maya.
I can't believe you're here...
I was the first one that *pinche pendeja* Lucille kidnapped.
Mom!
From Lucille's office--
A memento mori mushroom...
Lucille bred them, experimented with them, and harvested what's in them to use on us-- they're where her **chemicals** come from.

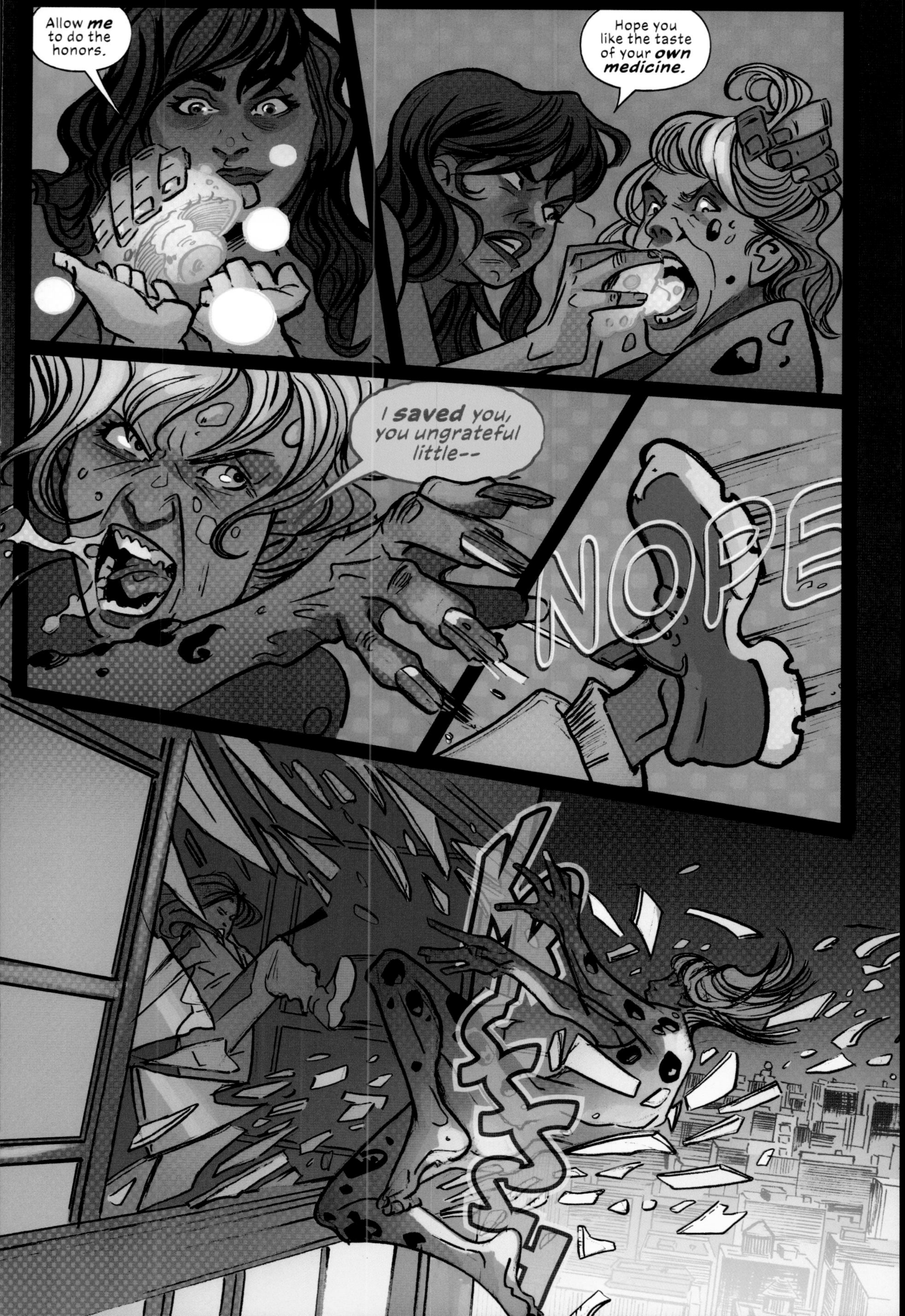
Allow me to do the honors.
Hope you like the taste of your own medicine.
I saved you, you ungrateful little--
NOPE

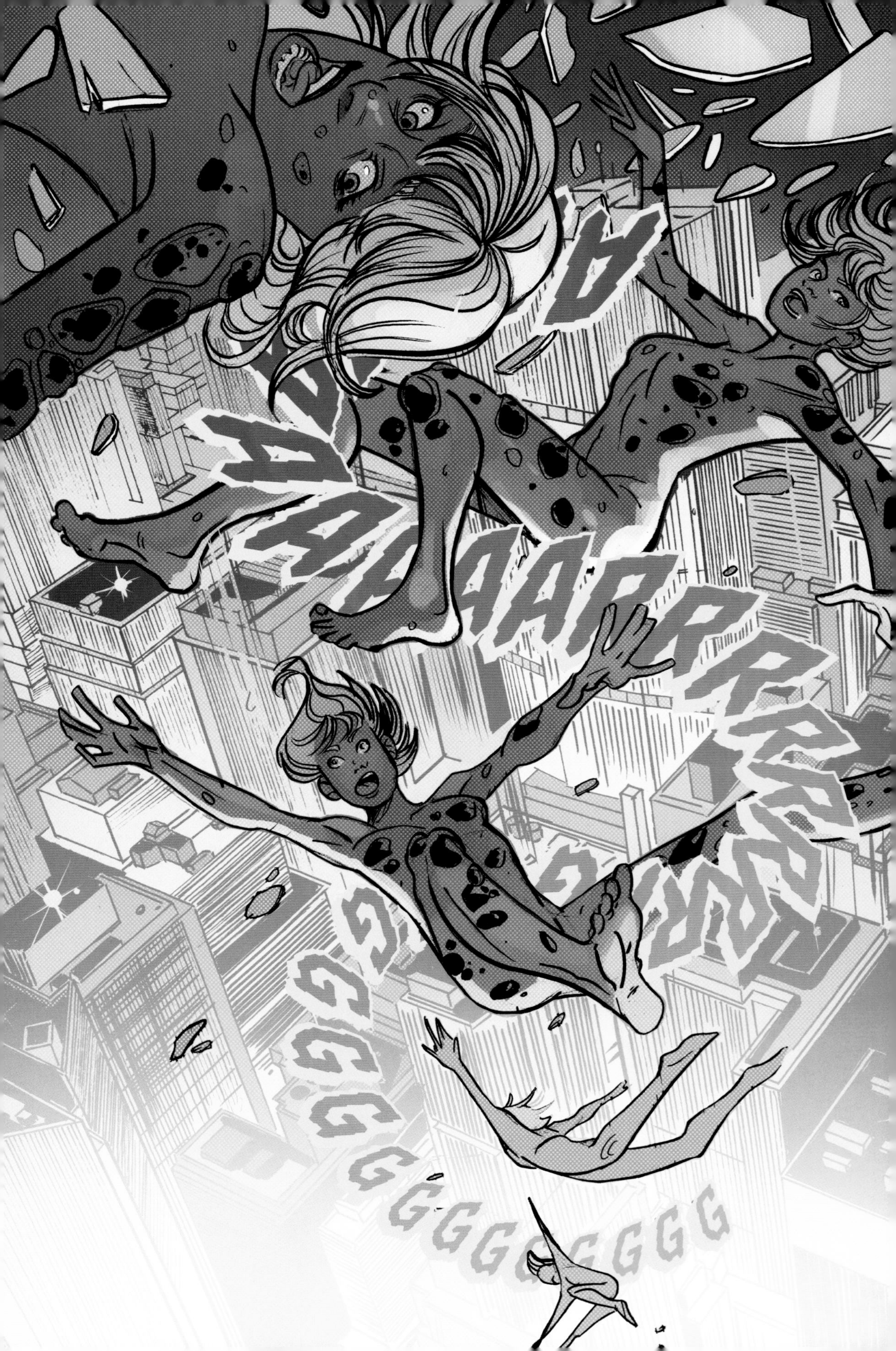
AAAAAARRRRRRGGGGGGGGGGGGGGGGG

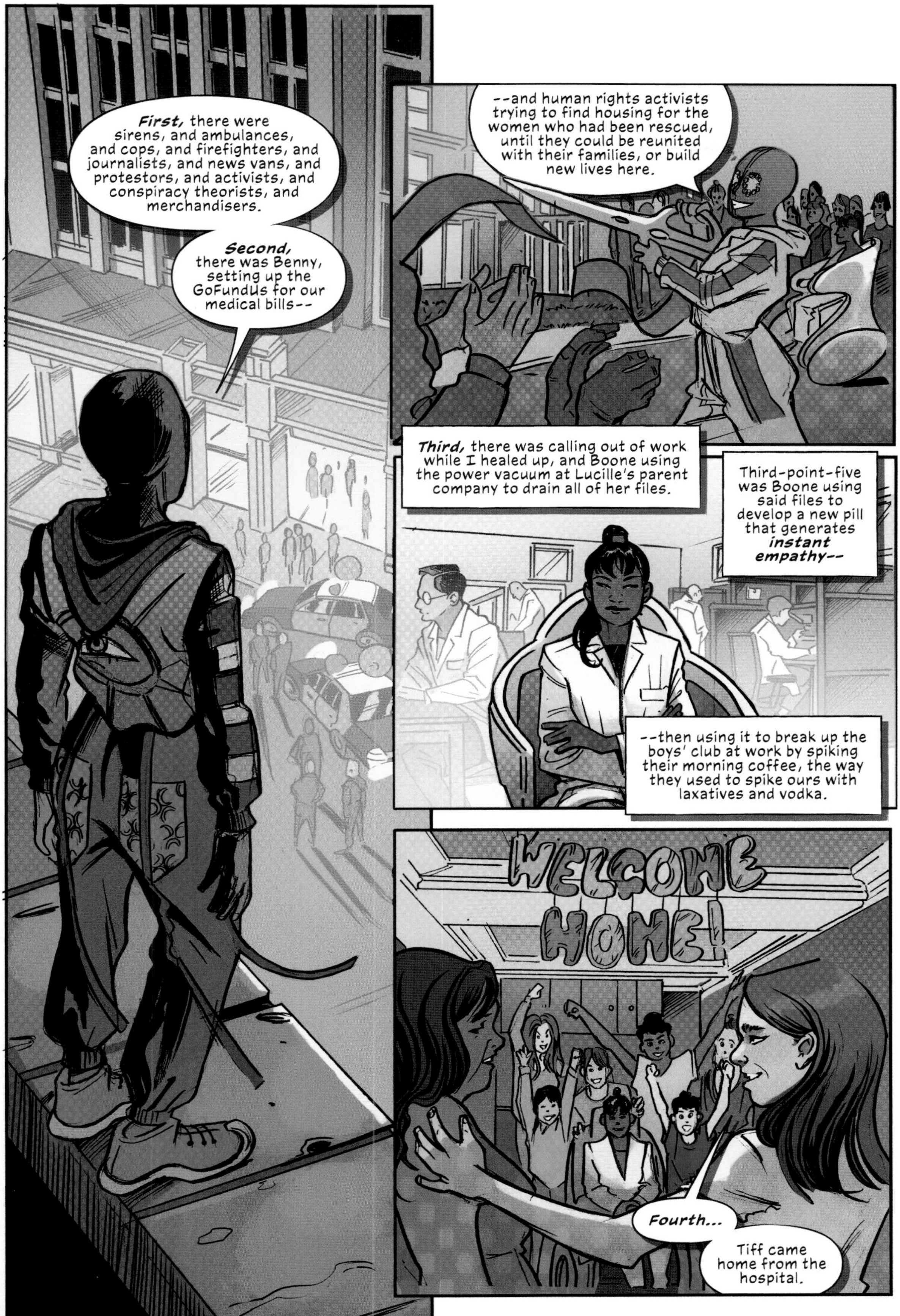
First, there were sirens, and ambulances, and cops, and firefighters, and journalists, and news vans, and protestors, and activists, and conspiracy theorists, and merchandisers.
Second, there was Benny, setting up the GoFundUs for our medical bills--
--and human rights activists trying to find housing for the women who had been rescued, until they could be reunited with their families, or build new lives here.
Third, there was calling out of work while I healed up, and Boone using the power vacuum at Lucille's parent company to drain all of her files.
Third-point-five was Boone using said files to develop a new pill that generates instant empathy--
--then using it to break up the boys' club at work by spiking their morning coffee, the way they used to spike ours with laxatives and vodka.
WELCOME HOME!
Fourth...
Tiff came home from the hospital.

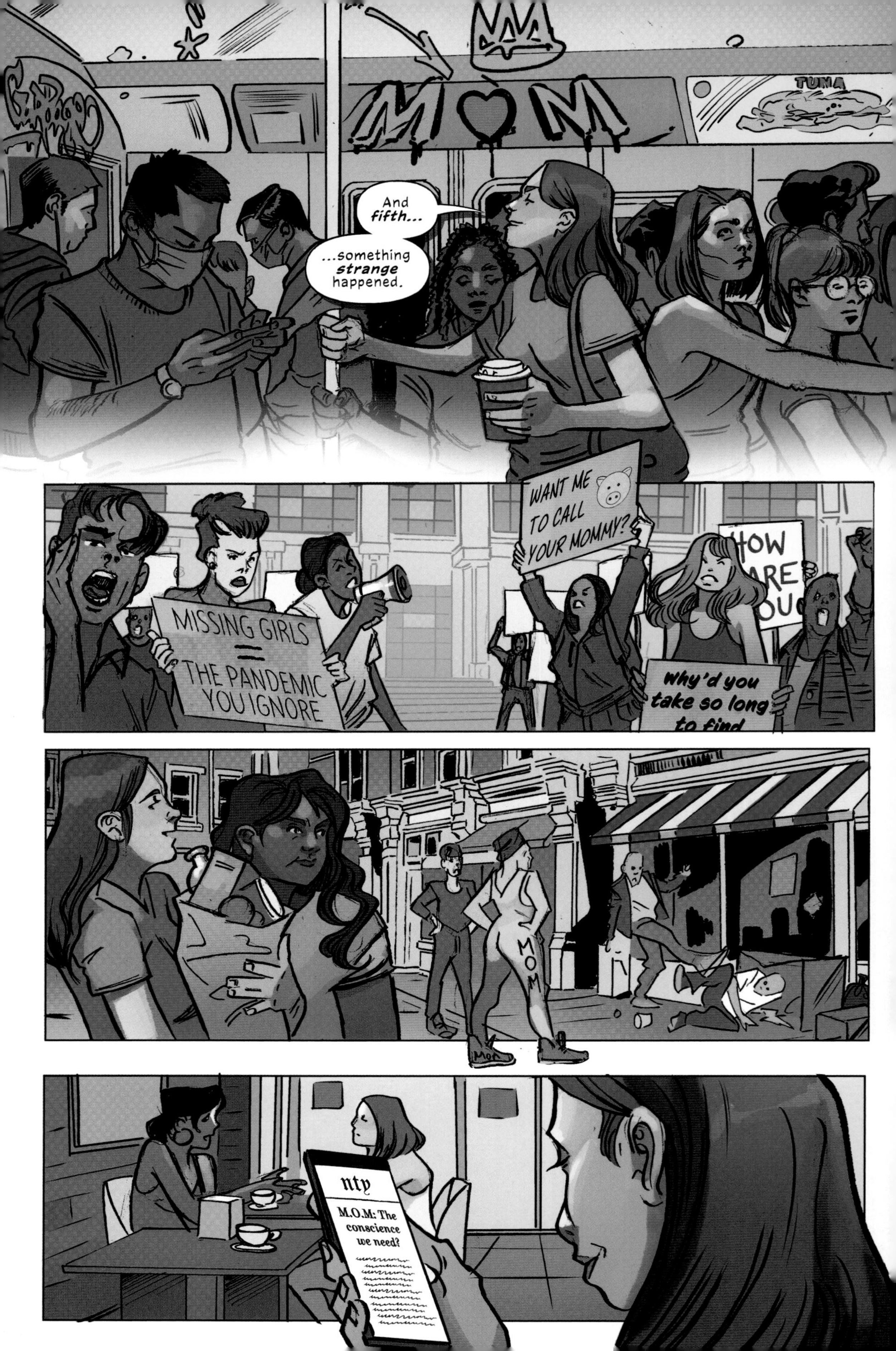
M♡M
TUNA
And fifth...
...something strange happened.
WANT ME TO CALL YOUR MOMMY?
HOW ARE YOU
MISSING GIRLS = THE PANDEMIC YOU IGNORE
Why'd you take so long to find
MOM
nty
M.O.M: The conscience we need?

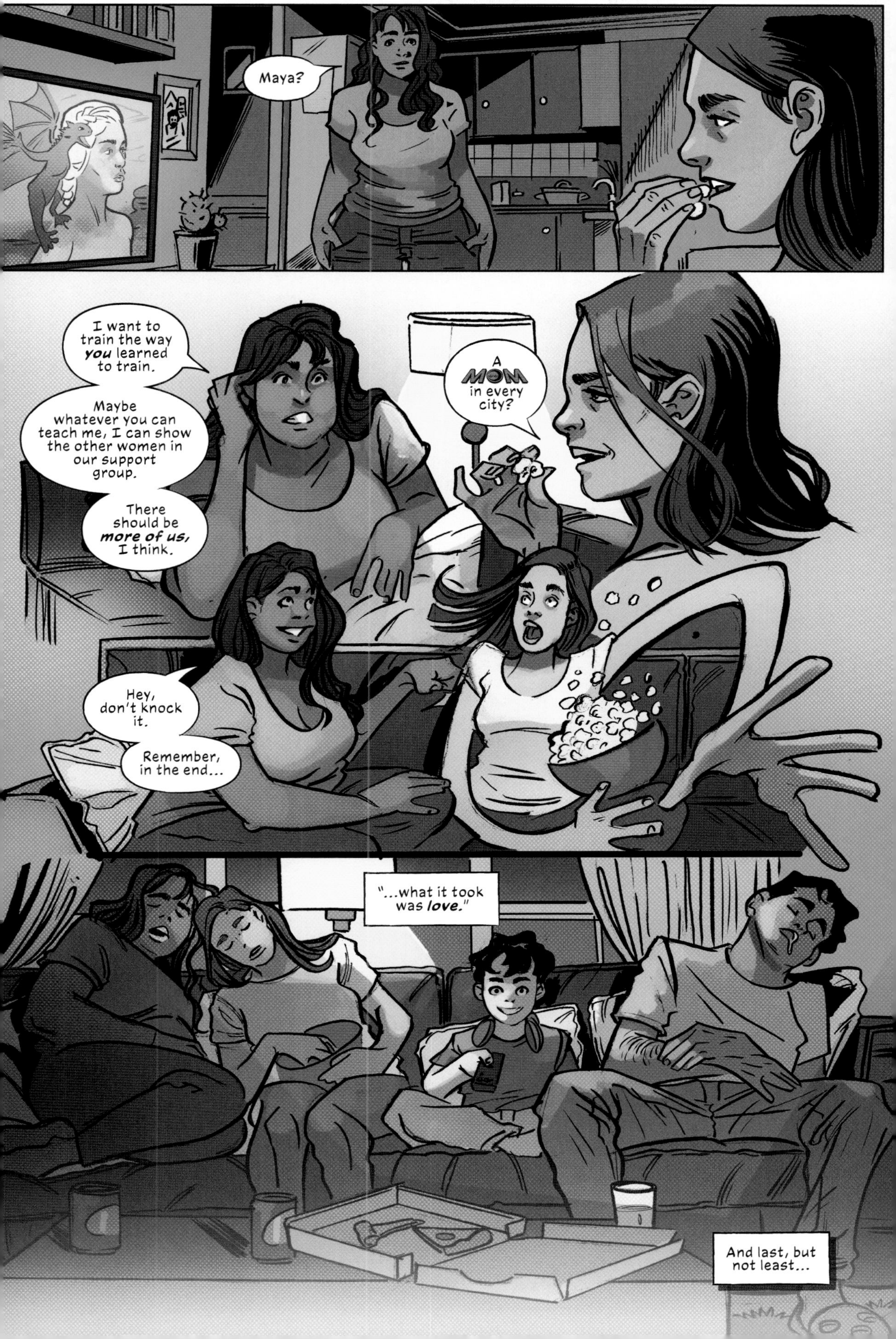
Maya?
I want to train the way *you* learned to train.
Maybe whatever you can teach me, I can show the other women in our support group.
There should be ***more of us,*** I think.
A MOM in every city?
Hey, don't knock it.
Remember, in the end...
"...what it took was ***love.***"
And last, but not least...

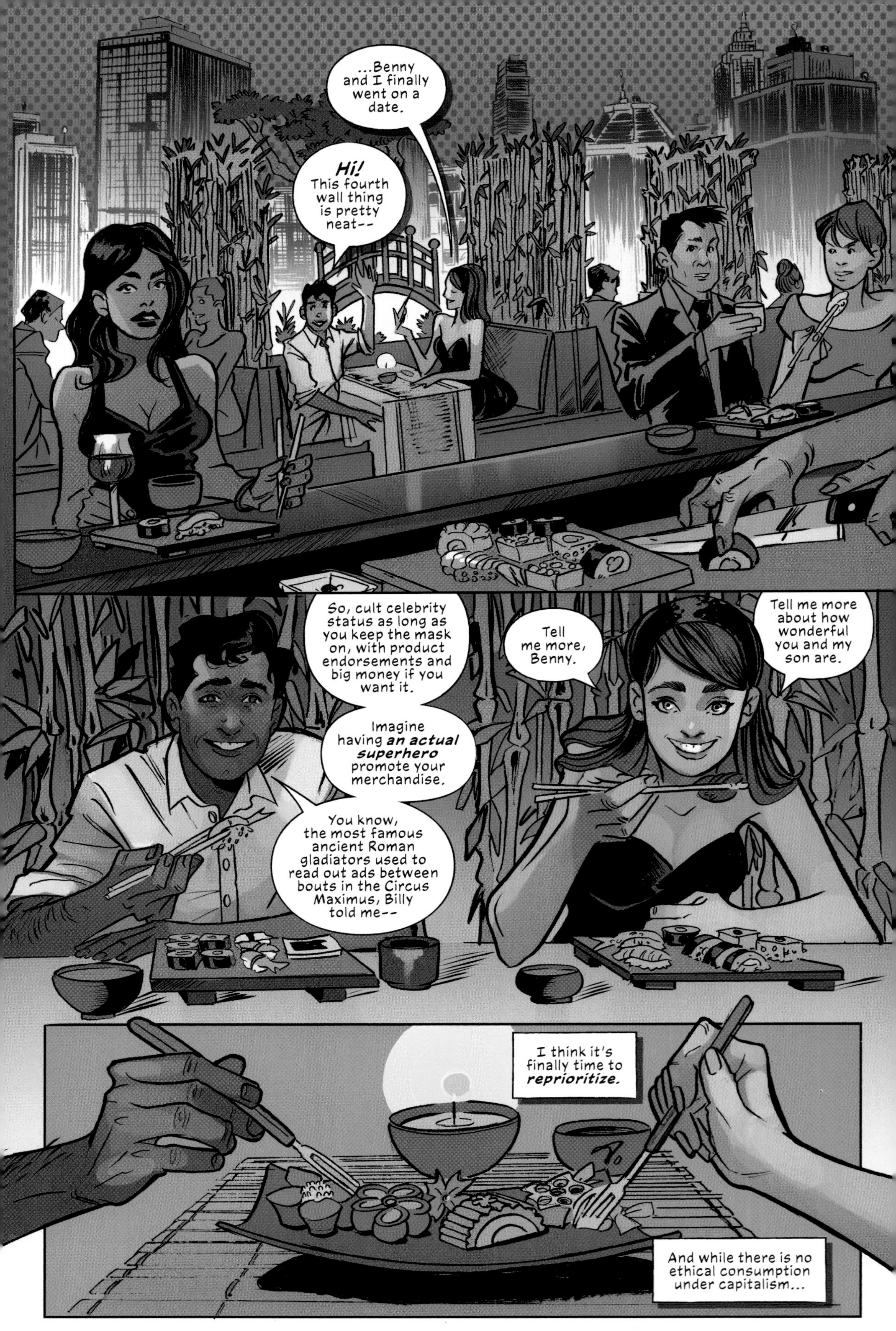

...Benny and I finally went on a date.
Hi! This fourth wall thing is pretty neat--
So, cult celebrity status as long as you keep the mask on, with product endorsements and big money if you want it.
Imagine having an actual superhero promote your merchandise.
You know, the most famous ancient Roman gladiators used to read out ads between bouts in the Circus Maximus, Billy told me--
Tell me more, Benny.
Tell me more about how wonderful you and my son are.
I think it's finally time to reprioritize.
And while there is no ethical consumption under capitalism...

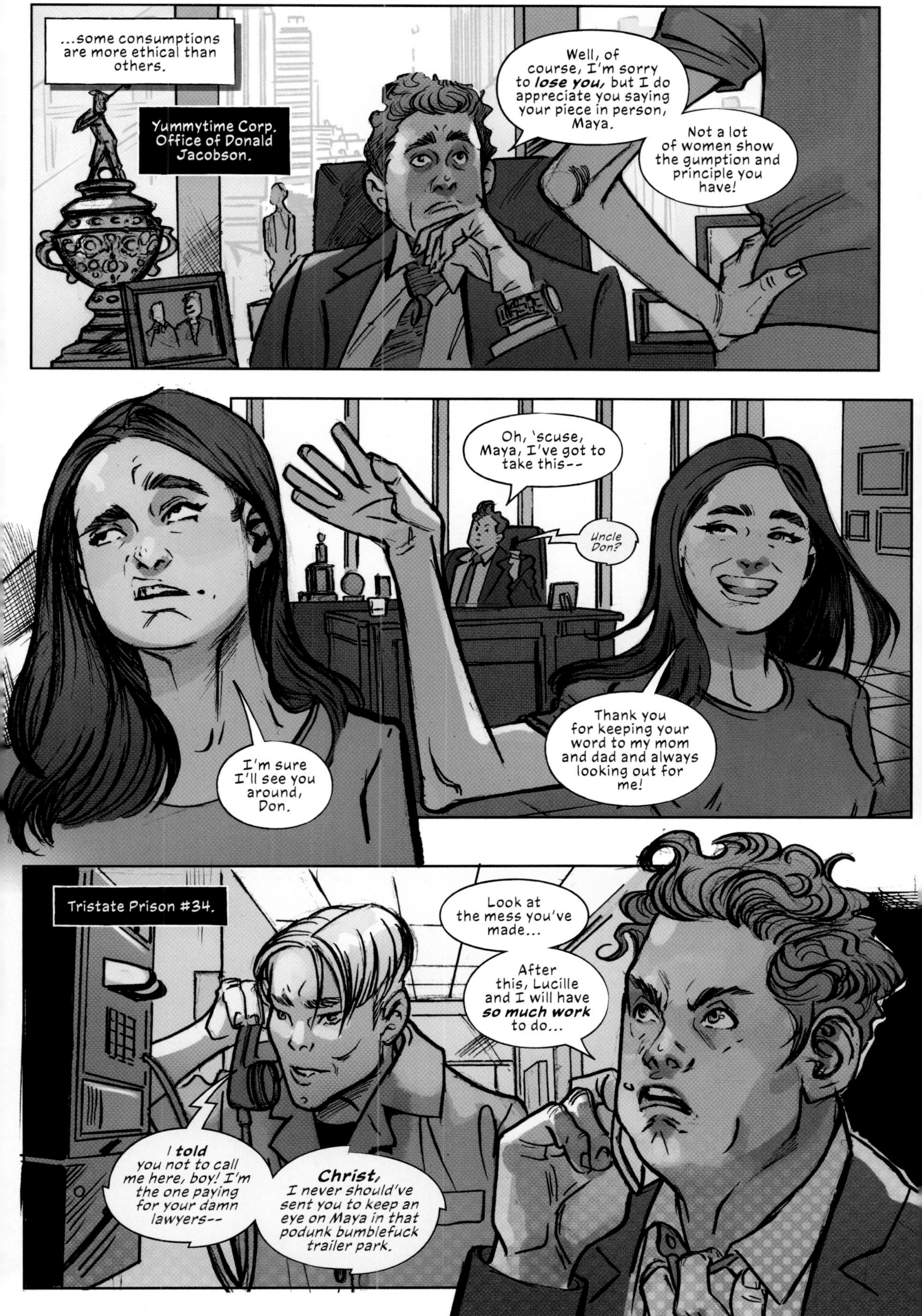
...some consumptions are more ethical than others.
Yummytime Corp. Office of Donald Jacobson.
Well, of course, I'm sorry to lose you, but I do appreciate you saying your piece in person, Maya.
Not a lot of women show the gumption and principle you have!
Oh, 'scuse, Maya, I've got to take this--
Uncle Don?
Thank you for keeping your word to my mom and dad and always looking out for me!
I'm sure I'll see you around, Don.
Tristate Prison #34.
Look at the mess you've made...
After this, Lucille and I will have so much work to do...
I told you not to call me here, boy! I'm the one paying for your damn lawyers--
Christ, I never should've sent you to keep an eye on Maya in that podunk bumblefuck trailer park.

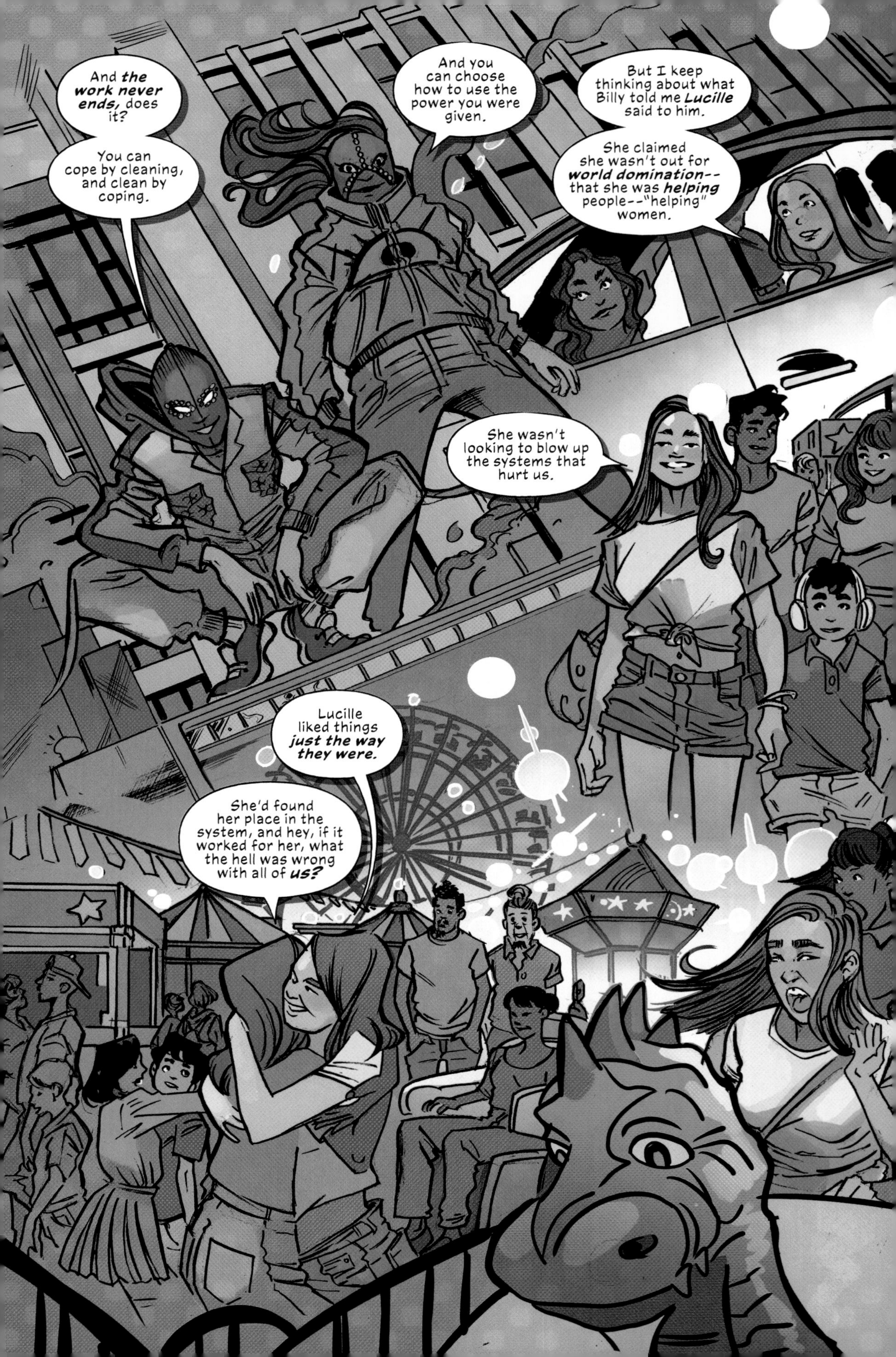

And *the work never ends,* does it?
You can cope by cleaning, and clean by coping.
And you can choose how to use the power you were given.
But I keep thinking about what Billy told me *Lucille* said to him.
She claimed she wasn't out for *world domination*--that she was *helping* people--"helping" women.
She wasn't looking to blow up the systems that hurt us.
Lucille liked things *just the way they were.*
She'd found her place in the system, and hey, if it worked for her, what the hell was wrong with all of *us?*

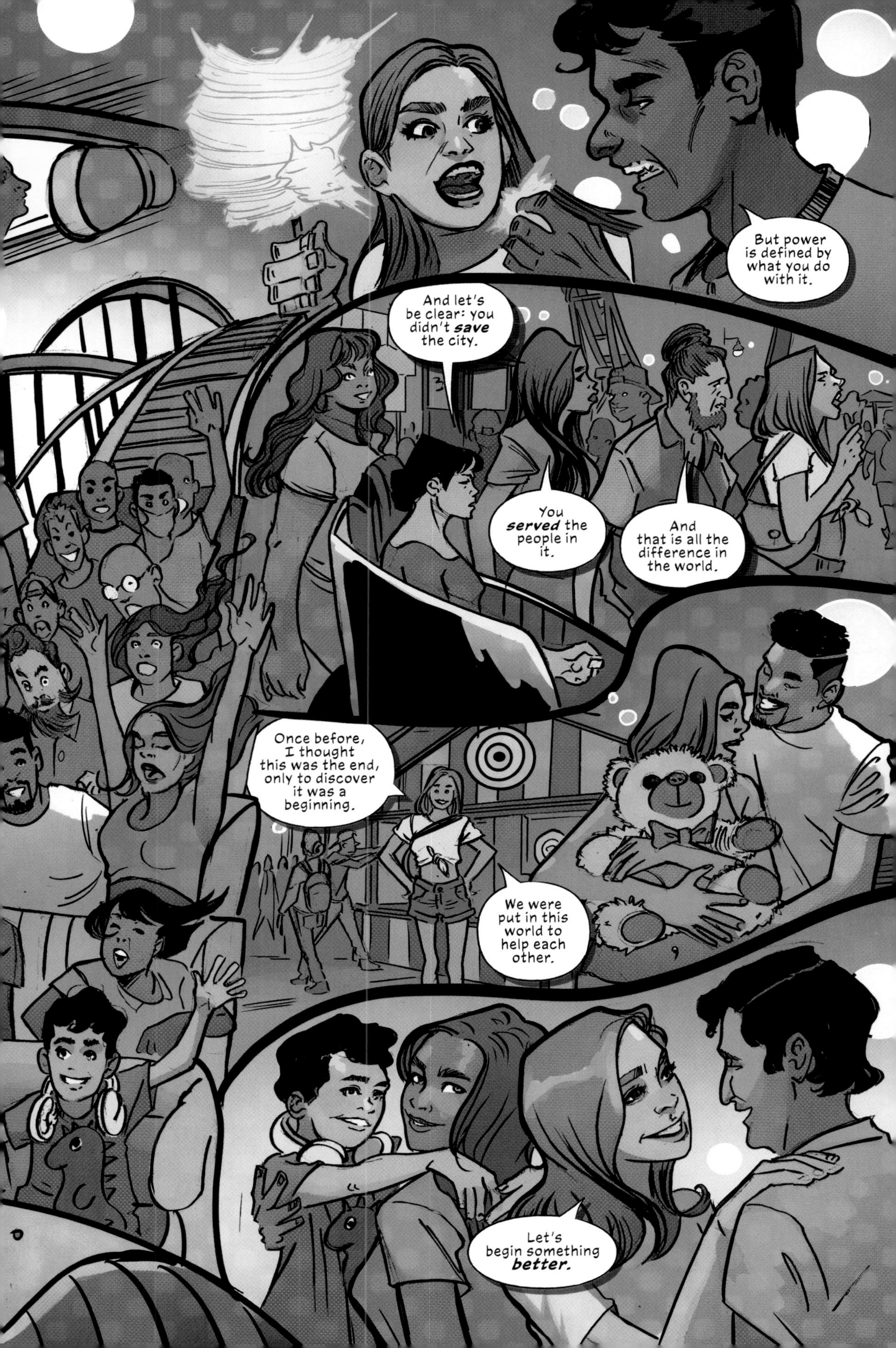
But power is defined by what you do with it.
And let's be clear: you didn't *save* the city.
You *served* the people in it.
And that is all the difference in the world.
Once before, I thought this was the end, only to discover it was a beginning.
We were put in this world to help each other.
Let's begin something *better.*

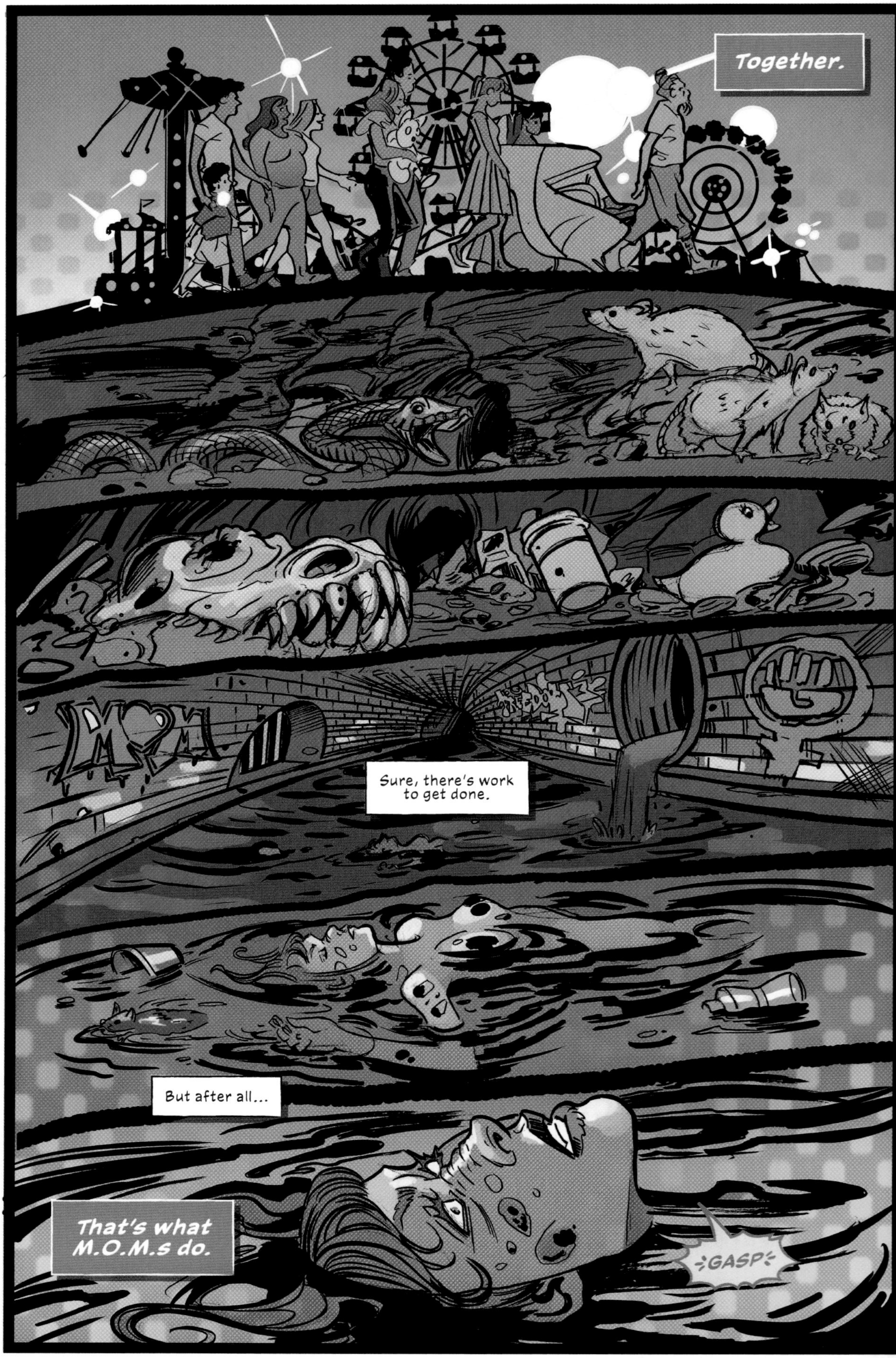
Together.
Sure, there's work to get done.
But after all...
That's what M.O.M.s do.
GASP

variant cover art by JEN BARTEL

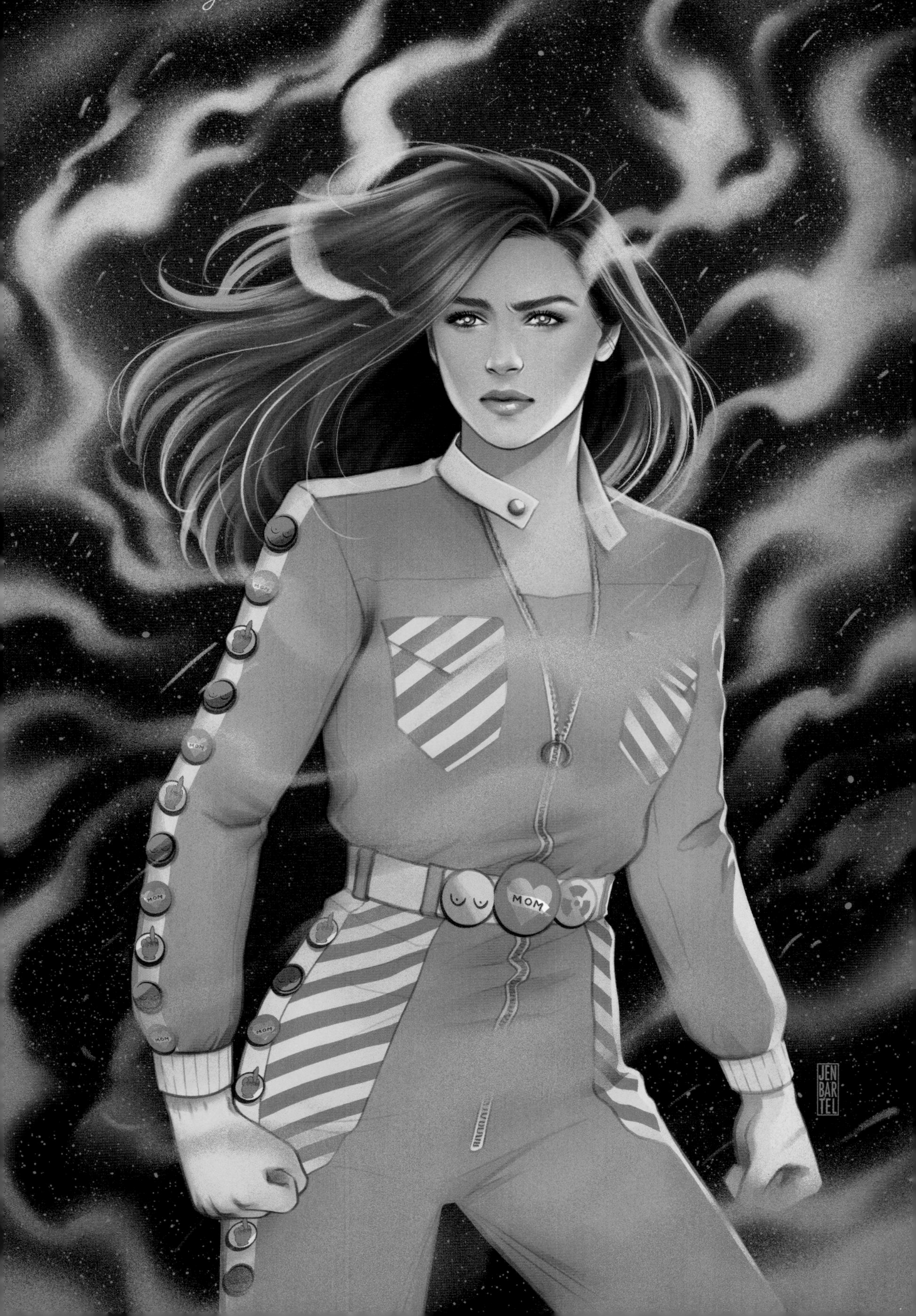
MOM
JEN BARTEL

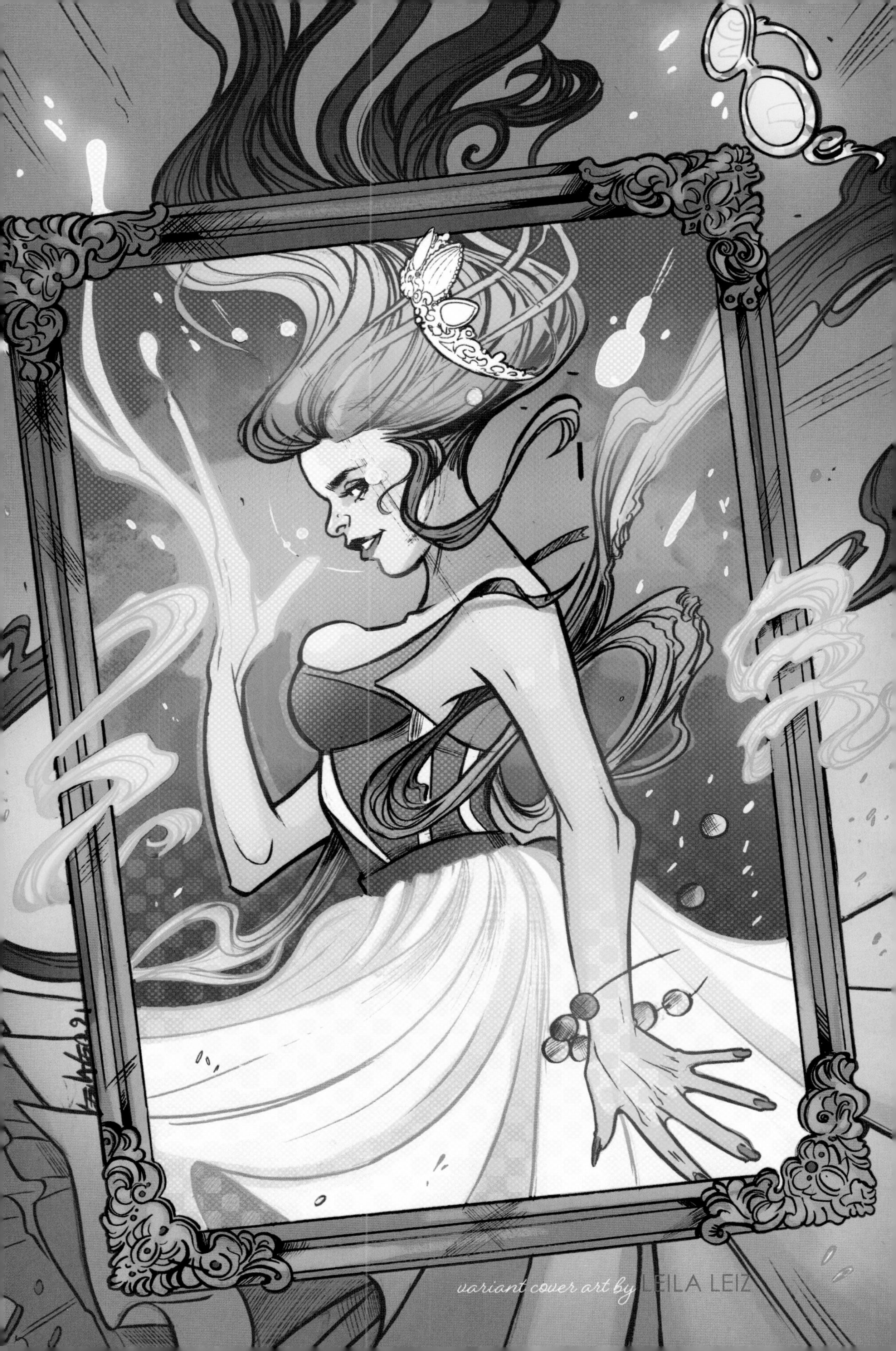

variant cover art by LEILA LEIZ

variant cover art by MIRKA ANDOLFO

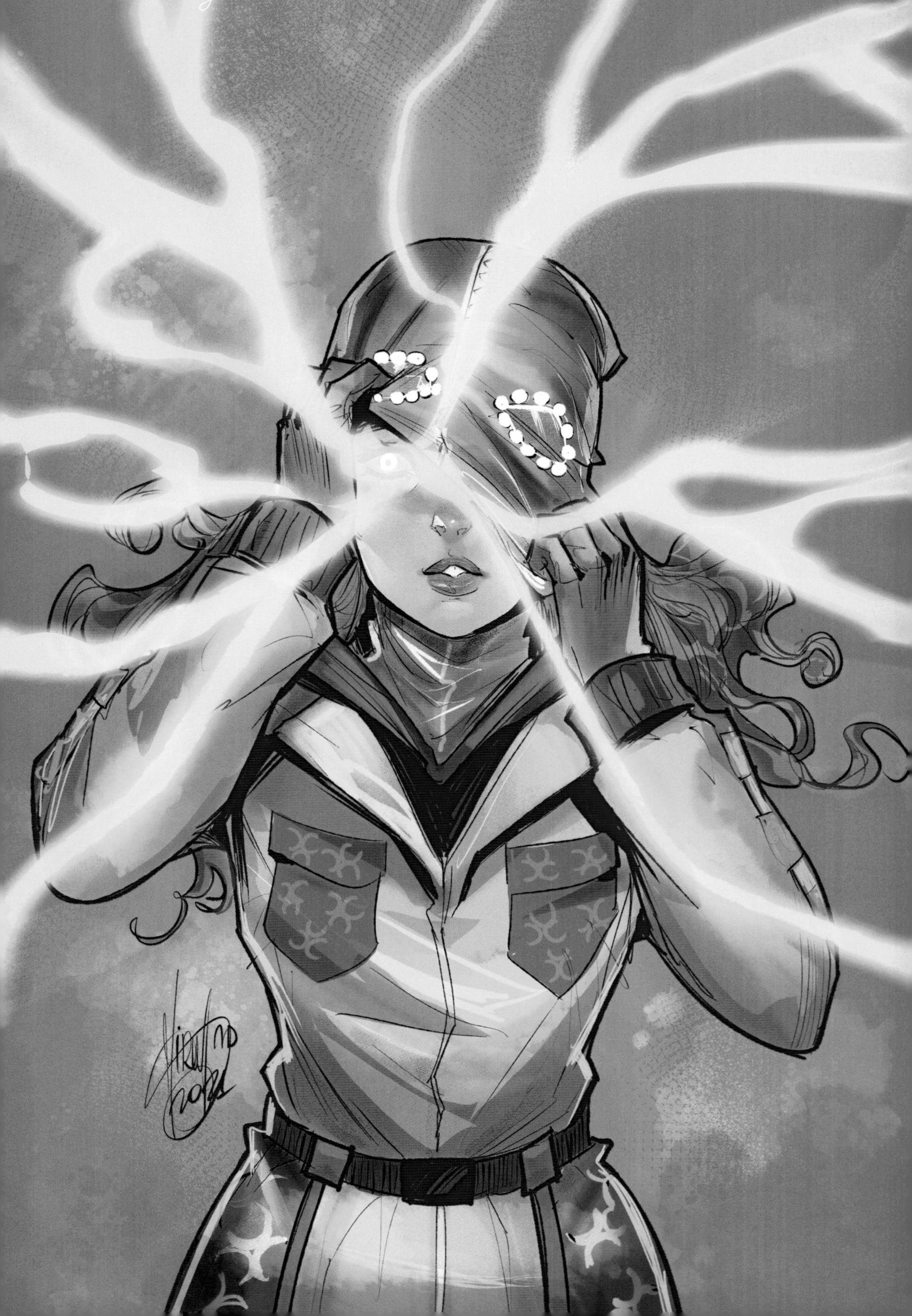

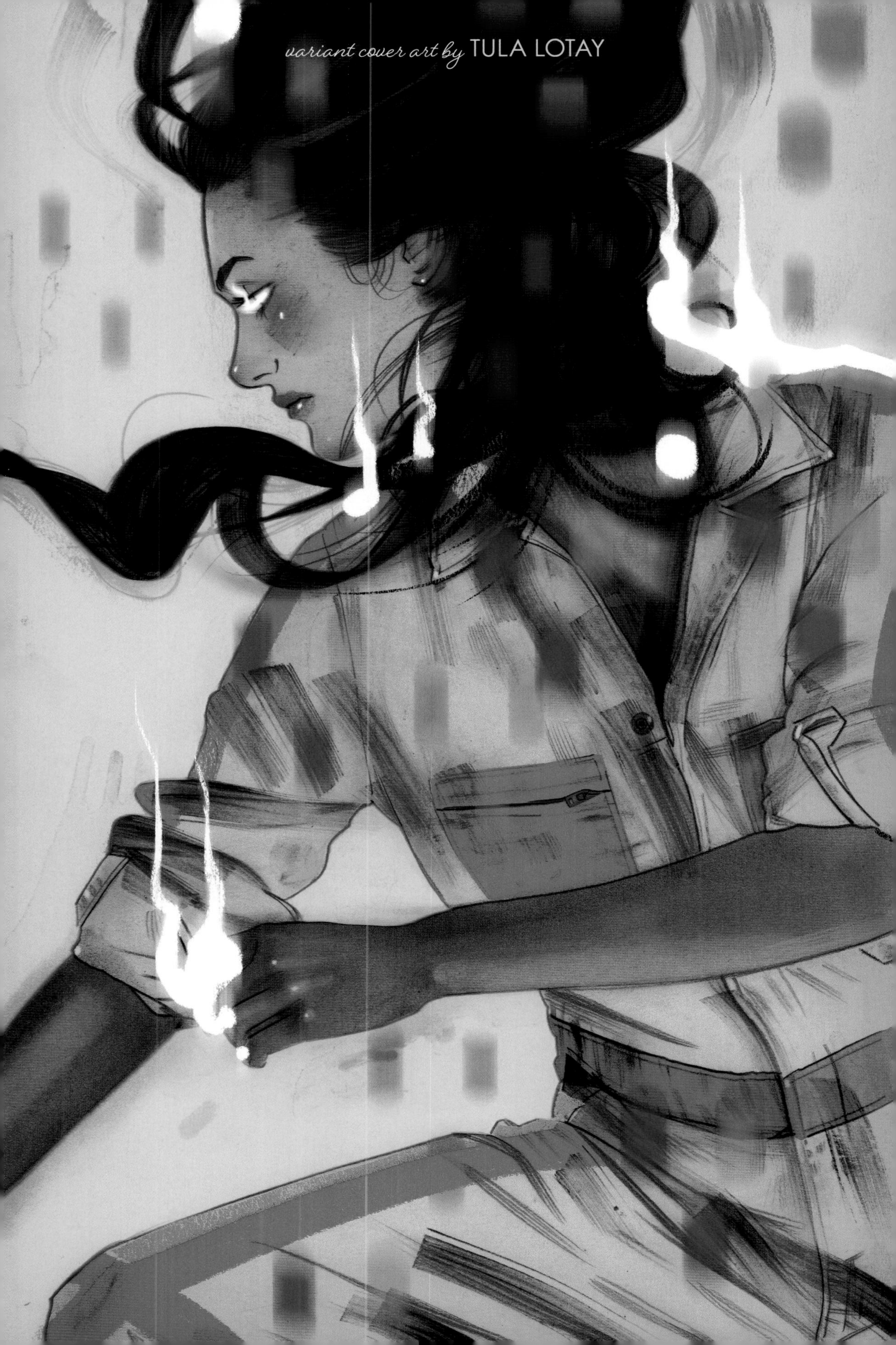

variant cover art by TULA LOTAY

variant cover art by CAT FERRIS

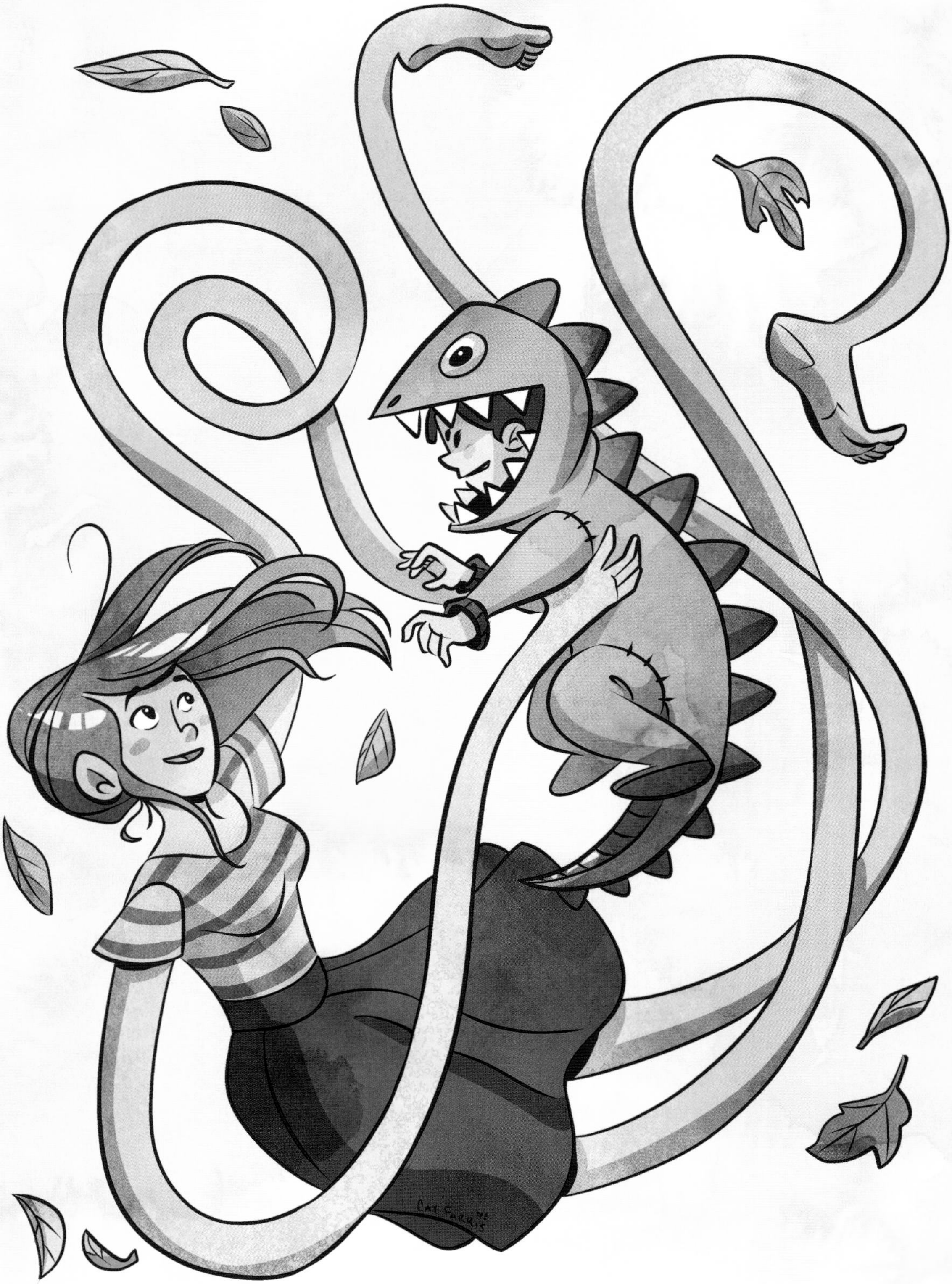
CAT FERRIS

variant cover art by LUANA VECCHIO

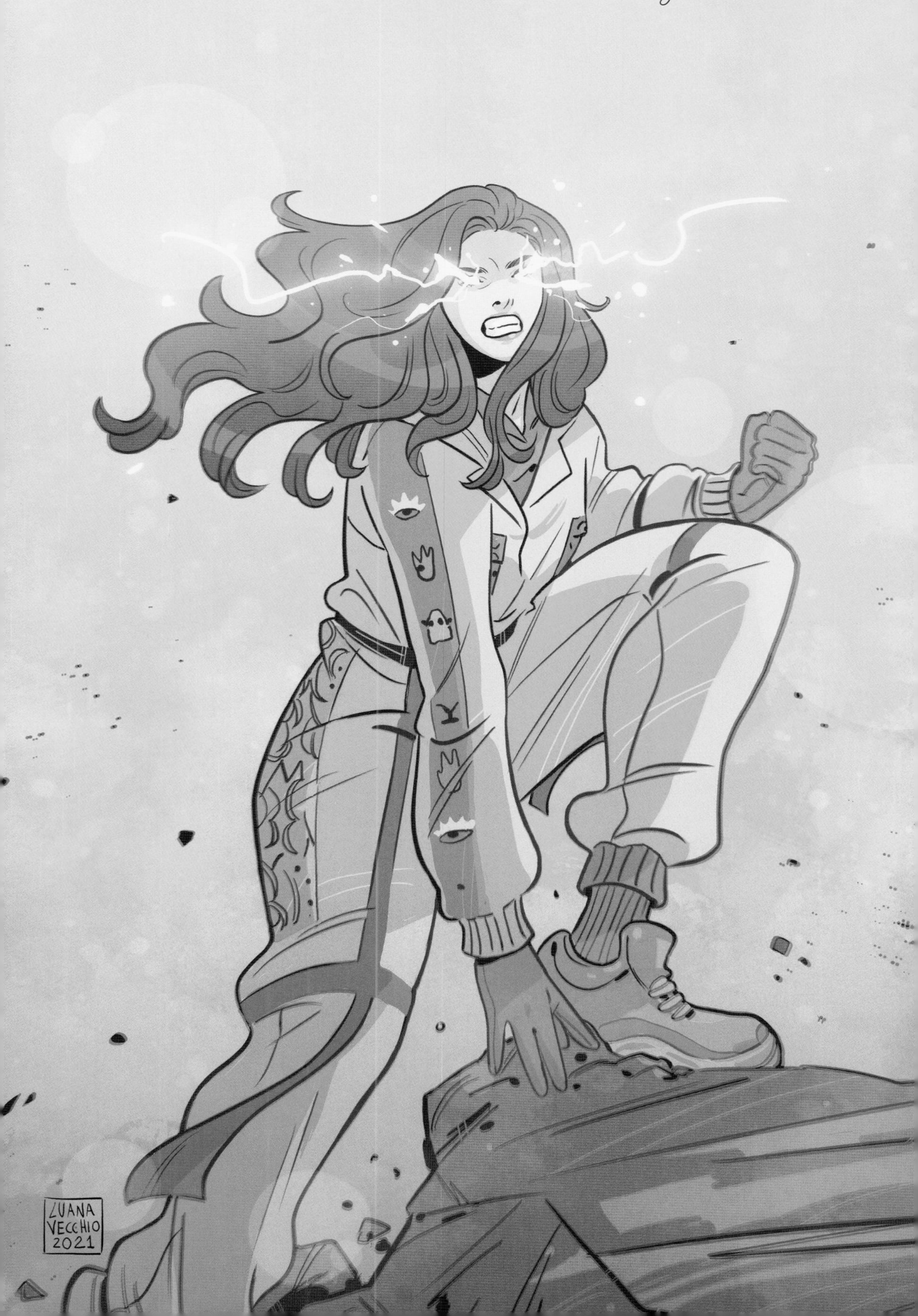
LUANA
VECCHIO
2021

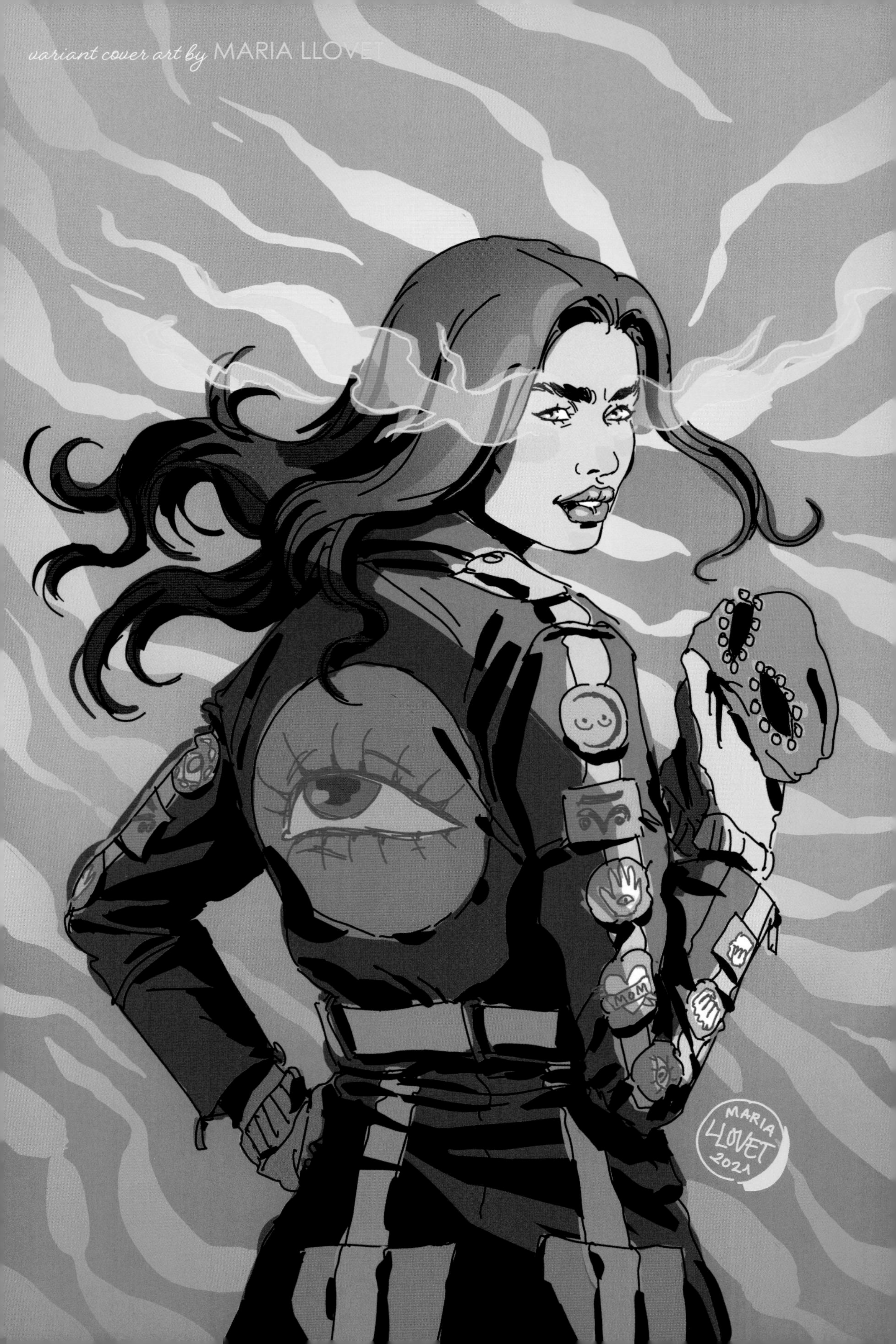
MARIA
LLOVET
2021
MOM
variant cover art by MARIA LLOVET

variant cover art by EMI LENOX

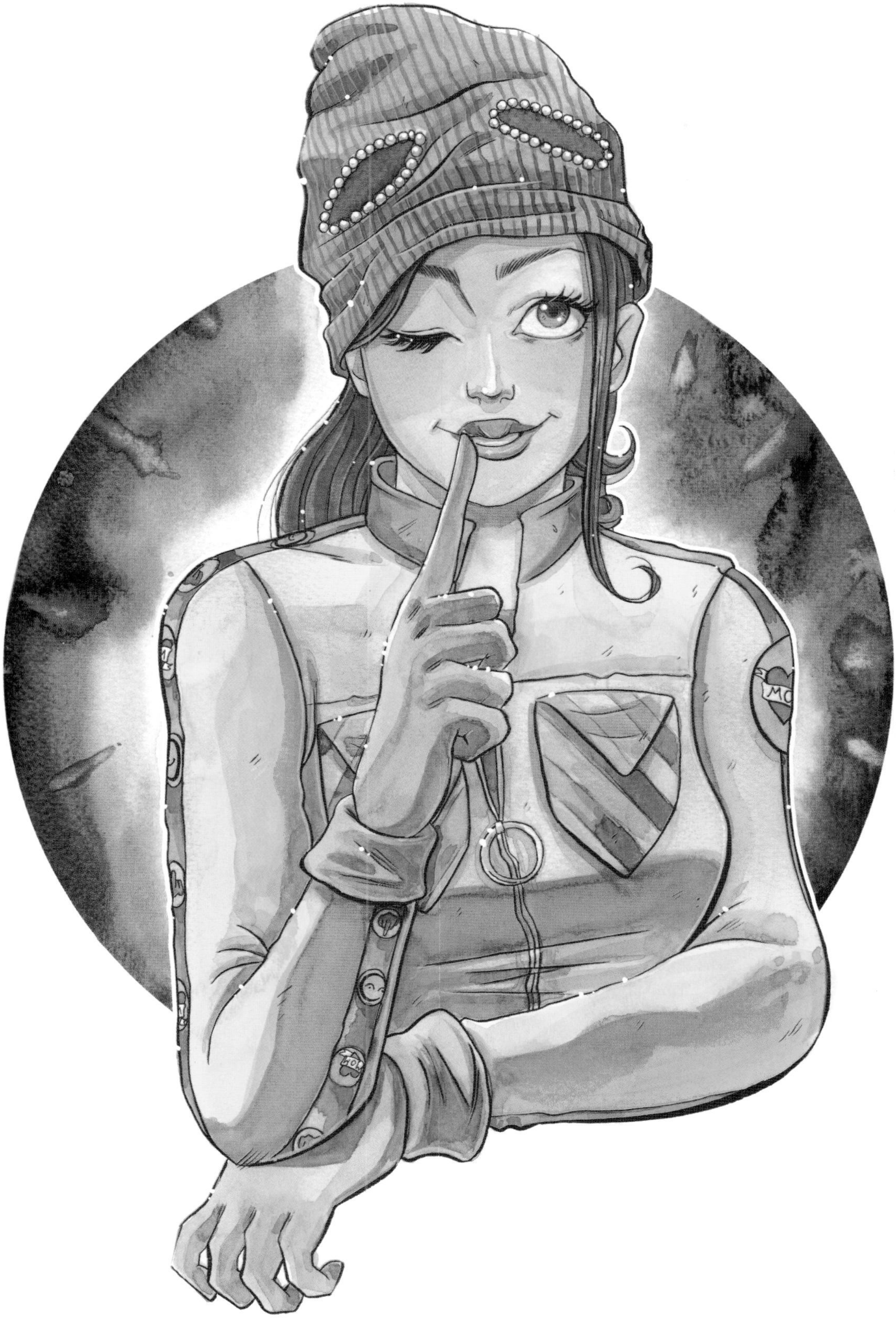

variant cover art by CAITLIN YARSKY

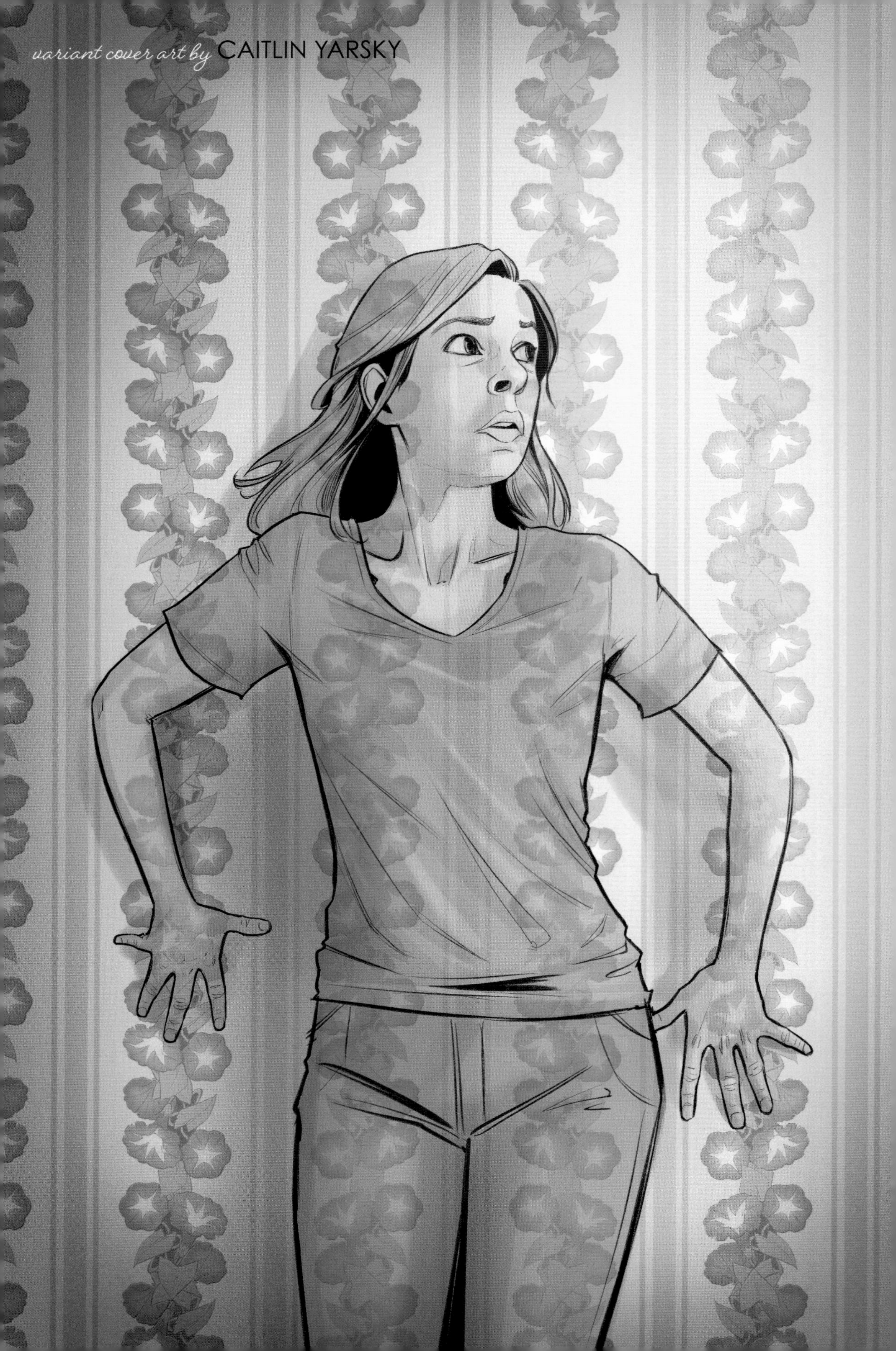

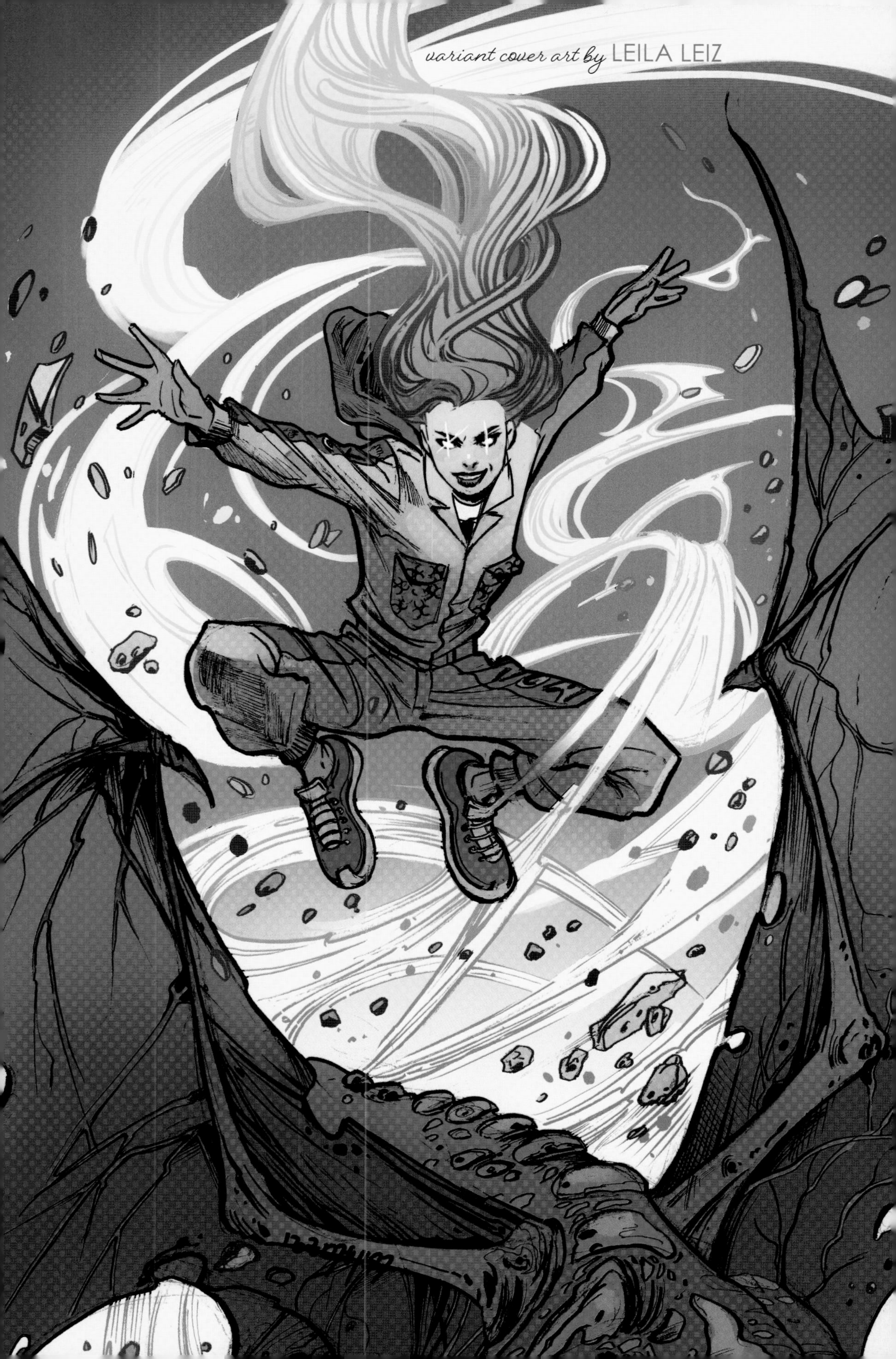

variant cover art by LEILA LEIZ

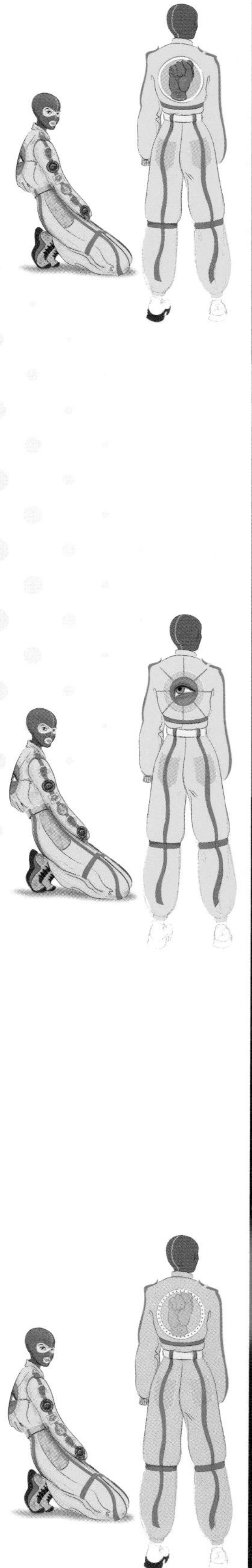

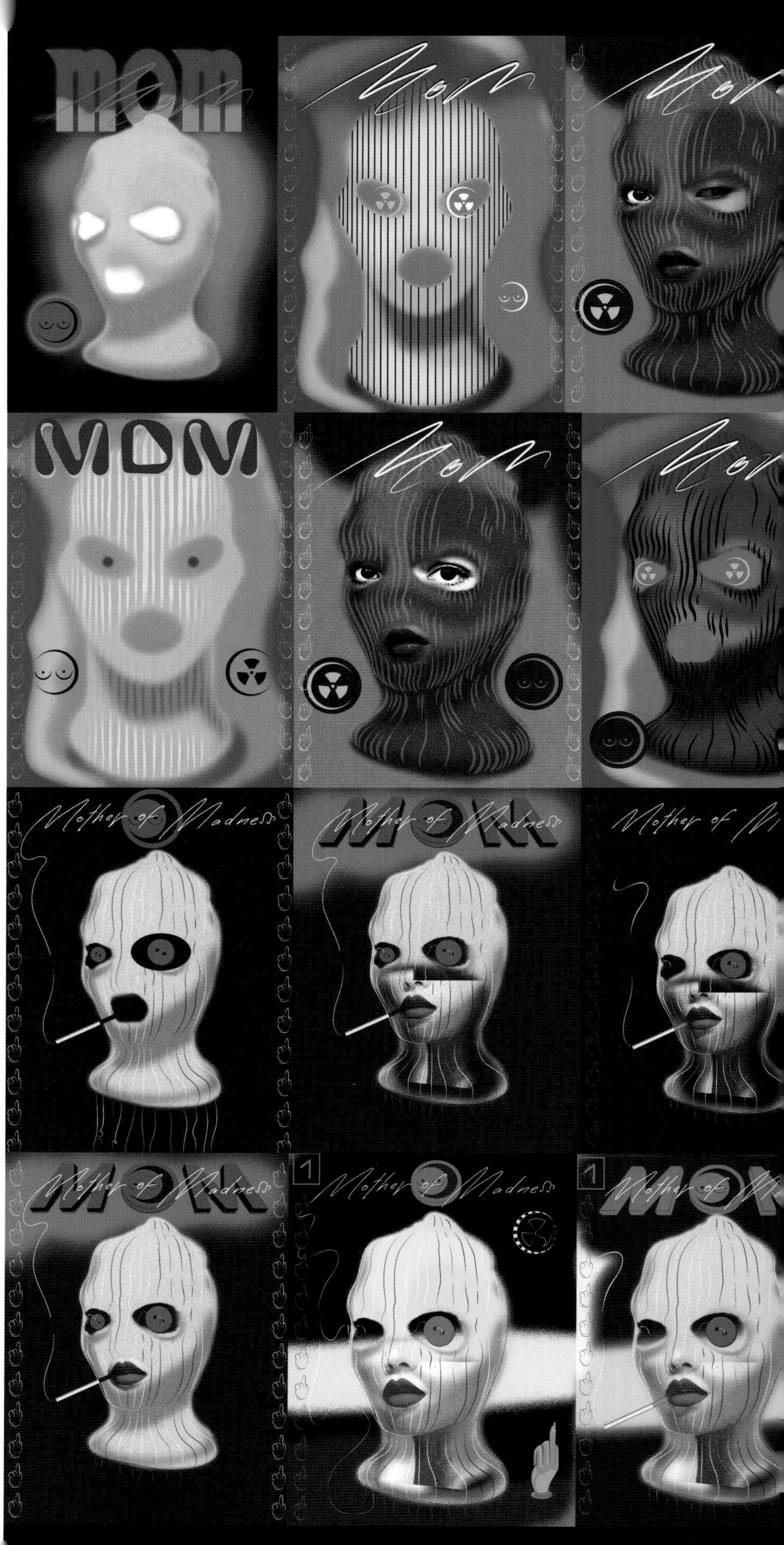
MOM
Mother of Madness

MDM
MDM
Mother of Madness
MoM

sketches by JO RATCLIFFE

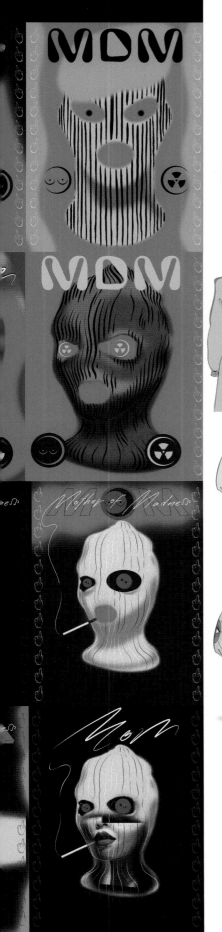

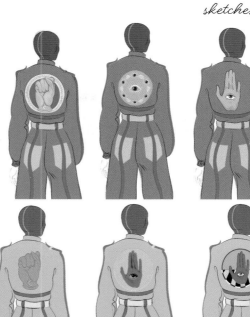

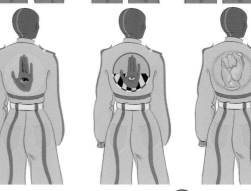

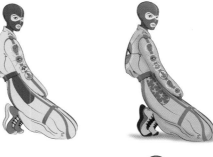

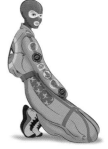

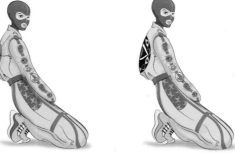

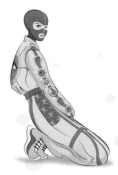

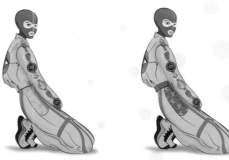

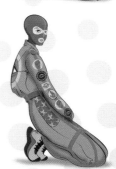

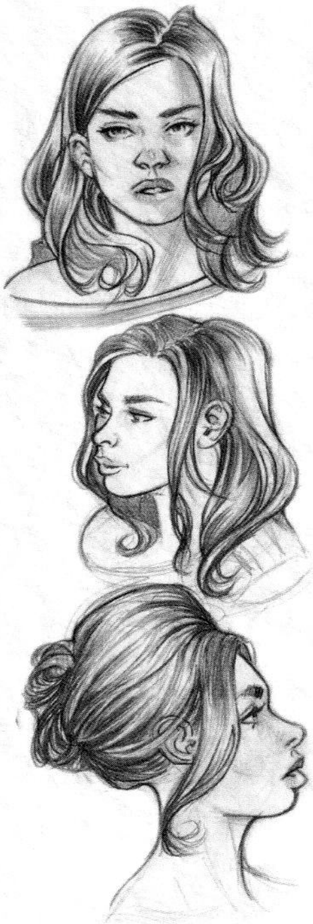

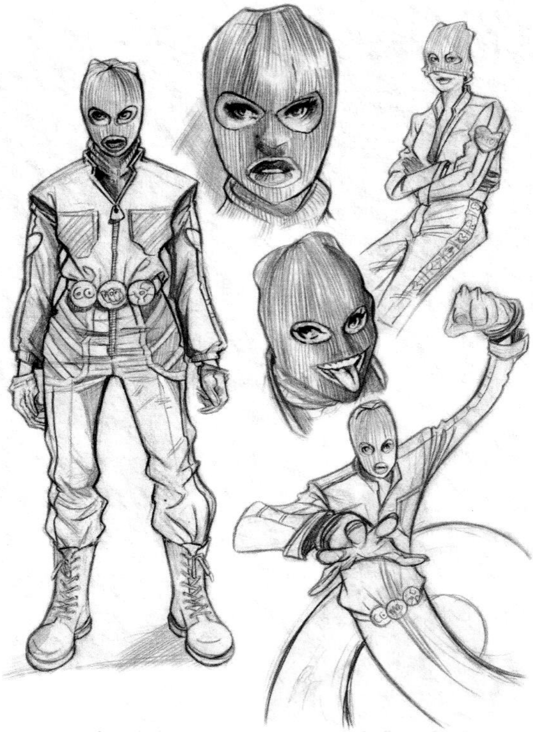

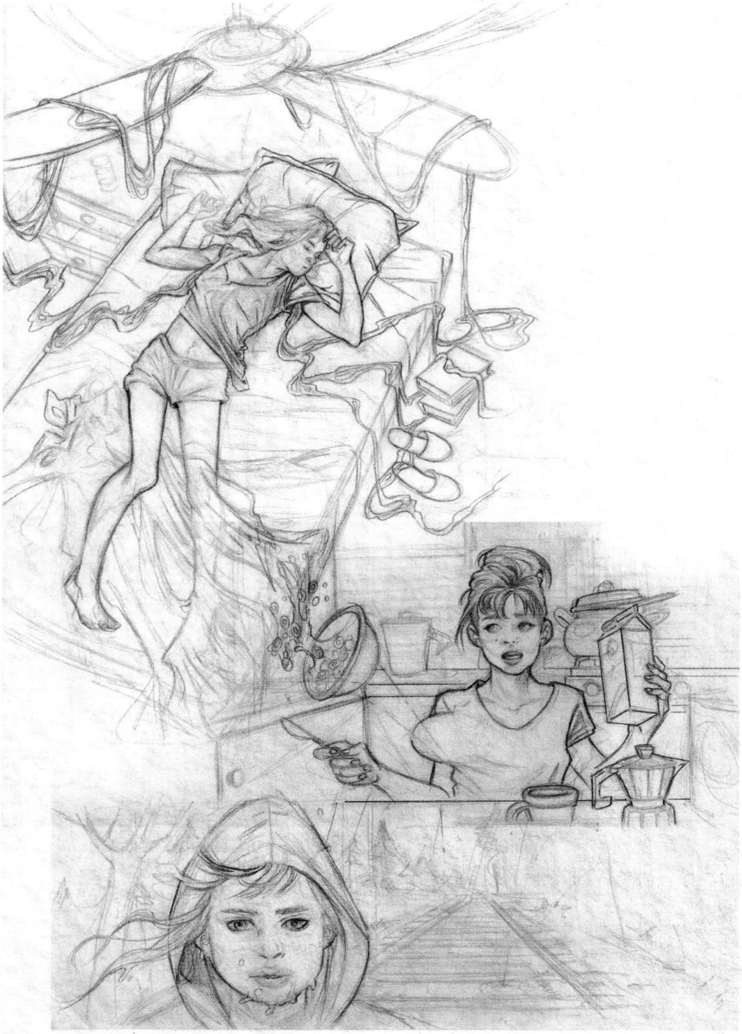

sketches by LEILA LEIZ

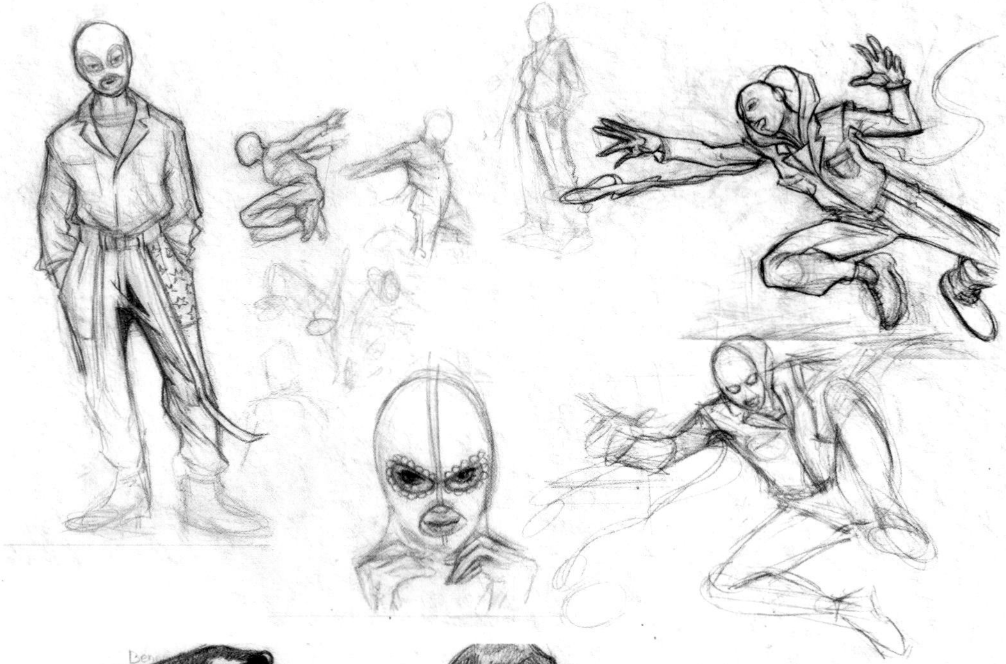

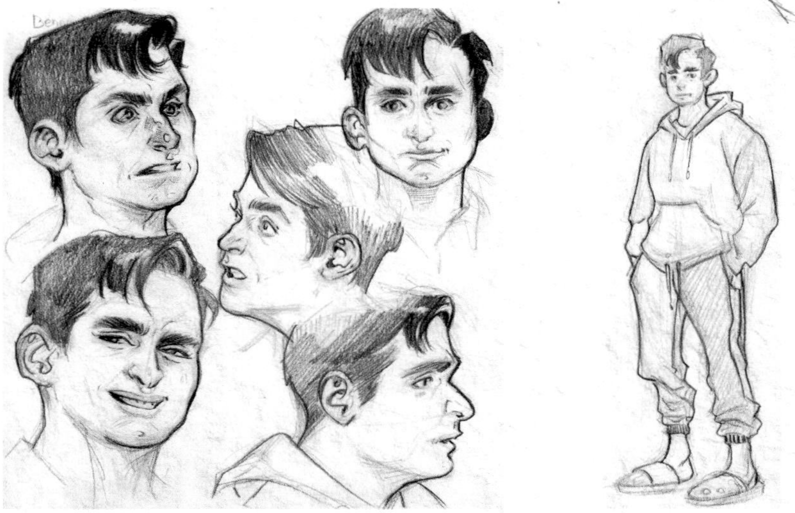

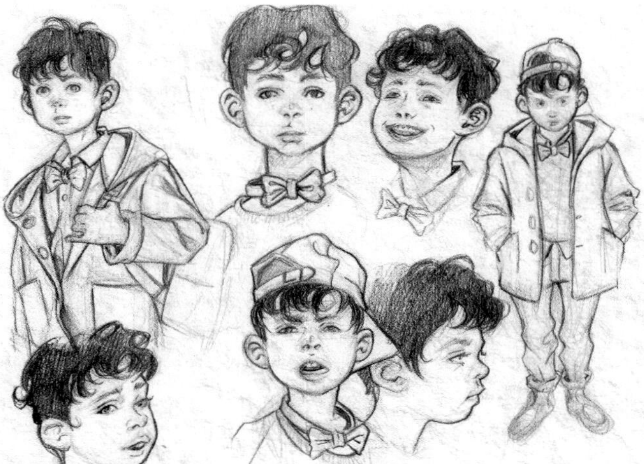

Maya's Powers

Maya's abilities are governed by her emotions and the hormones that cause them...

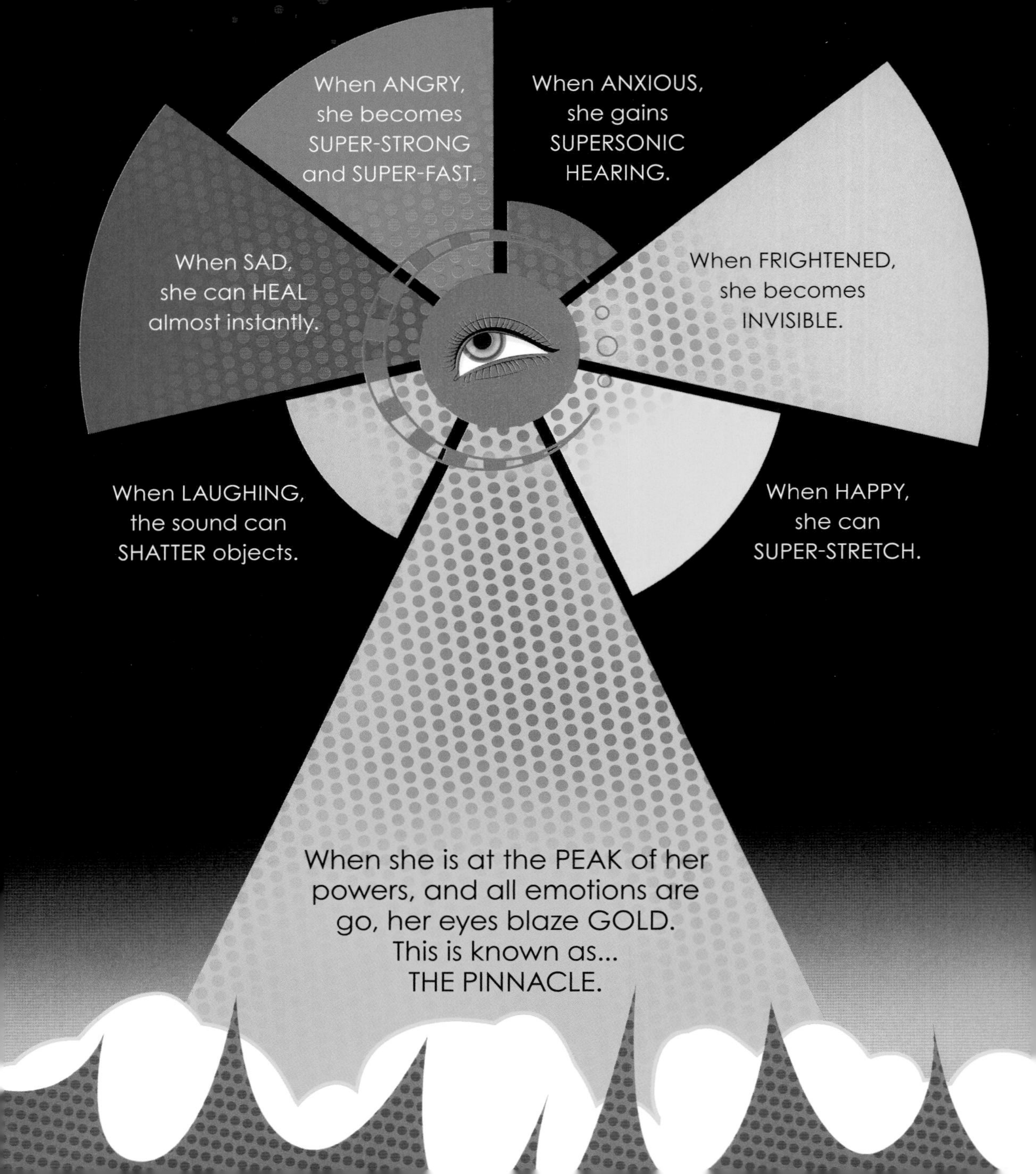

When ANGRY, she becomes SUPER-STRONG and SUPER-FAST.
When ANXIOUS, she gains SUPERSONIC HEARING.
When SAD, she can HEAL almost instantly.
When FRIGHTENED, she becomes INVISIBLE.
When LAUGHING, the sound can SHATTER objects.
When HAPPY, she can SUPER-STRETCH.
When she is at the PEAK of her powers, and all emotions are go, her eyes blaze GOLD. This is known as... THE PINNACLE.

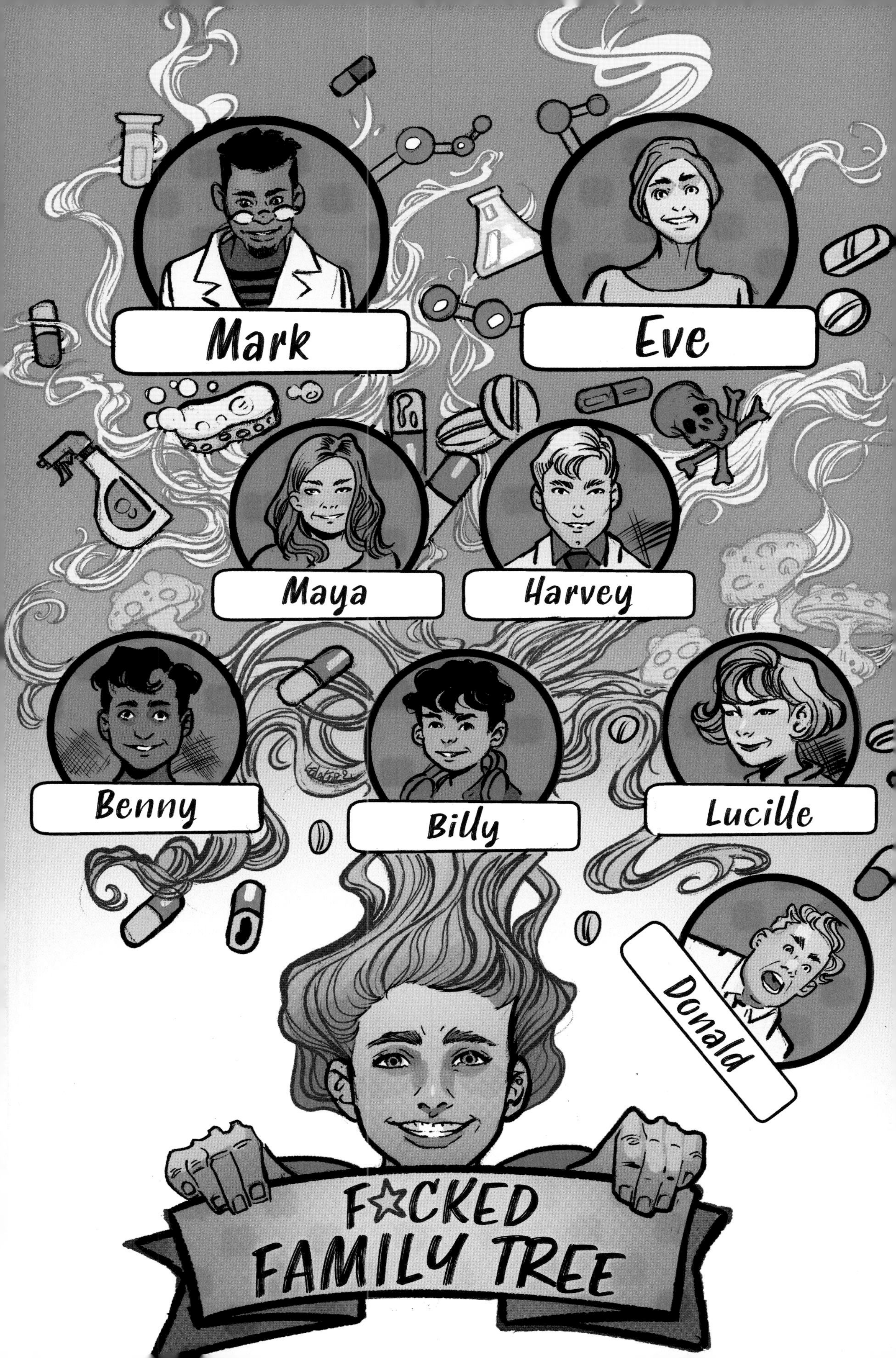

Mark
Eve
Maya
Harvey
Benny
Billy
Lucille
Donald
F☆CKED
FAMILY TREE

IF YOU OR SOMEONE YOU KNOW NEEDS SUPPORT, YOU DON'T NEED TO STRUGGLE ALONE. WE'VE INCLUDED A NUMBER OF ORGANIZATIONS FOR SHORT OR LONGER-TERM EMOTIONAL SUPPORT, ADVOCACY, COUNSELING, ADVICE, OR REFUGE IN THE UK AND USA.

IF YOU OR SOMEONE YOU KNOW IS IN IMMEDIATE DANGER OR IN NEED OF URGENT PROTECTION, CALL THE POLICE WITH **999** (UK) OR **911** (USA).

1. HATE CRIMES

A crime committed against someone because of their race, religion, beliefs, transgender identity, sexual orientation, or disability are hate crimes and should be reported immediately.

In the UK: Stop Hate Crime 24-Hour Helpline – 0800 1381625
https://www.stophateuk.org/

In the USA: STEP 1: Report the crime to your local police, and STEP 2: Quickly follow up this report with a tip to the Federal Bureau of Investigation (FBI). https://www.justice.gov/hatecrimes/get-help-now

2. DOMESTIC ABUSE

In the UK: National Domestic Abuse Helpline – 0808 2000 247 or visit www.nationaldahelpline.org.uk

In the USA: National Domestic Violence Hotline – 1-800-799-7233 or visit www.thehotline.org

Childhelp National Child Abuse Hotline – call or text 1-800-4-A-CHILD (1-800-422-4453) or visit https://www.childhelp.org/hotline

StrongHearts, supports Native American and Alaska Native women – 1-844-7NATIVE (762-8483) or visit www.strongheartshelpline.org

The Asian Pacific Institute on Gender-Based Violence – to access their directory of non-profit organizations offering support to Asian Pacific survivors visit www. apigbv.force.com

Ujima, the National Center on Violence Against Women in the Black Community – 1-844-77-UJIMA (85462) for information on resources, or visit www.ujimacommunity.org

Casa de Esperanza is a national resource center for organizations working with Latinas – 651.772.1611

WomensLaw provides basic legal information, referrals, and emotional support related to domestic violence, sexual assault, and stalking – https://hotline.womenslaw.org/public

3. RAPE, SEXUAL HARRASSMENT, AND SEXUAL ASSAULT

In the UK: The Rape Crisis National Helpline – 0808 802 9999 or visit www.rapecrisis.org.uk/get-help/want-to-talk (operated by Rape Crisis)

WomensLaw provides legal information, referrals, and emotional support related to domestic violence, sexual assault, and stalking – https://hotline.womenslaw.org/public

In the USA: RAINN (the Rape, Abuse & Incest National Network) – 1-800-656-HOPE (4673) or visit https://rainn.org/

Administered by the National Women's Law Center, the TIME'S UP Legal Defense Fund connects workers who face sexual harassment with attorneys – visit www.nwlc.org/legal-assistance

4. TRAFFICKING AND MODERN SLAVERY

In the UK: The Modern Slavery Helpline provides victims of modern slavery and trafficking – 08000 121 700 or visit www.modernslaveryhelpline.org

In the USA: The National Human Trafficking Hotline supports victims and survivors of human trafficking and those who suspect human trafficking 24/7 – 1-888-373-7888, text 233733, or visit www.humantraffickinghotline.org

5. LGBTQI+ RIGHTS AND AWARENESS

In the UK: Stonewall's Information Service Helpline, for lesbian, gay, bi, and trans individuals, and their allies – 0800 0502020 or visit www.stonewall.org.uk

The Mermaids Helpline, for transgender, nonbinary, and gender-diverse children, young people, and their families – 0808 801 0400 or visit www.mermaidsuk.org.uk

The Mindline Trans+ Hepline, for anyone identifying as transgender, non-binary or genderfluid, their families and communities – 0300 330 5468 or visit https://mindlinetrans.org.uk

In the USA: Trevor Project's Trevor Lifeline, crisis intervention and suicide prevention support for LGBTQ young people under 25 – 1-866-488-7386 or visit www.thetrevorproject.org

The Trans Lifeline, crisis and suicide prevention support for trans people – 1-877-565-8860 or visit www.translifeline.org

The NCLR (the National Centre for Lesbian Rights) Legal Helpline, for lesbian, gay, bisexual and transgender people, and their families facing custody, separation, divorce, immigration and asylum disputes – 800.528.6257 / 415.392.6257 or visit www.nclrights.org

6. ANTI-RACISM

BLACK LIVES MATTER

Black Lives Matter, a global anti-racist movement fighting to end structural racism – visit www.blacklivesmatter.com in the USA and www.blacklivesmatter.uk in the UK.

STOP ASIAN HATE

In the UK: End the Virus of Racism, a group of activists, artists, professionals, students, researchers and journalists working to establish the UK's first nonprofit dedicated to addressing systemic racism faced by people of East and Southeast Asian heritage – help by donating at https://bit.ly/3jOOeGN

In the USA: Stop AAPI Hate, a reporting center set up in response to escalating xenophobia and bigotry resulting from the COVID-19 pandemic – to find out more, report an incident of Asian Hate Crime or access safety and mental health toolkits visit www.stopaapihate.org

CIVIL RIGHTS

In the UK: Liberty works on the urgent human rights issues, including through its work defending women's, migrants', LGBT+, and protest rights – www.libertyhumanrights.org.uk

In the USA: The American Civil Liberties Union addresses everything from racial justice, immigration, and LGBTQ Rights, to national security, women's rights, and capital punishment – www.aclu.org

7. MENTAL HEALTH AND SUICIDE

Crisis Text Line – text HOME to 85258 (UK) or 741741 (USA) to connect with 24/7, high-quality text-based mental health support and crisis intervention, or visit www.crisistextline.org

In the UK: The Samaritans Crisis and Suicide Helpline – 116 123 or visit www.samaritans.org

The PAPYRUS HopelineUK, for young people under 35 experiencing thoughts of suicide – call 0800 068 4141, text 07860039967, or visit www.papyrus-uk.org

YoungMinds, for children and young people's mental health, and their parents and carers – text YM to 85258 or visit www.youngminds.org.uk

Wish, for women with mental health needs in prison, hospital and the community – 020 8980 3618 or visit www.womenatwish.org.uk

The CALM (the Campaign Against Living Miserably) Helpline, offers support to men – 0800 58 58 58 or visit www.thecalmzone.net

The Black, African And Asian Therapy Network (BAATN) – to access information and links to professional support visit www.baatn.org.uk

In the USA: The National Suicide Prevention Lifeline – 1-800-273-8255 or visit www.suicidepreventionlifeline.org

NAMI (the National Alliance on Mental Illness) HelpLine – 1-800-950-NAMI (6264) or visit www.nami.org

Face It Helpline, dedicated support for men – 651-200-4297 or visit www.faceitfoundation.org

Your Life Your Voice is Boystown USA's Helpline for children, parents and families struggling with self-harm, mental health disorders, and abuse – 1 (800) 448 - 3000 or visit www.yourlifeyourvoice.org

Ebony Magazine hosts a growing list of Black mental health resources by State – visit www.ebony.com/life/black-mental-health-resources

The National Asian American Pacific Islander Mental Health Association (AAMHPI) maintains a list of service providers for Asian Americans, Native Hawaiians, and Pacific Islanders in all 50 States – visit www.naapimha.org/aanhpiservice-providers

The Focus on You offers self-care and mental health support, run by a Latina therapist – www.thefocusonyou.com

WANTED

DEAD or ALIVE

CASH REWARD

WANTED FOR: THE MUSHROOM RISOTTO MASSACRE, SNEAKY CONSPIRACY, FEMALE MISOGYNY, BLATANT CORRUPTION, AGGRAVATED KIDNAPPING, "THERE CAN ONLY BE ONE," WHITE FEMINISM, UNLAWFUL EXPERIMENTATION, UNTESTED PHARMACEUTICALS, SMASHING THE GLASS CEILING ONLY TO PULL THE LADDER UP AFTER HER, AND OTHER ACTS OF VILE AND UNREPENTANT JERKERY.